See

Jesus

in the

Old Testament

By George Aaron Crabb

Table of Contents

DEDICATION

To Yeshua (Jesus).
Thank you for opening my eyes to see.
To see you in every part of the Old Testament.
Then beginning with Moses and with all the Prophets, He explained to them the things written *about Himself in all the Scriptures.*
(Luke 24:27 NASB)
I also dedicate this book to my beautiful bride Christina. You have been so wise and selfless. You are that Proverbs 31 wife.

ACKNOWLEDGMENTS

My mom and dad were saved during the Jesus Revolution. It was a time when the Spirit of God was burning in the hearts of young people. When that revival began to fade, my parents remained strong in the word of God and taught me to stay in the word of God.

CHAPTER ONE: THE WHOLE BIBLE

Jesus said to his Jewish disciples in Jerusalem:

"These are My words which I spoke to you while I was still with you, that all the things that are written about Me in the Law of Moses and the Prophets and the Psalms must be fulfilled." – Luke 24:44

Jesus expected his disciples to find him in the Tanakh – The Old Testament. The Jewish Bible today is in the same order that we saw Jesus say it:

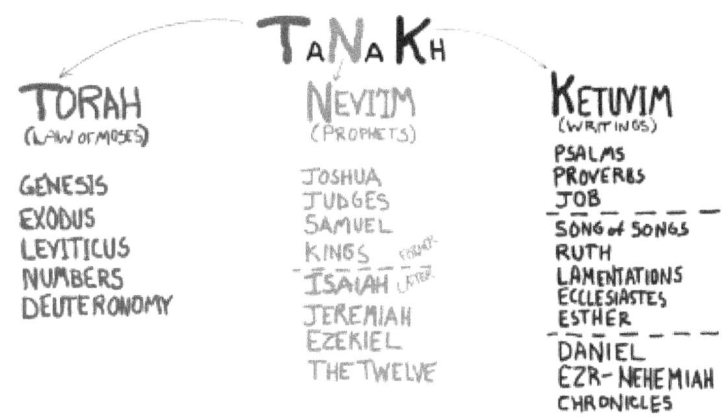

Jesus also said: *"You examine the Scriptures because you think that in them you have eternal life; and it is those very Scriptures that testify about Me"*

"For if you believed Moses, you would believe Me; for he wrote about Me."

(John 5:39,49 NASB)

Most Christians do not know much if anything about the Old Testament. Their pastors stay away from it just like they tend to stay away from the book of Revelation.

The Jesus Revolution or Jesus Movement of the 1970's was America's last great revival. A little place called Calvary Chapel, near Newport Beach, in southern California was a blessed church by God.

The pastor, Chuck Smith was a humble, local surfer who just wanted a small church of about two hundred people. However, God had other plans. This church went nuclear and spread all over the world.

God used Chuck Smith so powerfully during the last great revival called the Jesus Movement or better known as the Jesus Revolution. It is because he read and taught through the whole Bible.

Chuck was faithful to teach through the Old and New Testaments, over and over and the fruit of his ministry grew worldwide. Pastors have tried to figure out what his secret was to this great and powerful movement.

I have heard pastors say that it was because he took the hippies in and opened the doors of his church to them when most others did not. That was part of it for sure. But I can tell you another reason.

Chuck had a deep knowledge of God by reading all of God's word. And because of that, he was a loyal supporter of the Nation of Israel.

I know that pastors and theologians will not like what I just wrote.

It does not bother me because I do not live to please people, or the world. I am here to please God – the God of Abrahan, Isaac, and Jacob.

God promises to bless those who bless Israel. This is what Chuck did, and he did it when it was very unpopular among mainstream pastors. He even talked about how other pastors would write him letters about how it was wrong to support Israel. Obviously, those pastors were taught the long-standing lie that the church had spiritually become Israel after Jesus' first coming.

Calvary Chapel gave millions of dollars to help Israel.

Why?

Because Pastor Chuck taught to bless Israel and did so himself, and so God blessed his ministry powerfully. Out of his ministry, you can see men like Greg Laurie, Skip Heitzig, Jack Hibbs, Wayne Taylor and more. God used these men powerfully and they all have that same love for Israel that pastor Chuck had.

The reason Chuck knew God's plan with Israel, is because he knew God's words in the context of the whole Bible.

In the New Testament, you can see that both Romans chapter 11, Revelation chapters 7 and 14 tell of God's plan to rescue and save Israel in the end.

In fact, both the Old and New Testament tell of God's plan to save the Nation of Israel after he has a great harvest and saves His Gentile bride.

Paul wrote of the importance of declaring the whole council of God. This means that you need to know all of scripture to really know God.

You will hear many progressive types of Christians say, "Do not make an idol out of the Bible". They also say that being a real Christian is all about a relationship with God, knowing God in an intimate way.

I agree with that last statement because it really is about knowing God. It is also about trusting him, which means having faith in him.

But how do you know him, and have deep trust in him?

As you know, the most important part of a healthy relationship is effective communication. Listening to your spouse, your child, or your friend is paramount to knowing them.

So, how do you listen to God?

People claim that they have a word from the Lord, and believe they are modern day prophets and apostles. But can you really trust them?

If you are honest, the answer is no.

So how can you trust that you are hearing and listening to the voice of God? You do want that, and you want a close relationship with Him.

Here is how: Read the Whole Bible!

That is one of the main ways you develop the relationship you desire with God.

You might be saying, "Yeah, but I want to hear his voice out loud."

Then read your Bible aloud.

The whole Bible is his word to you, him speaking to you.

I know because the Bible itself proclaims this. It is all inspired by God and approved by him. It is perfect and without error, just as he is perfect and without error.

2nd Timothy 3:16 says: *"All Scripture is inspired by God and beneficial for teaching, for rebuke, for correction, for training in righteousness; so that the person of God may be fully capable, equipped for every good work."*

So, do you want to know God?

Then you must know his words.

You will get to know God more and see His plan clearly in this book as we walk through it in order, just like Yeshua (Hebrew for Jesus) did so, as he taught where he was found from Genesis to the last book of the Jewish Bible.

SEE JESUS IN THE OLD TESTAMENT

This will help you understand the rest of the Bible, the New Testament. It is like learning math. You must have the foundations in place, the beginning stuff or you will never fully understand it and use it for excellent work.

The first five books will give you the origins, the beginnings of God's relationship with humankind. God spends the first couple of chapters on creation but then spends the rest of it in relationship. He desires to know you and me; he loves you and me dearly.

Genesis, the book of beginnings, is about those relationships. Adam, Eve, Cain, Able, Enoch, Noah, Abraham, Isaac, Jacob, and Joseph were accounts about his love toward them and his Fatherly relationship with them.

The prophecies in the Old Testament alone will give you amazing insight into what has been fulfilled in Jesus, and what is yet to be fulfilled when he returns.

Pastors today say that they are not into prophecy because it is just a distraction from the real mission of loving people. But God is into prophecy, after all, one-third of the Bible is prophecy.

Not all of the prophecy has been fulfilled. This is exciting because you are still in the Bible. It is still alive, and you can see that you are still in those pages today.

For instance: Investigate the book of Ezekiel. In chapters 36 and 37 you can see how God brought Israel back to their own land from the four corners of the world. This was not the return from exile in Babylon and Persia because these scriptures speak of a united Israel. God told Ezekiel to take a stick and write on it Judah and then another stick and write on it Joseph. He then tells him to make them one in his hand and then explains to Ezekiel that it is the whole house of Israel. He tells him they are united, no longer the southern and northern kingdoms.

That did not happen until 1948 when Israel became a Nation again. Even in Jesus' days walking with his disciples, it was not the unified Israel.

But today, you can see it clearly. Just turn on the news feed and you will see a united Israel.

The Bible is the only book in history that dares to predict the future, and it happens just as it was written.

You can have confidence in the Bible because it is proven to be God's word, repeatedly. No other religion can honestly say that about their books or writings because they are counterfeit.

Did you know that the Secret Service has two main divisions?

One is of course to protect the President and other leaders of the United States government, but the other is to fight against counterfeit money.

So how do they train their members to spot counterfeits?

You might be thinking, "They must study many counterfeit bills."

No.

They study the real thing! They get to know the real, the true and genuine money so intimately that they really know it. They know every assorted color of paper fiber that is interwoven into the one-hundred-dollar bill. They know the hidden messages deep within the text and in the pictures on each bill.

That is exactly what you must do with God's word. This is how you deepen your relationship with him. Get to know him, not the false religions of this world. Know God, know how to see Jesus pictured in stories like Abraham and Isaac, Joseph, Moses, and Joshua. He is in there, but you must look to see him.

His words are sufficient for you. Jesus said, "Heaven and earth will pass away, but My words will not pass away" (Matthew 24).

His words are as good as gold! They are heavy and precious words that never pass away, never rusts, keeps their beauty and worth forever.

Did you know that gold is the only element on the periodic table that does not corrode? Everything in our world, on this earth, is rusting away or corroding. Scientists tell us that rust, corrosion, or oxidation is another word for burning up. So, everything in this present world is burning up, just as the Bible says.

However, there is one exception. There is one element on that periodic table that is not burning up.

Yes, it is gold. Gold never corrodes.

What is beautiful about that is that God's word tells that the foundations and streets of heaven are made of gold.

God's word is the same, and even greater than gold.

"Heaven and earth will pass away, but My words will not pass away." Those were Jesus's words, and they shine bright like gold forever and ever.

Treasure his words deep into your heart. Read, and feed on his words every morning, every day to help you. His words are like that Manna, (that bread from heaven) they nourish and sustain you.

The Bible also says, "Your word is a lamp to my feet and a light to my path" (Psalm 119).

Billy Graham would read five Psalms and one Proverb every morning. He did this because there are around 31 days in a month and 31 Proverbs and reading five Psalms would get you through the entire Psalms in a month.

Reading the Psalms opens your heart to worship God. The Proverbs give you practical wisdom for your life and your walk with the Lord.

As I am writing this very sentence, I just finished waking up at 4 am to thank God, then asked to be filled with the Holy Spirit, and studied his word. This has been a life-changer for me and my relationship with God.

Do it! Just make yourself, your lazy sinful self (I also struggle with laziness and sin), get up early and start the day with God. Thank him, talk to him, ask him to overflow you with His Spirit and then get into his word so he will speak to you.

So, what is this book about? What is the purpose of finding Jesus in the Old Testament?

First, Jesus himself did this! In Luke chapter 24, he did it twice on Resurrection Day.

He walked seven miles with two of his disciples, in disguise, form Jerusalem to a village called Emmaus, about a two-hour journey, and the Bible says he made clear where he was found in all the scriptures.

What were those scriptures?

The Tanakh, the Old Testament.

At the end of their journey with Jesus the two men ate with him and as soon as Jesus broke the bread and blessed it, they recognized him, and he vanished from their site.

Then they recollected how their hearts were burning within them as he spoke to them and showed them where he was found in the Old Testament.

Don't you want your heart to burn with the Spirit of God?

It is like the burning of love you have felt with your mom or dad, or someone you love dearly, and you see them after a long time of being away.

Another reason for drafting this book is the fact that most churches, most pastors today ignore the Old Testament. They also ignore and neglect the book of Revelation.

They tend to allegorize or over-spiritualize these books. They say, "Much of Genesis is not literal" and they say the same about the last book too, the book of Revelation.

The truth is these two books are the "Bookends," the beginning and the end of the Bible. If you can trick people into thinking the first and last book is just a story, or only symbolic, then you can make them believe anything.

The fact of the matter is this, God made sure we have had access to the beginning of his word and the end. It is just as Jesus, who is also the Word of God, said, *"I am the Alpha and the Omega, the first and the last, the beginning and the end." (Revelation 22)*

Jesus said those words at the very end of the Bible, near the end of the last chapter in Revelation. He is the author and finisher of our faith. He is the Word of God.

In this book you will see him in the ancient books of the Bible. You will be blessed deep within your heart and soul as you get to know the creator of all things. He created you, and he knows you through and through.

As to this salvation, the prophets who prophesied of the grace that would come *to you made careful searches and inquiries, seeking to know what person or time the Spirit of Christ within them was indicating as He predicted the sufferings of Christ and the glories to follow." (1st Peter 1:10-11 NASB)*

He loves you through and through. He has a great and loving plan for your life. This is where you gain hope and peace.

So, get ready to go on a journey of a lifetime, the journey of discovering, and seeing Jesus in the Old Testament.

CHAPTER TWO: LAW OF MOSES - TORAH

You have heard of the Law of Moses. You saw in your mind the famous Ten Commandments written on stone tablets. That is the law of God, and it has been used in Judicial laws for a long time. However, the phrase, "Law of Moses" has another meaning, and it was used in Jesus' time.

When you read, "Law of Moses" or simply, "Moses" as it referred to scripture, it meant the books of the Bible written by Moses.

These first five books were originally called the Torah. It is still called the Torah today in Israel.

These books are Genesis, Exodus, Leviticus, Numbers, and Deuteronomy.

The Torah, or first five books are also called the Pentateuch. This is if you are referring to the manuscripts written in the Greek. "Pente" means five in Greek, thus the first five books of the Bible.

The reason for the Greek and not Hebrew is because of the dominance of the Greek Empire around 300 BCE or BC (Before Christ's birth). They made everyone speak and write in Greek.

In fact, the Greek language and culture stuck, even into the next Empire, the Roman Empire.

Remember the sign above Jesus on the cross?

It said, "Jesus of Nazareth, King of the Jews." John 19:20 states that this was written in three languages – Hebrew, Latin, and Greek – and was put on the cross of Jesus.

Hebrew was the language of Jesus and his Jewish people. Latin was the Roman language. Greek was the common language of business and the Gentiles. It is likely that Jesus and his disciples spoke all three of these languages.

Greek was the most common language of that time. This is why the New Testament was written in Greek.

You may have seen the word, Septuagint in your studies of the Bible. This simply refers to the Scribes or scripture translators who were forced to write in Greek.

The term Septuagint, meaning "seventy," refers to the seventy-two translators—six from each of the twelve tribes of Israel—involved in translating the Torah from Hebrew to Greek in the third-century BC.

However, the first written words of the Bible were in Ancient Hebrew, sometimes called, Paleo Hebrew. These were picture words just like you see in other world languages. Our English alphabet derived from the ancient Hebrew.

For instance, the first two words in the Hebrew alphabet are: Aleph, and Bet. That is where the English word, "Alphabet" derived from, "Aleph Bet."

The letter Aleph is the "Father" of the Aleph-Bet, whose original pictograph represents an ox, strength, and leader.

What is interesting is that Aleph originally meant "Strength" or "Father".

Bet originally meant, "House" or dwelling place. So, the Hebrew Alphabet can mean, "My Father's House", which is awesome and something Jesus said.

Now that the "Nuts and Bolts," the history of the Torah is finished, let us look where we see Jesus in the Old Testament books.

Ready for it?

Wait for it!

Here it is.

He is in all of it.

Yes, Jesus is found in every book of the Old Testament.

From the very first book, the first chapter, to the very end to the book of Chronicles (The Jewish Bible, the Tanakh, during Jesus' time).

1st Chronicles 22: *"He shall build a house for My name, and he shall be My son and I will be his Father; and I will establish the throne of his kingdom over Israel forever."*

When the disciples asked the Lord Jesus to teach them to pray, He gave them a model prayer. He took them to David's prayer in Chronicles: "Thy kingdom come." That was in David's heart. These brief and simple words gather up the hopes of centuries.

Jesus will come again and that is our Great Hope!

Starting in the very first few words of the Bible you see the Father, the Son, and the Holy Spirit.

In fact, the very first word, "Beginnings" in the Hebrew spells out the gospel, the good news of Jesus Christ (Christ means Messiah in Greek).

You will see this in the next chapter in detail.

So why do all of this?

Because you will experience the stoke, the flame in your heart that only comes from God the Holy Spirit. Your heart will burn for God as you see Jesus in the Old Testament. Jesus taught it and those two on that road to Emmaus had burning hearts as he opened those Old Testament scriptures and showed them all of the places where he was found in them.

You can see it. Jesus talking about Noah, and how his name means "Rest," and that the Ark rested on that mountain named Ararat which means "The curse is reversed."

And what day did the Ark rest?

It rested on the 17th day of the same month that Jesus walked with those two on that road to Emmaus. It was three days after the 14th day of that same month, Passover. That is the same day that Jesus was crucified and died on that cross. So, three days after Passover is resurrection day and the same day Noah's Ark found rest, and the curse was reversed.

This is just one of the places you will be visiting in the Torah, the first five books written by Moses, and you will discover Jesus and his good news.

Jesus is in the story of Abraham and Isaac going up the mountain, that same mountain that later is called Calvary. The son carries the wood on his back to be the sacrifice, and the father carries a torch in his hand signifying the father's wrath.

Then in Joseph's story, you see something amazing.

Over twenty-five percent of the book of beginnings, the book of Genesis is given to that one man, Joseph.

Why?

Because he was a huge picture, a portrait, a type of Jesus Christ.

He had a miraculous birth; he was the father's most favored son. He was the favored son of Israel. He was despised and hated by his own brothers, yet the father sends him out of Hebron (Means alliance or fellowship), to his brothers, the shepherds of Israel.

They hated him and conspired to murder him. They sold him for pieces of silver and handed him over to the Gentiles.

Later, he was falsely accused, and sent down into that place of the condemned. It was there that he told the two who were condemned with him their fate, one is restored to the King, the other is cursed, in three days.

He was later raised up out of that place of the condemned and brought before the throne. He was the only one found worthy to reveal God's plan, which was a time of great harvest and then a seven-year time of great trouble.

He was then made the right-hand man to the throne. All had to bow down to him except for the one who sat on the throne.

He who sat on the throne gave him a Gentile bride.

Later, he collects a great harvest, and when that last piece of grain was harvested in that Gentile land, his bride was with him and then the seven-year period of great trouble came. It was a time of Jacob's trouble and overall the face of the earth.

It was during this time that he saves all of Israel. He forgives his brothers who told their father, Israel that a wild animal had devoured their long-lost brother many years ago. He loves and shows amazing grace to his brothers as he wept with each one of them, each of the tribes of Israel.

Do you see why God gave Joseph's story over one-fourth, or twenty-five percent of the book of Genesis?

His life was a preview of Jesus. It also shows you an outline of God's plan.

This is just the beginning, there is so much more.

Moses is also a picture and a type of Christ.

When Moses was born there was an evil king who ordered all the Hebrew baby boys killed. Just like Herod tried to kill baby Jesus when he heard that the new King of Israel had been born.

Moses was miraculously saved as a baby, and he was raised as a prince. He later humbled himself and went to his own people to deliver them. He was rejected the first time.

The New Testament backs all of this up.

In Acts chapter seven, Stephen gives a history lesson to the religious leaders of Israel just before he was martyred.

"And on the second *visit,* Joseph made himself known to his brothers..."

"This Moses whom they disowned, saying, 'WHO MADE YOU A RULER AND A JUDGE?' is the one whom God sent *to be* both a ruler and a deliverer..." Acts chapter 7 (NASB20)

Stephen, a New Testament Jewish follower of Jesus, gave two major examples of "Typology" or "Types of Christ" in the Old Testament.

That same chapter in Acts tells us that he was full of the Holy Spirit, so much so that his face shined like an angel.

"And Stephen, full of grace and power, was performing great wonders and signs among the people..." "And all who were sitting in the Council stared at him, and they saw his face, which was *like the face of an angel."*

Stephens face shined much like the afterglow that was on Moses' face after he came down the mountain, where he was in the presence of the LORD.

"...the sons of Israel would see the face of Moses, that the skin of Moses' face shone." (Exodus 34 NASB20)

Stephen was full of the grace and power from the Lord, Yahweh, the God of Abraham, Isaac, and Jacob.

You have the same opportunity as Stephen. In fact, you have the same access to God's power through his Spirit, just like Abraham, Isaac, Jacob, Joseph, Moses, Joshua, David, Debrah, Ruth, Mary, Peter, John, Stephen, and Paul. You only need to be willing as you trust and obey the Lord and his calling. Remember, those were mere men and women just like you and me.

If you are a woman, he will use you in the same powerful ways he used Ruth, Debrah, Mary the mother of Jesus, Elisabeth, Mary Magdelene, Priscilla, and more.

We can be used by God by humbling ourselves and increasing in his Spirit. God gives your insight into this in the Old Testament: *"Not by might nor by power, but by My Spirit,' says the LORD..." (Zechariah 4 NASB20)*

SEE JESUS IN THE OLD TESTAMENT

The Holy Spirit must empower you in order to do anything amazing for God. The Spirit always points you to Jesus. When you are filled with the Spirit, you too will point people to Jesus. He is the only way, the truth, and the life.

This is why the Old Testament points to Jesus. Jesus himself said it, *"These are My words which I spoke to you while I was still with you, that all the things that are written about Me in the Law of Moses and the Prophets and the Psalms must be fulfilled." (Luke 24 NASB20)*

I have heard of someone reading Isaiah 53 to a devout Jewish man or woman, and they interrupt saying, "Why are you reading about Jesus in the New Testament to me". Then the one reading says, "Oh no, I am reading from the Tanakh, from the Old Testament prophet Isaiah."

At that point, these beloved Jewish people have an awakening and often surrender their lives to their Jewish Messiah, Yeshua.

He is the LORD in the Torah, the first five books written by Moses describes through types, and prophecy. You see, Jesus is the promised one that the prophets spoke of. He is also the one the Psalms and Proverbs speak of.

Adam and Eve knew him.

Able pleased him with his offering.

Noah believed him, found grace in him, and built the Ark.

Abraham was his trusting friend.

Isaac loved his bride like him.

Jacob wrestled with him.

Joseph displayed his heart and life.

Moses himself spoke with him face to face and prophesied of him just before he died.

You see, the Torah, the first five books of the Bible speak of Jesus through and through.

It is like being in the forest and seeing all the trees pointing upward as if they are crying out to you to look up and see him. Their branches are like arms and hands raised as they worship the creator. They sway in worship when the wind blows through them.

In that same way every part of the Torah shouts to you, "Look at Jesus, see him, and receive him. You can be renewed and filled with his Spirit."

You too can be like a great tree that is planted by the living water. You can point upwards to Jesus in how you live, and how you love. The Holy Spirit always points to Jesus. The word of God also points to him.

CHAPTER THREE: GENESIS 1 – IN BEGINNING

Words and names in Hebrew have meaning. Noah's name means rest, and Moses name means drawn out of water.

So, the names tell a story and illustrate a picture in Hebrew.

Did you know that Hebrew letters themselves do the same thing?

Yes, they do.

Each of these original letters paint a picture and tell a story.

Old Hebrew or Paleo-Hebrew is the oldest form of Hebrew and each letter in the Paleo-Hebrew tells a story.

Baresheet (Biblical Hebrew: בְּרֵאשִׁית, Bərēʾšîṯ) is the first word in the Bible. The Jewish Torah, and the New Testament book of John, alludes to the Torah. It is typically translated as "In beginning."

This is what it looks like in Hebrew today:

בְּרֵאשִׁית

Not only can you see a picture in each letter, but the order of these ancient Hebrew letters tells an amazing story.

To get the true and original meaning you must refer to the original Hebrew called the Paleo-Hebrew.

The first letter of the Hebrew Alphabet is Aleph.

Aleph is the root word for aleph, meaning 'master', 'leader,' 'strength' particularly denoting a master of the Torah, which further alludes to God. It was the symbol of the Ox for strength.

The second letter is Beyt or Bet.

It speaks of a dwelling place and a shelter.

When you look at the two first letters of the Hebrew alphabet you see Aleph, Bet, and this is where you get the English word "Alphabet."

Jesus is called, "The Word" in the gospel of John.

This is amazing because God is the first and the last. Jesus himself said: *"I am the Alpha and the Omega, the first and the last, the beginning and the end." (Revelation 21, NASB)*

He is simply outside of time. God is not subject to time; time is subject to him.

So here we see the first two letters; the first is Aleph which means Father, and speaks of God, of his strength and Power. The second is Bet, and it speaks of a dwelling place.

In john chapter one you can see this:

In the beginning was the Word, and the Word was with God, and the Word was God. He was in the beginning with God. All things came into being through Him, and apart from Him not even one thing came into being that has come into being...And the Word became flesh, and dwelt among us; and we saw His glory, glory as of the only Son from the Father, full of grace and truth." (John 1, NASB)

Now look at the combination of the first two letters of the first word in the Bible. You can see "Father" in it when you use the Hebrew letters. Perhaps Jesus spoke of this while teaching the two on that road to Emmaus.

The "A" and the "B" together pronounce "Ab" which is short for "Abba" the Hebrew word for dad or father.

Abraham's name אַבְרָהָם means "High Father" - "ab" (אב).

So, the first two letters say to you and me "Father."

What is so beautiful about that is God is also called our Hiding Place. He shelters us. Read the Psalms and you will see this over and over.

He is your hiding place and whenever you are afraid you can trust him.

Jesus said, "Abide in Me." That word can also mean Dwell, or Shelter in me.

When you piece together the first word of the Bible, Baresheet you will see the good news of the Son of God, Jesus.

The first letter is: בְּ - Bet which means house or tent.

The second letter is: רֵ - Resh which means person, highest person, or head.

When you put Bet and Resh together it creates the word: בָּר - "Bar" which means, "Son."

The next letter is: א - Aleph which means leader, strength, God, first.

When you put these three letters together, Bet, Resh, Aleph together it creates the word: בְּרָא – Bara which means, to create and can also mean, "Son of God."

The next letter is: שׁ – Shin which means to consume, destroy, or teeth.

The next letter is: י – Yod which means, hand, hands, works, arm.

The last letter is: ת – Tav which means, covenant, mark, sign or cross in the ancient Paleo Hebrew.

When you put all these meanings together into one statement it reads:

BERISHEET

בְּרֵאשִׁית

"The SON OF GOD will be DESTROYED with his HANDS on the CROSS".

Perhaps Jesus pointed this out on the walk to the village of Emmaus on resurrection day in Luke chapter twenty-four.

But wait, there is more.

The original ancient Hebrew, the Paleo-Hebrew used pictures for words.

The first letter in Berisheet is: בְּ - Bet which means house or tent, was a picture of a tent or tabernacle. You can see the Tabernacle as Jesus who is out dwelling place.

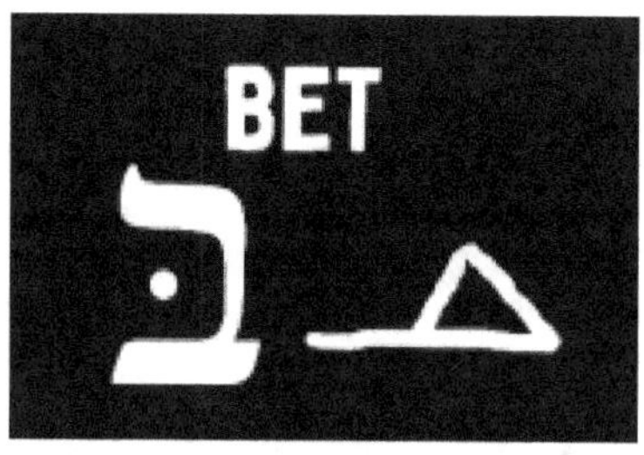

So, you can see how the first letter in Genesis was meant to be the illustration of a tent.

It is amazing because the tent is the same as "Tabernacle" or "Dwelling place." John chapter one says, "The Word was God…And the Word dwelt among us."

That word "dwelt" means "tabernacled" when you look-up that Greek word.

You could write that as the Word, Jesus or Yeshua tabernacled among us. It is like the word Immanuel which means, "God with us."

As you know, Hebrew reads form right to left not left to right like English.

So, look at the right side, at the second word of the Hebrew alphabet, Bet. It is a dwelling place, and the opening is pointing from right to left which speaks of looking to the future forever. The modern Hebrew looks like a shelter with a foundation below and a roof above.

The letter Bet in the Ancient Paleo Hebrew is clearly a drawing of a tent, and the opening is pointing from right to left. This tent speaks of the dwelling place of the Lord among his people, inside of the Tent of Meeting, the Holy of Holy place inside, where the Lord was speaking with Moses at the Mercy Seat.

Now let us take the first two letters and combine them. It creates the word Bar which means "Son" in Hebrew.

You have heard of the "Bar mitzvah", when a 13-year-old boy becomes a young man. The word Bar is son, and Mitzvah speaks of the Law of Moses. He becomes a "Son of the Law."

The second letter is: ר - Resh which means person, highest person, or head. So, Jesus is the person, the head of the tent or Tabernacle.

Now look at those two letters combined:

The next letter is: שׁ – Shin which means to consume, destroy, or teeth. It speaks of gnashing teeth.

You have heard of the elite special operations unit in Israel, Shin Bet.

That unit can be called "Defender Son," because it speaks of wrath, and judgement.

The original Paleo Hebrew showed it as teeth, as three teeth. Like teeth that devours their food. It was also known as a flesh hook as you can see in the picture. It was a three-point flesh hook.

The Shin is also where we get the "W" in English, and it is interesting that the word "Wrath" starts with a "W." God's wrath was poured out upon Jesus on the cross.

Now look at all of it together – remember Hebrew is read from left to right:

Now look at the last letter, at the far-left side of this word. It is the Tov which was always the cross in Ancient Hebrew. This is where we get our English letter "T."

It means a sign, a covenant, and the original shape was in fact a cross. Even in Ezekiel's time the "T" pronounced "Tav" was a sign, a symbol of a cross.

You can now see that the very first word of the Bible spells out the Good News of Jesus Christ.

The Bible opens with this message of him, and it closes with him. It is sealed with his promise.

You can have your heart sealed by him. He can dwell in your spirit and inside of your heart. If you have never received this good news, and you are not sure you are in him, in Christ you can receive this amazing gift right now.

To be born again, to become a child of God, through God the Son Jesus is the greatest thing anyone can ever do. It is simply by believing and trusting in Jesus, so simple that a young child can do this.

All you need to do is to pray, from your heart to God. This is business between you and God, the one who created you, and everything you have ever seen.

He loves you!

That is why he sent his only son, his perfect son down into this broken world, to die on the cross and shed his own blood for you. He then rose from the dead three days later in fulfillment of the ancient scriptures.

He is alive today, right now and he sees you.

So, if you would like to receive Jesus into your life, you can pray right now, from your heart to God.

Just repeat these words as your heart is bowed down to him. He loves you and he wants to bless you with a relationship for the rest of your life. So, repeat this prayer right now:

Dear God,

I know that I am a sinner

And I am sorry for my sin

Please forgive me

I believe Jesus died on the cross for me

I believe he shed his own blood for me

I also believe that he rose from the dead

I believe he is alive today

I choose to follow him from this moment forward

Thank you for loving me and forgiving me

I pray all this, in Jesus name

Amen.

Amen, my friend!

If you just prayed that and meant it, you are now a new child of God.

You may be feeling something amazing right now or you may feel nothing. It's not about your feelings but the promise of God in his word. You can trust in him.

If you have prayed that prayer and meant it, you are now his and he lives in your heart, and you live in him. In Christ, in his dwelling place forever.

Congratulations!

Be sure to be in fellowship with other believers and read your Bible daily. Get into a habit of waking up early every day to spend time talking with him (prayer), and reading his words.

I suggest reading John and continuing all the way to the end then starting at the beginning, in the book of Genesis.

If you need help reading and understanding the book of Revelation and the Old Testament, ask the Lord to help you.

You can also go to my channel on YouTube: The Whole Bible with George Crabb, and you can see a playlist called, "Revelation" and a playlist called, "How to find Jesus in the Old Testament."

You can watch it all for free and I know it will help you understand it and you will be blessed.

If this book has blessed you, please consider leaving a good review on amazon. Here is the QR code:

CHAPTER FOUR: GENESIS 3 – BRUISED HEEL

You have heard it said that the bruised heel in Genesis is about Christ. But how do you know for sure?

You can understand it through modern medical knowledge. You will see how that bruised heel prophecy makes perfect sense to a modern medical examination of a person's death and the position they died in.

You see it in Genesis chapter three. The scene is the Garden of Eden, where Adam and Eve have listened to the voice of the serpent, and they ate of the fruit of the tree that God told them not to eat from.

This is where sin and death entered the DNA of humankind.

God speaks to Adam, Eve, and the serpent, satan.

This is God himself telling satan, that he is going to bruise the Messiah, but the Messiah is going to destroy him.

The bruised heel has much more to it than you may realize.

First you can read what led up to this moment in a few verses from Genesis three:

Now the serpent was more cunning than any animal of the field which the LORD God had made. And he said to the woman, "Has God really said, 'You shall not eat from any tree of the garden'?"

The woman said to the serpent, "From the fruit of the trees of the garden we may eat; but from the fruit of the tree, which is in the middle of the garden, God has said, 'You shall not eat from it or touch it, or you will die.'" The serpent said to the woman, "You certainly will not die! For God knows that on the day you eat from it your eyes will be opened, and you will become like God, knowing good and evil."

When the woman saw that the tree was good for food, and that it was a delight to the eyes, and that the tree was desirable to make one *wise, she took some of its fruit and ate; and she also gave* some *to her husband with her, and he ate. (Genesis 3 NASB)*

You see, this is why Jesus called satan a liar and a murderer from the beginning.

Look at Jesus' very words:

They answered and said to Him, "Abraham is our father." Jesus said to them, "If you are Abraham's children, do the deeds of Abraham. But as it is, you are seeking to kill Me, a Man who has told you the truth, which I heard from God; this Abraham did not do. You are doing the deeds of your father." They said to Him, "We were not born as a result of sexual immorality; we have one Father: God." Jesus said to them, "If God were your Father, you would love Me, for I came forth from God and am here; for I have not even come on My own, but He sent Me. Why do you not understand what I am saying? It is *because you cannot listen to My word. You are of* your *father the devil, and you want to do the desires of your father. He was a murderer from the beginning, and does not stand in the truth because there is no truth in him. Whenever he tells a lie, he speaks from his own* nature, *because he is a liar and the father of lies." (John 8:39-44 NASB)*

Genesis three continues and now God enters the scene:

Then the eyes of both of them were opened, and they knew that they were naked; and they sewed fig leaves together and made themselves waist coverings.

Now they heard the sound of the LORD God walking in the garden in the cool of the day, and the man and his wife hid themselves from the presence of the LORD God among the trees of the garden.

Then the LORD God called to the man, and said to him, "Where are you?" He said, "I heard the sound of You in the garden, and I was afraid because I was naked; so I hid myself."

And He said, "Who told you that you were naked? Have you eaten from the tree from which I commanded you not to eat?"

The man said, "The woman whom You gave to be with me, she gave me some of the fruit of the tree, and I ate."

Then the LORD God said to the woman, "What is this that you have done?" And the woman said, "The serpent deceived me, and I ate."

Then the LORD God said to the serpent,

"Because you have done this,
Cursed are you more than all the livestock,
And more than any animal of the field;
On your belly you shall go,
And dust you shall eat
All the days of your life;
And I will make enemies
Of you and the woman,
And of your offspring and her Descendant;
He shall bruise you on the head,
And you shall bruise Him on the heel."
(Genesis 3 NASB)

God just made it very clear that the "Descendant" of the woman would bruise the serpent – satan's head. This speaks of his destruction as the bruised head is lethal.

This "Descendant" is none other than the Lord Jesus Christ or in Hebrew, Yeshua Hamashiach – it means the same thing.

Notice that he was the descendant of the woman, Eve, and not the man, Adam. This is so true because you can see that very first Christmas, when Jesus was born to Mary, he was conceived by the Holy Spirit. Joseph, who was Mary's husband had no sexual relations with her before Jesus was born. Isaiah prophesied this: *"Therefore the Lord Himself will give you a sign: Behold, the virgin will conceive and give birth to a son, and she will name Him Immanuel..." (Isaiah 7:14)*

Remember the Pharisees mocked Jesus who they claimed was born out of adultery: *"Abraham is our father." Jesus said to them, "If you are Abraham's children, do the deeds of Abraham. But as it is, you are seeking to kill Me, a Man who has told you the truth, which I heard from God; this Abraham did not do. You are doing the deeds of your father."*

They said to Him, "We were not born as a result of sexual immorality; *we have one Father: God." Jesus said to them, "If God were your Father, you would love Me, for I came forth from God and am here; for I have not even come on My own, but He sent Me. (John 8:39-42)*

God also said that satan would bruise the "Descendant" on the heel. This is not a permanent wound, because the Messiah was dead for three days.

Lividity

There is a medical term called "Lividity" and it is how medical examiners determine the position that a person died in.

They can conclude the position a person died in by the appearance of bruising. If someone died on their side, there will be bruising on their side. If someone died laying on their back, then there will be bruising on their back.

This is because the blood pools up at the lowest point of the dead body.

So, if one died upright, on a cross, then there would be bruising on the heel.

Jesus died upright, on the cross and therefore his heel was bruised. This fulfilled what God told satan thousands of years before the Messiah died on the cross.

Nicodemus and Joseph of Arimathea saw the bruised heel of Jesus when he was dead on that cross. These were the two righteous Pharisees who took care of the dead body of Jesus.

They both knew the scriptures well and may have seen that as one of the many prophecies Jesus fulfilled that day:

Joseph of Arimathea came, a prominent member of the Council, who was himself also waiting for the kingdom of God; and he gathered up courage and went in before Pilate, and asked for the body of Jesus. Now Pilate wondered if He was dead by this time, and summoning the centurion, he questioned him as to whether He was already dead. And after learning this from the centurion, he granted the body to Joseph.

Joseph bought a linen cloth, took Him down, wrapped Him in the linen cloth, and laid Him in a tomb which had been cut out in the rock; and he rolled a stone against the entrance of the tomb. (Mark 15:43-46)

Nicodemus, who had first come to Him by night, also came, bringing a mixture of myrrh and aloes, about a hundred litras weight. *So they took the body of Jesus and bound it in linen wrappings with the spices, as is the burial custom of the Jews. Now in the place where He was crucified there was a garden, and in the garden* was *a new tomb in which no one had yet been laid. (John 19:39-41)*

These men carefully wrapped Jesus dead body in clean linen. This is where the Shroud of Turin came from.

I used to be a critic of that shroud but if you research it, you will see it is legit. Researchers who were not believers in Jesus came together and studied the shroud. They all concluded that this was like nothing they had ever seen. They said the energy it would have taken to flash the image of that crucified, Jewish man on that linen, would have been greater than a Nuclear bomb flash.

The researchers also sampled the blood found at the pierced hands, feet, side, and yes, the head where the thorn crown was, and it was Jewish blood from the DNA test.

I am amazed that God had left that behind for us and for the world to see.

You can also see that they applied the Myrrh to Jesus dead body.

You recall Jesus' birth in Bethlehem, the wise men from the east gave gifts of Gold, Myrrh, and Frankincense.

What is even more amazing is that here you see the righteous Joseph wrapping Jesus dead body in clean wrappings.

At the birth of Jesus, another Joseph, who was also a righteous man, was wrapping baby Jesus in clean linen.

He was the husband of Mary, yet he had never had sexual relations with her. He had never defiled Mary, and he denied himself for the Son of God.

He was a man, a righteous man yet still a sinner and he gave this special woman to God.

Joseph of Arimathea also gave up his tomb to Jesus.

The Bible says that a dead man never defiled his tomb. It was also carved out of solid rock and never used. This speaks of Jesus being that precious stone, the corner stone.

Likewise, sinful man never defiled the womb of Mary. When Jesus was born, he burst forth out of that womb which was never defiled by dead, sinful men.

When Jesus rose again, he burst forth out of that tomb, like the womb. But this time he was born again, because he was the first fruits of life from the dead. He was the first fruits of new life. He made the way for you and me to be born again as children of God.

It is so amazing that God placed two very special men in Jesus' life. One at his birth, the other at his death and rebirth from the dead. Both righteous men were named Joseph.

Was that a coincidence?

Not at all. God meant for that to happen.

Not only was this Joseph, who was the husband of Mary sharing the same name as the Patriarch Joseph whose father was Jacob, but his father's name was also Jacob.

That's right. In the genealogy record, you can see this:

SEE JESUS IN THE OLD TESTAMENT

Jacob fathered Joseph the husband of Mary, by whom Jesus was born, who is called the Messiah. (Matthew 1:16 NASB)

God did this on purpose to show you how much he delighted in Old Testament Joseph. He did this because Joseph was a powerful foreshadowing and an illustration of Jesus.

After all, both were despised and rejected by their own, sold for pieces of silver, falsely accused, sent to the place of judgment, then raised up out of that place, made the right-hand to the throne, given Gentile brides, and saves Israel during the time of great trouble.

You will see that to a greater extent, in this book, in the chapter on Joseph as a type of Jesus.

Also, in Genesis 49 you will see that both Judah and Joseph had a prophecy from their father Jacob that showed a link to the Messiah. In fact, the early Rabbis were expecting Messiah son of Joseph. They thought that there would be two Messiah's. Messiah son of Joseph and Messiah son of David. What they did not realize is that it was always One Messiah, but two visits.

On the first visit he would be the despised and rejected, suffering servant. On the second coming, he is the powerful deliverer for Israel, the Lion of the tribe of Judah.

The New Testament points to both Joseph and Moses as types of Christ.

After Jesus died, rose again and ascended into Heaven, the church was growing, and many young Jewish men and women became followers of Yeshua – even if it meant losing their lives.

Stephen was one of them. Just before he was stoned to death, he was teaching the religious leaders a powerful message.

Stephen said this, by the power of the Holy Spirit, to these unbelieving Jewish leaders:

"The patriarchs became jealous of Joseph and sold him into Egypt. Yet God was with him, and rescued him from all his afflictions, and granted him favor and wisdom in the sight of Pharaoh, king of Egypt, and he made him governor over Egypt and his entire household.

Stephen continued:

"Now a famine came over all Egypt and Canaan, and great affliction with it, *and our fathers could find no food. But when Jacob heard that there was grain in Egypt, he sent our fathers* there *the first time. And on the **second visit**, Joseph made himself known to his brothers...*

"This Moses whom they disowned, saying, 'WHO MADE YOU A RULER AND A JUDGE?' is the one whom God sent to be *both a ruler and a deliverer with the help of the angel who appeared to him in the thorn bush. This man led them out, performing wonders and signs in the land of Egypt and in the Red Sea, and in the wilderness for forty years. This is the Moses who said to the sons of Israel, 'GOD WILL RAISE UP FOR YOU A PROPHET LIKE ME FROM YOUR COUNTRYMEN...'" (Acts 7 NASB)*

Joseph was made known on the second visit.

You can see that Moses identified himself as a type of Christ when he said, "God will raise up for you a Prophet like me..."

You can clearly see that the New Testament speaks of both Joseph and Moses as types and foreshadowing's of Jesus.

CHAPTER FIVE: NOAH – TYPE OF CHRIST

Noah was a picture, a portrait and type of Christ. He was preaching to that whole generation, he preached repentance, and at the same time he was preparing a place for him and his family, a dwelling place with many rooms. The door was open to the Ark, the saving place that was being prepared during that 120 years of preaching.

Did you know that Jesus is preparing a place right now? As he prepares this place for his own, the door is still open to enter that place with him.

Jesus said, "Come to Me, all who are weary and burdened, and I will give you rest." (Matthew 11:28)

Noah's name means "Rest."

The Ark rested on top of the mountain called Ararat.

Ararat means, "Curse Reversed."

Jesus directly said that the time around his return would be like the days of Noah and of Lot.

What were those days like?

Noah's time is described in the scriptures as a time of violence yet a time when people are getting married. Hmm...that sounds a lot like today.

Sounds a "Lot" like today – no pun intended. Lot's time was speaking of Sodom and Gomorrah, a time of great sexual perversion. This was expressed in the fact that the men of that city wanted to have sex with the two angels who arrived to take Lot and his family away before the wrath of God fell on that place.

In both cases, God was "catching away" or saving his people before a great time of tribulation and judgment.

This time of great trouble will be felt worldwide, and the flood of Noah was worldwide. Nothing would have lived if God had not saved a remnant.

Luke 17

And just as it happened in the days of Noah, so will it also be in the days of the Son of Man: people *were eating, they were drinking, they were marrying,* and *they were being given in marriage, until the day that Noah entered the ark, and the flood came and destroyed them all. It was the same as happened in the days of Lot: they were eating, they were drinking, they were buying, they were selling, they were planting,* and *they were building; but on the day that Lot left Sodom, it rained fire and brimstone from heaven and destroyed them all."*

Noah was a righteous man, and he preached for over one hundred years but only his seven family members believed him.

Revelation chapter one shows seven churches.

Noah was preparing a place for his loved ones, for a long time, just like Jesus is preparing a place for you.

Noah did not know the day or the hour that God would have them enter through the open door of the Ark. Then one day, suddenly and unexpectedly God called him and his family up, through that open door and then God shut it.

This is when that great flood, that tribulation period began. It was God's judgment poured out on a wicked, perverted, and violent generation. Just before that door was made shut, they were mocking Noah, and they could have even said, "Where is the promise of this Great Flood Noah?"

Progressive Christians today speak this way. Many of them are saying, "Where is the rapture?" Or "Where is the promise of his coming?"

But suddenly, Noah and his family were gone, safe in the Ark and about to float above the Earth.

If you are a believer in Jesus, you too are safe in Christ. He will either take you home to be with him if you die, or if he returns while you are still alive, you will be caught up, safe with him in that place he has been preparing for you.

Jesus spoke much about this.

John 14 (NASB)

"Do not let your heart be troubled; believe in God, believe also in Me. In My Father's house are many rooms; if that were not so, I would have told you, because I am going there to prepare a place for you. And if I go and prepare a place for you, I am coming again and will take you to Myself, so that where I am, there *you also will be..."*

Noah prepared this saving place, a place with many rooms, for those who he knew and those that knew him. This speaks of his family, and you who believe and trust in Jesus are his family.

In fact, the Bible uses a beautiful phrase, "In Christ". You can see this revealed over and over in the New Testament. In fact, it is repeated 89 times.

God uses this phrase to show you that you are in Him, you are under his wing so to speak, no longer on your own. You are clothed in his righteousness if you belong to Christ. You abide in him. Your dwelling place is in him, even when you mess up.

This should give you great comfort as a believer because when God the Father sees you, he sees his perfect Son Jesus' righteous standing, not your imperfect flawed life. This is because you are in Christ as a born-again believer. You are now a child of God, who has been born into his family.

In the Ark you can see a family: Noah, his bride and six others.

In the book of Revelation, you see Jesus with seven churches. This is how it was with Noah. He was the preacher of righteousness and prepared a place for his bride and his family. Then, when it was finished, God had them go into it and God shut the open door.

You can also see an open door in the book of Revelation. The church of Philadelphia has an open door and is spared from the hour of trial coming to the whole world. This speaks of the seven-year tribulation period and how this church is spared, or you could say caught up to be with the Lord.

"Behold, I have put before you an open door which no one can shut, because you have a little power, and have followed My word...Because you have kept My word of perseverance, I also will keep you from the hour of the testing, that hour which is about to come upon the whole world, to test those who live on the earth..." (Revelation 3)

John also sees this open door to Heaven right after Jesus addressed the seven churches. It was put into that order for a reason. It was stated after these things.

"After these things I looked, and behold, a door standing *open in heaven, and the first voice which I had heard, like* the sound *of a trumpet speaking with me, said, "Come up here, and I will show you what must take place after these things." (Revelation 4)*

After what things?

The church age. Because those seven churches paint a picture of the entire church history. This is like Jacob's prophecy over his twelve sons in Genesis chapter forty-nine.

Jesus referenced the time of Noah as to what the world would be like near his return. They were eating, drinking, and getting married. This speaks of a time of celebration and peace before the storm. However, it was also a time of violence all over the earth. It speaks much of what we see today.

Interestingly in Genesis six, the original Hebrew word used for violence is "Hamas."

It is incredibly interesting that God chose to destroy the world of that time.

In Genesis chapter 6, God explains why:

Genesis 6

SEE JESUS IN THE OLD TESTAMENT

Now the earth was corrupt in the sight of God, and the earth was filled with violence(Hamas). And God looked on the earth, and behold, it was corrupt; for humanity had corrupted its way upon the earth.

Then God said to Noah, "The end of humanity has come before Me; for the earth is filled with violence (Hamas) because of people; and behold, I am about to destroy them with the earth. Make for yourself an ark.

This is the original Hebrew word that God used for violence: חָמָס, Hamas, pronounced: "khaw-mawce". Yes, this the same word the demonic terrorist organization uses.

The meaning of this original Hebrew word is violence, wrong, cruelty, injustice.

This is what the world saw on Octobre 7th, 2023 in Israel. It was the same kind of violence that God saw just before the flood of Noah.

This is what you and I are seeing today, as I am writing this book. Columbia University in New York started protesting Israel and allied themselves with Hamas.

These dark protests spread to nearly all the universities and colleges around the world. This is a huge sign of the times because Jesus referenced the days of Noah as to what the world would look like near his return.

Hamas was voted in by the Palestinian people in Gaza. Israel gave all control over to the Palestinians in Gaza and left them with great infrastructure, but all they did was dig tunnels of terror, and shot lethal rockets at the people of Israel.

October 7th, 2023, saw this diabolical, demonic group, attack the people of Israel in a way not seen since the Holocaust of World War II. These evil people have the personality and spirit of satan inside of them. They are deceivers, liars, and murderers.

They were taking Meth just like the Nazis took it under Hitler. Thousands of them rushed in through the blown-up fence, and through tunnels to slaughter the innocent women, children, and men.

They had no mercy. They murdered children in front of the parents and parents in front of their children. They invented horrible ways to torture and murder. They were fulfilling the demonic will of their father, satan.

So, immediately the university students in the United States and throughout the world began to show their allegiance to Hamas. They held banners that said, "By any means necessary".

What they mean is they want Israel destroyed by any means. In other words, what Hamas did was justified to them. This is so evil.

They also cried out, "From the river to the Sea, Palestine will be free". They are saying from the Jordan river to the Mediterranean Sea, Palestine will be free of Israel. What they are saying is that they want Israel to be wiped off the map.

This is a huge fulfilment of what Jesus said about knowing the signs of the times and seasons.

Many pastors today say, "We don't focus on prophecy because it just distracts you from the real mission of loving others and serving".

This is not what Jesus said. He was rebuking the religious leaders of his time for not knowing the signs and prophecy of his first coming. The same could be said of the religious leaders today.

I have served on different Elder boards in different churches, attended many Pastors and leaders conferences and I can tell you that there has been a great shift away from the expectation of Jesus' return.

Pastors today are saying that Jesus' return is delayed, and they say this because they misinterpret the scripture. They claim that we must make disciples of all ethnic groups around the world first, then Jesus can come.

Really?

So, let me get this straight, God is leaving it all on our shoulders to usher him back?

No.

The fact of the matter is this, the gospel has been preached and disciples have been made throughout the world, to all ethnic groups.

Not only that, but you can see in the book of Revelation that God sends an Angel who flies around the world proclaiming the gospel to all tribes, peoples and languages. This happens during the tribulation period, before Jesus touches down on this earth.

These same people do not believe that Revelation is a future event but that it was all fulfilled by 70 A.D.

Emperor Domitian sent John to the Island of Patmos no sooner than 95 A.D. and in the book of Revelation Jesus calls it "Prophecy", it was not written before or around 70 A.D.

You see, God has given us prophecy and he expects you and me to be students of it. Prophecy fills up around thirty percent of the whole Bible.

Why would anyone neglect around one-third of the Bible?

You and I know better, and that is one of the reasons I am writing this book.

May the Lord help us.

Make no mistake my friend. Jesus will help us and rescue you and me. It is called the rapture, and it means being caught up to him.

Remember Noah's Ark, the place he prepared for his bride and family members. The door was open to them, and they went in and were together and they were floating above the earth during a time of great trouble on this earth.

1st Thessalonians 4

For the Lord Himself will descend from heaven with a shout, with the voice of the archangel and with the trumpet of God, and the dead in Christ will rise first. Then we who are alive, who remain, will be caught up together with them in the clouds to meet the Lord in the air, and so we will always be with the Lord. Therefore, comfort one another with these words.

Right after this passage, you see the tribulation period start. Remember these chapters were installed by the translators. This was originally one continuous passage:

1st Thessalonians 5

For you yourselves know full well that the day of the Lord is coming just like a thief in the night. While they are saying, "Peace and safety!" then sudden destruction will come upon them like labor pains upon a pregnant woman, and they will not escape.

This passage written by Paul, parallels the story of Noah leading up to the flood.

But Noah and his family found grace in the site of the Lord, and they were caught up together above the destruction below.

These are words of comfort for you and me. So let us comfort one another with these words.

The apostle Peter tied the flood of Noah and the future time of tribulation together. He pointed out that they will be similar in this passage:

2nd Peter 3

Know this first of all, that in the last days mockers will come with their mocking, following after their own lusts, and saying, "Where is the promise of His coming? For ever since the fathers fell asleep, all things continue just as they were from the beginning of creation." For when they maintain this, it escapes their notice that by the word of God the heavens existed long ago and the earth was formed out of water and by water, through which the world at that time was destroyed by being flooded with water. But by His word the present heavens and earth are being reserved for fire, kept for the day of judgment and destruction of ungodly people.

Then Peter follows this up with great hope and speaks of being patient and how important it is to be ready.

The Lord is not slow about His promise, as some count slowness, but is patient toward you, not willing for any to perish, but for all to come to repentance.

CHAPTER SIX: CHRISTOPHANIES

Abraham had close visits with his friend, Yahweh, the LORD.

The Lord was pleased with Abraham.

Why?

Because Abraham believed and trusted God, so God accounted it as righteousness. That means he had confidence in and trusted God.

Genesis 18

Now the LORD appeared to Abraham by the oaks of Mamre, while he was sitting at the tent door in the heat of the day.

When he raised his eyes and looked, behold, three men were standing opposite him; and when he saw them, *he ran from the tent door to meet them and bowed down to the ground, and said, "My Lord, if now I have found favor in Your sight, please do not pass Your servant by."*

In that passage you can clearly see that Abraham was visited by the Lord himself.

This is called a Christophany.

So you might be asking, "What is a Christophany?"

The word Christophany is a combination of two Greek words: *Christos* which means Christ and *phainein* which means to appear. When you combine them together you get Christophany which means Christ appears.

It is described as a pre-incarnate visit of Jesus Christ. Incarnate means in the flesh. Like when you go to a Mexican food restaurant and order Carne Asada, you know the word "Carne" means meat or flesh.

So, a Christophany is a visit from the Lord Jesus Christ before he was born in the flesh at Bethlehem.

He often appears as the angel of the LORD, the LORD of Heaven's Armies or the Captain or Commander of Heavens Armies.

When you see angel of the LORD, the Lord in all caps it is a placeholder for Yahweh or YHWH. The abbreviated form, YHWH is called the Tetragrammaton which is the covenantal name of God in the Hebrew Bible. It is written with the four consonants: **Y**odh **H**e **W**aw **H**e. This Tetragrammaton is the Greek word for the four letters.

Another pre-incarnate account is when the Angel of the LORD or Yahweh found Hagar near a spring in the desert, *So the angel of the LORD said to her, "Return to your mistress, and submit to her authority." The angel of the LORD also said to her, "I will greatly multiply your descendants so that they will be too many to count." (Genesis 16:9-10 NASB)*

He not only encouraged her, but he promised to increase her descendants which is something only God could do, not something angels do. This was Yahweh himself speaking to this heartbroken woman.

Hagars response to him confirms this: *Then she called the name of the LORD who spoke to her, "You are a God who sees me"; for she said, "Have I even seen Him here and lived after He saw me?" (Genesis 16:13 NASB)*

The words she used shows you that she had an encounter with the Lord, in the physical form and this can be called a "Christophany".

The first encounter was of course Adam, and then Eve. Then Enoch walked and talked with the LORD and one day he just walked right into Heaven with him without dying. He had such a close relationship with the LORD, that he simply was taken alive, and it was the first rapture in the Bible.

Then we see Abraham having a visit from the LORD.

Jesus himself confirms that Abraham saw him and that he was before Abraham: *Your father Abraham was overjoyed that he would see My day, and he saw* it *and rejoiced." So the Jews said to Him, "You are not yet fifty years old, and You have seen Abraham?" Jesus said to them, "Truly, truly I say to you, before Abraham was born, I am." (John 8:56-58 NASB)*

Jacob had a special encounter with the LORD, and you can see it here in Genesis:

Genesis 32

Then Jacob was left alone, and a man wrestled with him until daybreak. When the man saw that he had not prevailed against him, he touched the socket of Jacob's hip; and the socket of Jacob's hip was dislocated while he wrestled with him. Then he said, "Let me go, for the dawn is breaking." But he said, "I will not let you go unless you bless me." So he said to him, "What is your name?" And he said, "Jacob." Then he said, "Your name shall no longer be Jacob, but Israel; for you have contended with God and with men, and have prevailed." And Jacob asked him and said, "Please tell me your name." But he said, "Why is it that you ask my name?" And he blessed him there. So Jacob named the place Peniel, for he said, "I have seen God face to face, yet my life has been spared."

"I have seen God face to face..." that tells you everything you need to know about this being a Christophany. I can't wait to see the replay of this in Heaven. Imagine it, wrestling with the LORD.

You can see that the prophet Hosea points to Jacob having an actual physical wrestling match with the LORD himself. After this God gave Jacob a new name, Israel. Israel means governed by God.

Hosea 12

And in his mature strength he contended with God.
Yes, he wrestled with the angel and prevailed;
He wept and implored His favor.
He found Him at Bethel,

And there He spoke with us,
And the LORD, the God of armies,
The LORD is His name.

Can you imagine wrestling with the LORD? He must have laughed as Jacob was struggling to defeat him. Yet, the LORD was gentle with him just as a loving father is with his own son.

I raised a son who was much like Jacob. He is the most strong-willed boy I have ever known. He would rather die than do what he is told. I love him dearly and yes; he has tried to defeat me many times in wrestling matches. Of course, he would fight me, but as his father I was not out to destroy him but correct him.

The LORD dislocated Jacob's hip not to hurt him but to help him. He did this in the same way a good shepherd would break one of the legs of a wondering, rebelling lamb. If that lamb does not learn in a big way, it will continue to wonder off and eventually the wolves would kill it.

So, the LORD himself gave Jacob the same tough love to save him from himself and the evil one.

He does the same thing for you and me. If you belong to him, you will experience God's tough love at times. This may seem harsh when you go through it, but you will look back and thank him for it. God loves you and only does what is best for you.

Joshua had an encounter with the angel of the LORD or the Captain of Heavens Armies:

Joshua 5

Now it came about when Joshua was by Jericho, he raised his eyes and looked, and behold, a man was standing opposite him with his sword drawn in his hand, and Joshua went to him and said to him, "Are you for us or for our enemies?" He said, "No; rather I have come now as captain of the army of the LORD."

And Joshua fell on his face to the ground, and bowed down, and said to him, "What has my lord to say to his servant?" And the captain of the LORD'S army said to Joshua, "Remove your sandals from your feet, for the place where you are standing is holy." And Joshua did so.

What I love about this passage is how Joshua asks him, "Are you for us or for our enemies?" And this captain of the army of the LORD replied, "No". The Lord simply says no, without explanation.

What identifies this appearance as the LORD is the fact that Joshua fell on his face to the ground, bowed down, and said, "What has my lord to say to his servant?"

If this was an angel, he would have immediately said do not do that. Every angel knows better than to allow anyone to worship them, especially after seeing what happened to Lucifer.

Then he tells him to remove the sandals from his feet because the place where he was standing was holy. That is what the LORD said from the burning bush with Moses.

Look at Gideon's encounter with the pre-incarnate Jesus:

Judges 6

11 Then the angel of the LORD came and sat under the oak that was in Ophrah, which belonged to Joash the Abiezrite, as his son Gideon was beating out wheat in the wine press in order to save it *from the Midianites.*

12 And the angel of the LORD appeared to him and said to him, "The LORD is with you, valiant warrior." Then Gideon said to him, "O my lord, if the LORD is with us, why then has all this happened to us? And where are all His miracles which our fathers told us about, saying, 'Did the LORD not bring us up from Egypt?' But now the LORD has abandoned us and handed us over to Midian."

14 And the LORD looked at him and said, "Go in this strength of yours and save Israel from the hand of Midian. Have I not sent you?"
(Judges 6:11-14 NASB)

This passage is awesome. You can see a clear conversation between Gideon and the Angel of the LORD. If you compare verse 12 and verse 14 you can see it.

Verse 12 says "the angel of the LORD said to him", and verse 14 says "the LORD looked at him and said…have I not sent you?"

If you look closely, you can see that the angel of the LORD and the LORD are the same person speaking to Gideon. He appeared to him, then sat down with him and spoke to him in conversation. He appeared to him in the physical form.

Typically, when you see the phrase "**The angel** of the LORD" it speaks of God. If it says, "**an angel** of the LORD" it speaks of a messenger, which is just an angel.

There is another appearance that is different yet very powerful.

It is in the book of Daniel.

Many consider the fourth person in the fiery furnace with Shadrach, Meshach, and Abednego a Christophany: *Then Nebuchadnezzar the king was astounded and stood up quickly; he said to his counselors, "Was it not three men that we threw bound into the middle of the fire?" They replied to the king, "Absolutely, O king." He responded, "Look! I see four men untied and walking about in the middle of the fire unharmed, and the appearance of the fourth is like a son of the gods!" (Daniel 3:24-25 NASB)*

These three men were thrown into this extremely hot furnace because they refused to bow down and worship the golden image that king Nebuchadnezzar had set up. He made a law that all had to bow down to the 90-foot-high Golden image whenever the music was played.

These three young men refused to bow down and stayed upright. Imagine it, thousands of people face down toward the image, as the king demanded, and you see three men still standing up like a sore thumb.

Imagine it in the context of today. Imagine the whole world under the rule of Islam and they erect a huge image to their god Allah. Then they make a law that when you hear the Friday prayers singing from the public speakers, you are required to bow with your face to the ground and toward Mecca.

Imagine it. You and your two friends are at the world leaders conference, in a huge stadium, and the prayers begin. Millions go prostrate, face down in submission and obedience. However, you and your two friends remain standing upright in front of these powerful leaders. The cameras are recording live on every possible new channel and social media platforms.

You and your friends know the cost, that it will require your very lives if you do not submit. You believe in Jesus, and you will not conform to this world.

Suddenly, the head of this world governing force yells out, "Bow down now".

But you and your friends refuse to submit.

The leader orders an immediate public execution. They have a huge burning man size statue set up with a jail cell inside and it is ready to be lit. The leader orders it lit, and you can feel the heat of the flames from where you stand, about a football field away.

You can see the flames and the glow of the sizzling hot coals at the base of the fire. The evil leader orders the secret service agents to throw you and your two buddies into the hottest part of the fire. The hardened men, who took you to the edge of the flame, began to burn but you and your friends are perfectly fine.

Those large men suddenly caught fire and died.

You and your buddies are in awe that nothing bad is happening to you.

Suddenly, you see the Son of God, the LORD standing with you. He is smiling and he is brighter than the white-hot flames of the burning wood.

Then the people noticed their leader was in awe that there were four of you walking around in the flames.

Then you and your friends walk out, completely unharmed and the cords around your wrists were burnt to ashes.

You notice that there is no damage to your clothing, or your hair. In fact, you do not even smell like smoke. You realize that this was due to the LORD being there and protecting you and your friends.

This is what it was like for Shadrach, Meshach, and Abednego. They walked with the LORD just like Enoch did, and they were saved from death.

CHAPTER SEVEN: MELCHIZEDEK

Many believe that this High Priest named Melchizedek was a Christophany – a visit of Jesus Christ before his birth. The New Testament book of Hebrews makes it clear that Melchizedek was at a minimum a type and a picture of Jesus Christ. The book of Hebrews tells you that he had no mother or father and that he was the king of Salem (Peace), and Priest of God.

Hebrews 7

For this Melchizedek, king of Salem, priest of the Most High God, who met Abraham as he was returning from the slaughter of the kings and blessed him, to whom also Abraham apportioned a tenth of all the spoils, was first of all, by the translation of his name, king of righteousness, and then also king of Salem, which is king of peace.

Without father, without mother, without genealogy, having neither beginning of days nor end of life, but made like the Son of God, he remains a priest perpetually.

Hebrews makes it perfectly clear that this Priest from the city of Peace represented Jesus Christ.

The author of Hebrews also points to him not having a father or mother, without a genealogy, no beginning of days or end of life, but made like the Son of God. These parts of the scripture make many believe that this speaks of Jesus himself.

I will not say it only because the Bible does not say it. At a minimum he is like Christ, a powerful type of Christ.

After all, the scripture did say, "made like the Son of God". Like is the same as saying a "type of".

You can find him mentioned in Genesis 14, Psalm 110, and throughout the book of Hebrews.

We first see this mysterious person in Genesis, as he brings bread and wine to Abraham and then Abraham offers him a tenth or a tithe.

Genesis 14
And Melchizedek the king of Salem brought out bread and wine; now
he was a priest of God Most High. And he blessed him and said,
"Blessed be Abram of God Most High,
Possessor of heaven and earth;
And blessed be God Most High,
Who has handed over your enemies to you."
And he gave him a tenth of everything..."

Abraham gave a tenth to him. You know that in the Old Testament, the first tenth of your income, crops, whatever God has blessed you with was his. Many think this was giving a tenth away, but it was already his. Anything more than the tenth was considered giving to God.

This points to Melchizedek as a picture of God, because Abraham gave a tenth to him.

Jesus quoted Psalm 110, as speaking about himself. This is a Psalm of David, written around 1000 years before Jesus was born. In it you see this Melchizedek priest emerge once again.

Psalm 110
The LORD says to my Lord:
"Sit at My right hand
Until I make Your enemies a footstool for Your feet."
The LORD will stretch out Your strong scepter from Zion, saying,
"Rule in the midst of Your enemies."
Your people will volunteer freely on the day of Your power;
In holy splendor, from the womb of the dawn,
Your youth are to You as the dew.
The LORD has sworn and will not change His mind,
"You are a priest forever
According to the order of Melchizedek."
The Lord is at Your right hand;
He will shatter kings in the day of His wrath.

He will judge among the nations,
He will fill them with corpses,
He will shatter the chief men over a broad country.
He will drink from the brook by the wayside;
Therefore He will lift up His head.

In Matthew, Jesus directly quotes this Psalm as describing himself:

Now while the Pharisees were gathered together, Jesus asked them a question: "What do you think about the Christ? Whose son is He?" They said to Him, "The son of David." He said to them, "Then how does David in the Spirit call Him 'Lord,' saying,
'THE LORD SAID TO MY LORD,
"SIT AT MY RIGHT HAND,
UNTIL I PUT YOUR ENEMIES UNDER YOUR FEET"'?
Therefore, if David calls Him 'Lord,' how is He his son?" No one was able to offer Him a word in answer, nor did anyone dare from that day on to ask Him any more questions. (Matthew 22:45 NASB)

Wow, the wisdom of Jesus is so amazing. He simply used his own word that he gave to David 1000 years earlier and silenced his critics.

He simply showed them how David wrote about him, inspired by the Holy Spirit saying, "The LORD says to my Lord: Sit at my righthand...". Jesus is at the righthand of the Father. You see that his enemies become his footstool and later you see that he is a Priest forever after the order of Melchizedek.

You can see that this mysterious priest is at a minimum a type and picture of Jesus.

The High Priest was always a foreshadowing of Jesus. In the Holy Place of the Tabernacle or Temple it was his job to keep the seven-golden lampstands full of olive oil to keep it burning bright and hot. When that Menorah was fully lit and full, the Holy Place shined brightly, and it gave the people hope.

The Seven Golden Lampstands was symbolic of the Church, the bride of Christ. You can see this displayed in the book of Revelation, chapter one: *"...the seven lampstands are the seven churches".*

Jesus said to John, it is the Church. Yes, the church is not perfect and still sins. However, the true church belongs to Jesus, and he loves her as a groom loves his bride.

So, Jesus being the Great High Priest not only takes loving care of the Seven Golden Lampstands, but he also carries over his Heart the 12 tribes of Israel.

That's right. The Gold breastplate, with 12 precious stones was worn by the High Priest in that Holy Place, and these twelve stones represented each of those 12 tribes. All of them.

Jesus did not take that breastplate off and dispose of it when he created the mostly Gentile church. He did not call the twelve precious stones the church. In fact, he kept them over his heart the entire time.

Imagine it. When the High Priest pours the olive oil into the Seven Golden Lampstands, you are seeing a picture of Jesus filling the Churches with the Holy Spirit. The Spirit was always represented by the olive oil. So, this caused the lamps to shine brighter and hotter in the presence of the Lord.

What happens when those Lamps shine brighter from the pouring of the oil?

The brighter the light the more those precious stones look beautiful and bright. Those precious stones have a warm glow and even warm up the heart of the Lord. This is his will, that the church would love and receive the long-lost brother, Israel.

This is especially true today when entire generations of world leaders are shaking their fists at God, and Israel.

Both Joseph and Moses were major types of Christ. They both had Gentile brides and were in the Gentile land, when God had them save all of Israel during a time of trouble.

Remember those precious stones are still over Jesus' heart today.

In the Bible, Melchizedek, has a Biblical Hebrew name: מַלְכִּי־צֶדֶק, and it means "King of Righteousness," or "my king is Zedek". He was the King of Salem and Priest of El Elyon (often translated as "Most High God").

Jesus is called the Prince of Peace, and you that this mysterious priest and king from Salem. Salem means peace and he was the king over it. Some have suggested this was Jerusalem before it was officially called Jerusalem. Jerusalem means City of Peace. The Hebrew word is pronounced, Yerushalayim (Hebrew: יְרוּשָׁלַיִם). The "shalayim" speaks of Shalom or peace.

His name means King of Righteousness. What a fitting name for Jesus who is our righteousness.

Hebrews continues to use Melchizedek in reference to Jesus over and over. His name is brought up 8 times in this book alone. Look for yourself:

Hebrews 5

So too Christ did not glorify Himself in becoming a high priest, but it was *He who said to Him, "YOU ARE MY SON, TODAY I HAVE FATHERED YOU"; just as He also says in another* passage, *"YOU ARE A PRIEST FOREVER ACCORDING TO THE ORDER OF MELCHIZEDEK."*

God clearly calls Jesus His Son, and a forever Priest after the order of Melchizedek. This is powerful and it goes all the way back to Abraham.

Hebrews continues to compare Jesus and Melchizedek:

"He became the source of eternal salvation for all those who obey Him, being designated by God as High Priest according to the order of Melchizedek."

You can see him called High Priest once again. Remember this priest was in Abraham's time which was hundreds of years before Moses and Aaron. You know how Jesus is our Great High Priest who is our mediator between humankind and God. He keeps and takes care of that Seven Golden Lampstands, and he keeps the Twelve Precious Stones of Israel over his heart.

Joseph kept his brothers over his heart as he was in command of Egypt. He was the right-hand man to the throne, all had to bow the knee to him except he who sat on the throne. He had a beautiful new Gentile family, yet those precious brothers, who sold him down the road, were still over his heart.

Even before he saw them, he forgave them, he loved them and missed them dearly. When he saw them again, he wept. He wept because he loved them and wanted close fellowship with them again.

Hebrews 6

This hope we have as an anchor of the soul, a hope *both sure and reliable and one which enters within the veil, where Jesus has entered as a forerunner for us, having become a high priest forever according to the order of Melchizedek.*

That scripture "This hope we have as an anchor for the soul" has been in my home, on the wall for a long time now. Jesus is our anchor, firm and secure and no one can move that connection you have in him.

Did you know that the symbol for the early church was the anchor? Yes, before the fish it was the anchor. If you look carefully at the anchor, you can see a cross in it.

That passage also said, "which enters within the veil, where Jesus entered as a forerunner for us, having become high priest..." this speaks of that massive Temple Veil that separated the Holy Place, from the Holy of Holy Place.

During Jesus time, they would tie a rope around the ancle of the High Priest when he was to enter underneath of the Veil and into the Holiest Place (keep in mind that anchors have ropes). He went under that massive curtain to sprinkle the blood of the sin offering on the lid of the Ark, which was the Mercy Seat.

Many of these priests would die in that place. The designated high priest had bells on the hem of his priestly garment and if the other priests stopped hearing the bells they would pull him out and find him dead.

This is why they cast lots to see who the lucky one was each year. Remember John the Baptist's father Zechariah? The lot fell on him to be the acting High Priest and enter under the Temple Veil. You can see it spelled out in the New Testament gospel of Luke:

Luke 1

In the days of Herod, king of Judea, there was a priest named Zechariah, of the division of Abijah; and he had a wife from the daughters of Aaron, and her name was Elizabeth.

They were both righteous in the sight of God, walking blamelessly in all the commandments and requirements of the Lord. And yet they had no child, because Elizabeth was infertile, and they were both advanced in years.

Now it happened that while he was performing his priestly service before God in the appointed order of his division, according to the custom of the priestly office, he was chosen by lot to enter the temple of the Lord and burn incense. And the whole multitude of the people were in prayer outside at the hour of the incense offering. Now an angel of the Lord appeared to him, standing to the right of the altar of incense. Zechariah was troubled when he saw the angel, and fear gripped him. But the angel said to him, "Do not be afraid, Zechariah, for your prayer has been heard, and your wife Elizabeth will bear you a son, and you shall name him John.

Zechariah must have thought, "This is it; I am a dead man." He likely was there when one of the other priests died inside the Holy of Holy place.

Legend says that the Veil before the Most Holy Place was 40 cubits (60 feet) long, and 20 (30 feet) high, and it had the thickness of the palm of the hand. So, the Veil was so heavy, that, in the exaggerated language of the time, it needed 300 priests to lift it.

When Jesus died on that cross, the massive Temple veil was torn from top to bottom. This goes right along with the Hebrew passage how he was the forerunner entering under the veil.

He is our Great Anchor for our souls, anchored in that most Holy Place.

This means we have direct access to that Holiest place with God as people who are in Christ.

CHAPTER EIGHT: ISAAC – TYPE OF CHRIST

Abraham and Isaac has been a sore subject for many Bible critics. They hate the picture of Abraham holding the knife high as he was ready to plunge it into his son Isaac.

However, if you look at this account through the lens as a preview of one of the greatest moments in history, the cross, then you will be overjoyed when you see this story unfold.

Imagine it. Abraham hears from the Lord:

Genesis 22

"Take now your son, your only son, whom you love, Isaac, and go to the land of Moriah..."

Was Isaac his only son?

No. Remember Ishmael was his other son.

So why did God say, "Take now your son, your only son"?

Because God was painting a picture for you and me. Jesus was called the only Son of God.

Not only that, but Isaac was the son of the promise. Ishmael was not. In the New Testament, you can see that Ishmael represents the flesh and Isaac the Spirit: *"And you, brothers and sisters, like Isaac, are children of promise. But as at that time the son who was born according to the flesh persecuted the one who was born according to the Spirit, so it is even now". (Galatians 4:28-29 NASB)*

You and I who are in Christ, are in his likeness. In fact, the name, "Christians" was given to the early followers of Jesus as a mocking word meaning, "Little Christs".

God tells this Father Abraham to take his only son, whom he loves to the land of Moriah.

Did you know that this is the very first mention of LOVE in the Bible?

Yes, it is the first mention of love and when you see a first mention it is monumental. It also speaks of Abrahams deep love and connection with his son of the promise, Isaac.

So, the very first mention of love has to do with a father and his son, going to a mountain, to offer his only son as a sacrifice. Sound familiar?

In that first verse you also can see God tell Abraham to take him to the land of Moriah.

Where is Moriah?

It is the land that became known as Jerusalem.

Genesis 22

So Abraham got up early in the morning and saddled his donkey, and took two of his young men with him and his son Isaac; and he split wood for the burnt offering, and set out and went to the place of which God had told him.

The passage continues, and you see a donkey and two of his young men. Remember Jesus had two of his disciples, go and get the donkey for him on Palm Sunday. It was days before he became the ultimate sacrifice on that same hill.

You also see Abraham splitting the wood. The cross was made of wood.

Next you see "the third day", and Abraham tell his young men that he and his son will return to them. Remember Jesus told his young men who followed him, that he would die and in three days would be raised from the dead. In other words, he would return to them alive after being the sacrifice.

On the third day Abraham raised his eyes and saw the place from a distance. Then Abraham said to his young men, "Stay here with the donkey, and I and the boy will go over there; and we will worship and return to you."

Abraham said, ***"we will worship and return to you"***. As the scripture continues in Genesis 22 it becomes clearer that this is gospel, the message of the cross:

And Abraham took the wood for the burnt offering and laid it on his son Isaac, and he took in his hand the fire and the knife. So the two of them walked on together.

The father took the wood and laid it on his son. Wow. Jesus had the wood cross laid upon his shoulders and willingly carried it up this same mountain called Calvary.

The father carried the fire and the knife in his hand. The fire speaks of God's wrath, and the knife speaks of how Jesus was pierced on his side. The wrath had to be paid, and Jesus took the wrath of His Father fully for you and me.

Then it says, the *"two of them walked together"*. Remember Jesus was talking to his father on this same mountain when he said, "Father, forgive them…"

Look at what Isaac asks his father as they ascend this mountain: *Isaac spoke to his father Abraham and said, "My father!" And he said, "Here I am, my son." And he said, "Look, the fire and the wood, but where is the lamb for the burnt offering?"*

Isaac looks around and sees no lamb for the burnt offering, and wonders what is going on. Abraham gave him a prophetic answer saying, *"God will provide for Himself the lamb for the burnt offering"*.

It was around 2000 years later, John the Baptist sees Jesus arrive at the Jordan river and announces, "Behold, the Lamb of God who takes away the sin of the world".

Jesus is the Lamb.

Yes. Figuratively he is called the Lamb.

Remember it was the blood of the Lamb placed on the doorposts of the homes in Egypt that saved them from death.

Also, when one wanted to go to the Temple to worship God, the only requirement was to present the lamb to the priest at the entrance. It had to be an unblemished, perfect lamb. The priest would examine the lamb, not the person who came to worship, only the lamb.

After he examined the lamb, and it was found worthy, the worshiper was free to enter in and worship God.

This is so important. Remember this when you feel like you are not worthy to worship God. You may have sinned, and feel like God had had enough and has now rejected you. You might be telling yourself this, or others are saying it to you or about you. Perhaps one of satan's minions could be saying to you, "Look at what you did".

Satan will first tempt you into sinning and then after you sin say to you, "How could you do this to God, he is done with you".

All you need to say is this, "That is a good reminder, I am completely unworthy, but the Lamb is worthy, and I will freely worship him".

You and I are not worthy, as sinners, to enter the Temple, into the Holy Place and into the Holy of Holy Place. Jesus, the Lamb is worthy. He is without blemish, perfect, and righteous before the Father and we as believers are in Him forever.

This is what grace is all about. If you are honest, you still sin, and your own work cannot make it right. The closer your relationship is to the Lord Jesus, the more you realize your need.

So, we left off with Isaac asking his father, where the lamb was for the burnt offering. He saw the wood, the fire, the knife, and realized the most important thing was missing, the lamb.

If you do not have the Lamb, you will end up being the sacrifice that must be paid. But God provided the Lamb, he Himself.

Now look at Abrahams response:

Abraham said, "God will provide for Himself the lamb for the burnt offering, my son."

Did you see that?

God will provide for Himself the Lamb. His own son, his only son, whom he loved, Jesus. He is the Lamb of God himself.

The next scene continues to look like the scene of the cross. They make it to that place, the same place where Jesus was crucified over 2000 years later, and it looks the same:

Then they came to the place of which God had told him; and Abraham built the altar there and arranged the wood, and bound his son Isaac and laid him on the altar, on top of the wood.

Jesus was laid on top of the wood too. He was bound and nailed to that wood to be the payment for your sin and my sin. Jesus could have blinked his eyes and all who were crucifying him would have instantly died.

But he wanted to be bound and nailed to that wood. He came to this earth for this very mission. In that same way, you see Isaac being obedient to his father. He knew that his father was good, and that God was good. He trusted his father with his very life.

This was the same mountain we see in Jerusalem today. Mount Moriah is still there, and it was there that Jesus died on the cross. It was the place that God had shown Abraham, and it was the place where he was bound to the wood.

And Abraham reached out with his hand and took the knife to slaughter his son. But the angel of the LORD called to him from heaven and said, "Abraham, Abraham!" And he said, "Here I am." He said, "Do not reach out your hand against the boy, and do not do anything to him; for now I know that you fear God, since you have not withheld your son, your only son, from Me."

Here again, you can see the angel of the LORD. Remember from two chapters ago, when you see, "the angel of the LORD", it is likely speaking of the Lord himself, a Christophany, a preincarnate visit of Jesus.

Abraham was obedient and he trusted God. He knew that Isaac would somehow live and return home with him. This all speaks of what the Father and the Son did on that same mountain. This is amazing.

The Lord said to Abraham, "I know that you fear God, since you have not withheld your son, your only son, from Me".

He said it again. He said that Isaac was his only son.

Now, look at what happens next.

Isn't this exciting?

You get to read this story, and you can do it from the comfort of your home and go back in time, over 4000 years ago and see Jesus in the Old Testament.

This next seen shows you how God will provide the sacrifice:

Then Abraham raised his eyes and looked, and behold, behind him was a ram caught in the thicket by its horns; and Abraham went and took the ram and offered it up as a burnt offering in the place of his son.

A ram caught in the thicket by its horns.

A ram is a mature male sheep. Jesus was a 33-year-old man, a mature Jewish man who was called the Lamb of God by his cousin John.

Also, you can see it was caught in the thicket, the rams head was stuck by its horns. This speaks of the crown of thorns pushed down on the head of Jesus.

Being caught in the thicket also speaks of the stone that the builders rejected.

When Solomon's temple was being built the cornerstone was rejected according to history. It was tossed out, and caught in the thicket as it grew around it. Then the builders later realized that this was the Chief Cornerstone, and they quickly reached out to it and placed it in the Temple.

Abraham took the Ram as the sacrifice instead of his own son. This relieved him and Isaac. You too, can be relieved and take what Jesus offers if you have not. He is the gift from God, the payment for your sins. All you must do is receive him.

And Abraham named that place The LORD Will Provide, as it is said to this day, "On the mountain of the LORD it will be provided."

He named that mountain, there in Jerusalem; The LORD Will Provide. This is the name for Golgotha, or Calvary today. When you visit the Holy Land, when you travel to Israel and see Jerusalem, you will see that place, and remember on that mountain it was provided.

My dream is to stand on the Mountain of the Lord, the very mountain where Jesus paid the price at Golgotha, the very place where Jesus was crucified.

I want to stand there and talk with the Lord and feel his presence knowing that this place is special to him.

You can go there and see it.

You will see it in a later chapter, in Ezekiel and how it lines up: The Mount of Olives, the East Gate, Dome of the Tablets, and traditional Golgotha or Calvary.

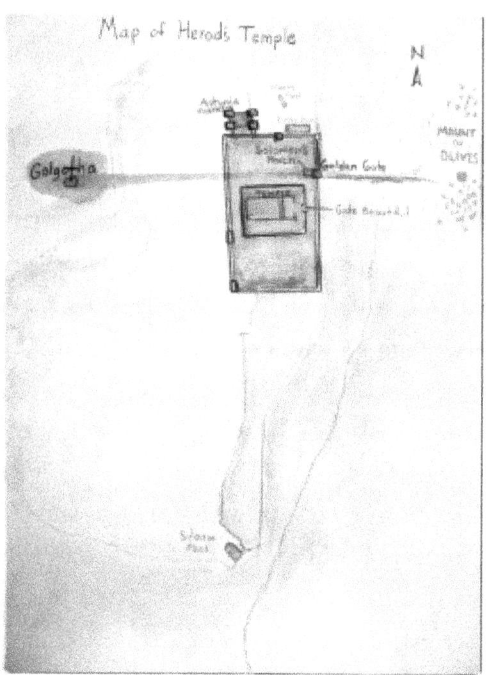

Perhaps I will lead a group to do this. I am scheduled for a pastors trip to Israel January of 2025. I will keep you posted on my YouTube channel: The Whole Bible with George Crabb.

Also, if you are enjoying this book, please consider leaving a positive review as this will help spread the good news that Jesus is in the Old Testament.

Here is the QR code to link you to amazon:

The proper name for that special place is Yahweh Yireh, Yahweh will Provide.

"...as it is said to this day, "On the mountain of the LORD it will be provided."

Genesis 22 finishes up with, "as it is said to this day...". Yes, it is still said to this day, and it is marvelous.

On the mountain of the LORD, it will be provided.

What will be provided?

What was provided?

Jesus, the Lamb of God who was slain, to take away the sins of the World. That is what was provided, and it was the most Magnanimous moment in history.

Isaac's Bride

The pattern of many Christ types is repeated in the Old Testament. You see story after story of a Type of Christ receiving his bride, and often she is a Gentile and then he saves Israel. For instance: Joseph with Asenath, Moses with Zipporah, then later Boaz with Ruth. All these real people in history were foreshadowing's of Jesus and his bride.

That is how God makes it clear, by repeating it over and over. It is like the one-thousand-year reign of Christ found in Revelation chapter 20 where God has it say "Thousand years" six times in seven verses. When something is repeated like that, it is not a coincidence or allegorical, it is on purpose.

In Abraham and Isaac's story, you will see this repeated story of the Bride of Christ as you see him send out his unnamed servant who was the head of his household to find a bride for his son Isaac.

It is assumed that this unnamed servant is Eliazar.

Eliezer means: "My God, the helper" or "Comforter", this speaks of God the Holy Spirit. He is called a helper and a comforter.

Jesus makes this connection about the Spirit:

But the Comforter, which is the Holy Ghost, whom the Father will send in my name, he shall teach you all things, and bring all things to your remembrance, whatsoever I have said unto you. (John 14:26)

Father Abraham has his mysterious unnamed servant show up in Genesis 24. But it seems to be on purpose because the Holy Spirit also does not speak of himself but points to Jesus.

"...when He, the Spirit of truth, has come, He will guide you into all truth; for He will not speak on His own authority, but whatever He hears He will speak; and He will tell you things to come. He will glorify Me, for He will take of what is Mine and declare it to you." (John 16:13-15)

In this Genesis chapter, the father dispatches his unnamed servant, who is the Helper or Comforter

The word "Helper" is mentioned 17 times in the Bible. The very first mention of it speaks of Eve, because God said Adam needed a helper.

The first family speaks of the trinity. You see a Father who was Adam, the son, Seth, and a helper, Eve.

Adam was also a type of Christ. Jesus said, when you have seen me you have seen the Father. Adam was made in God's image. He had no father except for God. Adam was put into a deep sleep (like Jesus' death), he was pierced on his side (Jesus was pierced on his side on the cross). And when that happened, the church, the bride of Christ was birthed.

How was the church given help? From the Spirit. The church is filled with the Holy Spirit.

Jesus himself called the Spirit the Helper. You can see it right here: *"But the Helper, the Holy Spirit whom the Father will send in My name, He will teach you all things, and remind you of all that I said to you. (John 14:26 NASB)*

The Holy Spirit searches for the bride of Christ and it is he who brings new believers to the Bridegroom.

Abraham was a picture of the Father God and Isaac His only Son, whom he loved. You just saw a powerful painting of that in Genesis chapter twenty-two.

Now, you are about to see what has happened after the death of Jesus on the cross, and his resurrection from the dead.

What happened?

His church, his bride, was found and is still being found today every time someone opens their heart to the Bridegroom Jesus. The Holy Spirit draws people to Christ.

So, the sequence of events is the birth of the promised one, the cross, the resurrection, the ascension to the Father, and the bride being found.

In this next chapter in Genesis, you are going to see that unfold.

Genesis 24

"...you will go to my country and to my relatives, and take a wife for my son Isaac."

She had to be part of his family. You and I are made children of God, part of the family of God when we have been born again to him. This happens through faith and by his grace in his Son Jesus Christ.

Then Abraham said, *"Beware that you do not take my son back there".*

Jesus is with the Father now and he has left to prepare a place for us, his bride. He will not return here until he finished preparing that place for you and me. He will not return here to earth until it is made new for his kingdom.

Also, in this passage you can see that Abraham's servant brings gifts for Isaac's bride to be. The Holy Spirit gives you gifts as well when you have been born again into God's family.

Isaac's bride Rebekah performs good work for the Servant of the father's house. She serves him water and his camels. She did this work with great joy and gratitude. We as Christians get to do wonderful work for the Lord, through the power of the Spirit.

Then when her work was done, the helper, like the Spirit, takes her away to the see her husband. She was caught up onto the Camel and taken away to the son of the promise.

In that same way the Bride of Christ, the Church will be caught up to be with the Lord forever. Because of the mark of the Holy Spirit in you, God will take you and me up to him when we die or when he returns.

SEE JESUS IN THE OLD TESTAMENT

CHAPTER NINE: JOSEPH – TYPE OF CHRIST

2076-1966 BC Before Christ

Over twenty-five percent of the book of Genesis, the first book of the Bible, the book of beginnings is dedicated to one man, Joseph.

Why?

Because Joseph was a portrait of Jesus.

You may have heard it, "He was sold for silver, hated by his own, and then becomes the second in command."

But there is so much more.

In fact, Joseph's story reveals God's plan from Jesus' first coming all the way through his second coming and beyond.

What? You might be asking, "Are you sure about that?"

Yes.

And you will see it in this chapter.

Psalm 81

Blow the trumpet at the new moon,
At the full moon, on our feast day.
For it is a statute for Israel,
An ordinance of the God of Jacob.
*He established it as a **testimony in Joseph***
When he went throughout the land of Egypt.

The word, "Testimony" in the Tanakh (Old Testament), is always used in reference to God Himself.

How was Joseph a testimony of Jesus?

The following list shouts it out to you:

He had a miraculous birth.

He was the father's most favored son.

He was despised and rejected by his own.

He was sent out of Hebron (means alliance or fellowship).

His own conspired to murder him.

He was sold for pieces of silver.

He was handed over to the Gentiles.

He was falsely accused.

He was sent down to the place of the condemned though innocent.

He tells the fate of the two prisoners condemned with him.

In three days one lives, and the other was cursed to death.

He was later raised out of that place of judgment.

He was brought before the throne.

He was the only one found to reveal the sealed plan of God.

Every knee had to bow except for he who sat on the throne.

He is given a Gentile bride.

He gathers a great harvest before the 7 years of famine or trouble.

The seven-year period of trouble was over all the face of the earth.

During that time, the sons of Israel will come to him bowed down.

He will then reveal to his brothers that HE IS ALIVE.

He will forgive them and show great mercy and grace to them.

They will weep together, individually with him (like Zechariah 12).

He will explain to them that he fulfilled God's plan.

He will save Israel.

He will unite his new family to his old as One forever.

He will give them the best of the land.

Who was just described, Joseph or Jesus?

In that list you may have noticed it started out in the past tense, present tense and then in the future tense. This was done on purpose, to show that the past tense were those things which were fulfilled by Jesus. The present tense are those things which are taking place now, and the future tense are those things which will take place after these present things.

Now we can go into Joseph's story in detail. God is into these kinds of details because he put them there for us so that we can understand books like Revelation.

Past

Both Joseph and Jesus had miraculous births. Both, Rachel and Mary were Israel's most favored woman.

Rachel looks a lot like Mary. God favored her because he granted her a son. Mary was highly favored by God, after all, she was chosen to give birth to the Messiah Jesus.

Genesis 30:22

Then God remembered Rachel, and God listened to her and opened her womb. So she conceived and gave birth to a son, and said, "God has taken away my disgrace." And she named him Joseph, saying, "May the LORD give me another son."

During that time of Mary, many of the young Israeli women were hoping that they could be the one to give birth to the expected Messiah.

Israel was expecting him.

Most of the people, including the religious leaders, were expecting the Messiah. This is evident in the scriptures because when Jesus was riding on the donkey, through the East Gate the people were crying out, "Save us now, Hosanna, Hosanna, blessed is he who comes in the name of the Lord."

The religious leaders were often asking Jesus if he was the Messiah, and so they asked because they thought he could be him. In fact, some of them knew he was.

Both Joseph and Jesus were the Father's most favored son.

Genesis 37:3

Now Israel loved Joseph more than all his other sons, because he was the son of his old age; and he made him a multicolored tunic.

He was highly favored and loved by his father. Jesus was loved by his Father in Heaven as you can see when John baptized him: *After He was baptized, Jesus came up immediately from the water; and behold, the heavens were opened, and he saw the Spirit of God descending as a dove and settling on Him, and behold, a voice from the heavens said, "This is My beloved Son, with whom I am well pleased."(Matthew 3:16-17 NASB)*

Yet, being the most loved and favored son made his brothers hate him. They were envious of him. Just look at Joseph's story:

Genesis 37

And his brothers saw that their father loved him more than all his brothers; and so they hated him and could not speak to him on friendly terms.

Then he shared to his envious brothers how they were bowing down to him through his prophetic dreams. This enraged them even more.

Then Joseph had a dream, and when he told it to his brothers, they hated him even more. He said to them, "Please listen to this dream which I have had; for behold, we were binding sheaves in the field, and behold, my sheaf stood up and also remained standing; and behold, your sheaves gathered around and bowed down to my sheaf."

Imagine it. They were already envious and hated him. And now he tells his older brothers that in his dream, he saw their sheaves of grain bowing down to his upright sheaf: *Then his brothers said to him, "Are you actually going to reign over us? Or are you really going to rule over us?" So they hated him even more for his dreams and for his words.*

They were livid. Perhaps they tore their clothing in anger and rage. We see this same type of anger when Jesus tells the High Priest Caiaphas, that he himself indeed was the Messiah, the Son of God and that he would see him at the right hand of the power.

Jesus basically told this most powerful, religious leader that he will have to bow down to him. Caiaphas was so livid; he tore his clothes and wanted him dead: *And the high priest said to Him, "I place You under oath by the living God, to tell us whether You are the Christ, the Son of God." Jesus said to him, "You have said it yourself. But I tell you, from now on you will see the Son of Man sitting at the right hand of power, and coming on the clouds of heaven." Then the high priest tore his robes and said, "He has blasphemed!" (Matthew 26 NASB)*

This is like the scene with Joseph and his brothers. They hated him and they could not speak peacefully to him.

Then Joseph has another dream.

Then he had yet another dream, and informed his brothers of it, and said, "Behold, I have had yet another dream; and behold, the sun and the moon, and eleven stars were bowing down to me."

Now Joseph tells his brothers his second dream from God, and it is the same theme yet a different picture. This time it is the sun, moon, and eleven stars bowed down to him.

This time his father Israel or Jacob hears it, and he rebuked him and then he gives us insight into what the sun and moon and the eleven stars mean.

"...Am I and your mother and your brothers actually going to come to bow down to the ground before you?"

Jacob just interpreted a New Testament scripture for you and me. You see, in the book of Revelation, the sun, moon and twelve stars. From what you see in Genesis, you can interpret the meaning. This is why it is so important to realize that the Bible interprets the Bible.

Look at Revelation chapter twelve: *A great sign appeared in heaven: a woman clothed with the sun, and the moon under her feet, and on her head a crown of twelve stars; and she was pregnant, and she cried out, being in labor and in pain to give birth. (Revelation 12 NASB)*

Genesis tells you that this speaks of Israel. Yes, Israel is mentioned in the book of Revelation. Then it continues to speak of Jesus who is an Israeli. Yes, Jesus is Jewish, and born of Israel.

Revelation twelve continues to tell the story of birth of Jesus and how satan wanted to kill him through Harod: *And the dragon stood before the woman who was about to give birth, so that when she gave birth he might devour her Child.*

The woman in that passage was Mary who gave birth to the Messiah. Now you see a direct connection between Rachel and Mary. Remember Israel or Jacob called the sun and moon himself and his wife Rachel.

Revelation twelve continues to give an overview, a big picture view of Israel, Mary, Jesus' birth, death and resurrection, and how he was caught up to the Father: *And she gave birth to a Son, a male, who is going to rule all the nations with a rod of iron; and her Child was caught up to God and to His throne. (Revelation 12 NASB)*

Now let's head back to Genesis where you are seeing these amazing comparisons, these similarities between Joseph and Jesus.

Genesis 37

And Israel said to Joseph, "Are your brothers not pasturing the flock in Shechem? Come, and I will send you to them." And he said to him, "I will go." Then he said to him, "Go now and see about the welfare of your brothers and the welfare of the flock, and bring word back to me." So he sent him from the Valley of Hebron, and he came to Shechem.

Joseph said, "I will go". He showed perfect obedience to his father.

He was sent out of fellowship (Hebron means alliance or fellowship) with his father to the sons of Israel who hated him. Both Joseph and Jacob knew the sons of Israel had a deep hatred toward Joseph, but they both agreed to do this.

This speaks of the Father and Jesus doing the same thing. You see, God sees way past the present and he sees all the way to the moment when all of Israel will be saved.

Joseph went after his brothers and found them at Dothan

He comes to his brothers who were the shepherds of the father's flock, and he finds them leading the flock in Dothan. (Dothan means laws and customs).

This is the way Jesus found the shepherds of Israel, the religious leaders were leading the flock of God, the people of Israel into the laws and customs only. They forgot about the heart of the law which is love. They were to love the Lord God with all their hearts, minds and souls and to love their neighbors as themselves. This was not happening when Jesus found these shepherds.

This is how Joseph found them at Dothan; he found them in the laws and customs.

The next few verses in Genesis 37 show how Joseph's brothers, the shepherds of the father's flock plotted to kill him. The Religious leaders plotted to kill Jesus in that same way.

When they saw him from a distance, and before he came closer to them, they plotted against him to put him to death.

They conspired to murder him. They conspired against him to kill him. This is exactly what they did with Jesus: *"...the Pharisees went out and conspired against him, as to how to destroy him"* (Matthew 12:14).

Genesis 37

They said to one another, "Here comes this dreamer! Now then, come and let's kill him, and throw him into one of the pits; and we will say, 'A vicious animal devoured him.' Then we will see what will become of his dreams!"

This is an amazing part of Joseph's story because this is what the Religious leaders said about Psalm 22, where it says, *"They pierced my hands and feet"*. They changed it after Jesus time because it spoke of him.

So, what did they change it to say?

*"Dogs are all around me, a pack of villains closes in on me **like a lion [at] my hands and feet.**"*

The Masoretic Text is the Old Testament manuscript and was written hundreds of years after Christ.

It was primarily copied, edited, and distributed by a group of Jewish men known as the Masoretes between the 7th and 10th centuries of the Common Era (CE) or Anno Domini (AD). The oldest known complete copy, the Leningrad Codex, dates from the early 11th century CE or AD.

However, the Dead Sea Scrolls are the oldest manuscripts, and you can see it written this way in Psalm 22:

A company of evildoers have enclosed me.
They have pierced my hands and feet.

Remember Joseph's brothers plotted and conspired to kill him. And what was their lie to their father Israel?

...will say, 'A vicious animal devoured him.'

This is what Israel has been told for a long time now. But Psalm 22 does not say that. The Dead Sea Scrolls have proven it.

Wow. The goodness of God to reveal the location of those scrolls in 1947.

Joseph's story continues to show the story of Jesus even to our time today. It is not over. God still has a great and awesome plan to save Israel, just like he did in the story of Joseph.

Now, back to this unfolding story:

Genesis 37

So it came about, when Joseph reached his brothers, that they stripped Joseph of his tunic, the multicolored tunic that was on him

They stripped him of his tunic. This was to shame him, and it speaks of what happened two-thousand years later at the cross.

Jesus was stripped of his tunic: *And they stripped Him and put a red cloak on Him (Matthew 27:28-30)*

The soldiers were mocking Jesus, and they put a scarlet red tunic on him. They did this to Jesus to mock him as King. Joseph's brothers were doing the same thing when they said, *"...we will see what will become of his dreams".*

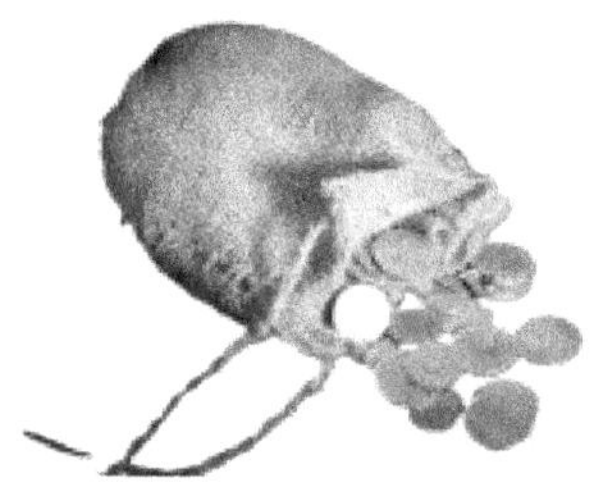

Genesis 37

He was sold for silver

And Judah said to his brothers, "What profit is it for us to kill our brother and cover up his blood? Come, and let's sell him to the Ishmaelites...so they pulled him out and lifted Joseph out of the pit, and sold him to the Ishmaelites for twenty shekels of silver

He was sold for silver, and it was his brother Judah who thought of it.

Then one of the twelve, whose name was Judas Iscariot, went to the chief priests and said, "What will you give me if I deliver him over to you?" And they paid him thirty pieces of silver. (Matthew 26:14-15)

The name Judas is derived from the name Judah.

Is that a coincidence?

Not at all. Only God himself could have placed all of these details in Joseph's story, two-thousand years before it came to pass in Jesus' life.

This was also prophesied about through Jeremiah, at least five-hundred years before Christ: *"Then was fulfilled what had been spoken by the prophet Jeremiah, saying, "And they took the thirty pieces of silver, the price of him on whom a price had been set by some of the sons of Israel..." (Matthew 27:9)*

He was sold as a slave for twenty pieces of silver. Jesus was sold for thirty pieces of silver by Judas. Judas and some of the religious leaders, the shepherds of Israel set this price together.

Twenty pieces was the going rate of a slave in Joseph's time and thirty pieces of silver was also the price of a slave during Jesus' time.

Jesus said: *"...whoever wants to become prominent among you shall be your servant, and whoever desires to be first among you shall be your slave; just as the Son of Man did not come to be served, but to serve, and to give His life as a ransom for many." (Matthew 20:26-28 NASB)*

Joseph was sold for silver, as a slave to the Ishmaelites. They were handing him over to the Gentiles because they were not to shed the blood of their own brother. This is what was happening with Jesus.

The religious leaders could not Judicate the death penalty anymore because it was taken away from them by the Romans. So, they handed Jesus over to the Gentiles.

During the first part of the first century, the Roman Emperor Caesar Agustus had had enough of the Jews and finally removed the judicial authority from them at the ascension of Caponius. Jewish historian Josephus recorded this transfer of power: *"part of Judea was reduced into a province, and Caponius, one of the Equestrian order of the Romans, was sent as a procurator, having the power of life and death put into his hands by Caesar!"*

In the minds of the Jewish leadership, this event signified the removal of the scepter or national identity of the tribe of Judah because they could no longer give the death penalty.

But God promised in his prophecy that the scepter or right to rule shall not depart from Judah until Shiloh or Messiah comes. This could not happen until Messiah.

In their view the prophecy was not fulfilled.

However, there was a young man named Yeshua in Hebrew, or Jesus in the Greek, who had already arrived in Israel. He was born of the young Jewish woman who was also a virgin. She just happened to be of the tribe of Judah.

He already taught in the Temple, at the age of twelve and the religious leaders were amazed at his wisdom.

So, these leaders had the ruler staff taken away from them and Shiloh had come. He was in their midst. He fulfilled the prophecy.

What prophecy? The prophecy that Jacob, or Israel told around two-thousand years before the time of Jesus.

In Genesis 49, Jacob tells his boys to gather around him and he prophesied over each one of them. When he told Judah his prophecy, for his tribe, it was all about the Messiah.

Genesis 49
"The scepter will not depart from Judah,
Nor the ruler's staff from between his feet,
Until Shiloh comes,
And to him shall be the obedience of the peoples"

The name Shiloh was synonymous with the title Messiah. This was well known during the time of Jesus.

The scepter was the tribal identity, associated with the right to impose capital punishment. As you saw, it had departed from the kingdom of Judah, early in the first quarter of the first century.

The historian Josephus was from the time of Jesus and points out that the Sanhedrin had no authority over capital cases: *"After the death of the procurator Festus, when Albinus was about to succeed him, the high-priest Ananius considered it a favorable opportunity to assemble the Sanhedrin. He therefore caused James the brother of Jesus, who was called Christ, and several others, to appear before this hastily assembled council, and pronounced upon them the sentence of death by stoning. All the wise men and strict observers of the law who were at Jerusalem expressed their disapprobation of this act...some even went to Albinus himself, who had departed to Alexandria, to bring this breach of the law under his observation, and to inform him that Ananius had acted illegally in assembling the Sanhedrin without the Roman authority." (Antiquities 20:9 written by Josephus)*

You just saw Jesus of Nazareth and his brother James as historical figures, but Josephus also declares that the Sanhedrin had no authority to pass the death sentence upon any man

This is why they went to Pilate. They handed Jesus, their own Jewish brother, over to the Gentiles to be put to death. They simply wanted him to be gone, out of their lives forever.

In that same way, the brothers of Joseph wanted him out of their lives, but they would not kill him.

So, he was bound and taken away by these Gentiles.

Joseph then was under the hand of this Captain of the Guard, named Potiphar.

He was the picture of Pontius Pilate, after all he was also a Captain of the Guard, so to speak.

The wife of Potiphar later falsely accused joseph, and he was sent to the place of Judgement or the place of the condemned.

Imagine it, he was treated as guilty even though innocent. Even Potiphar must have known that. He must have suspected his wife of telling lies. But he still sent him away as guilty. He sent him down into that place of the condemned.

Jesus was innocent. Even Pilate knew this, but he was all about his own reputation more than he was about doing what was right.

Genesis 39

So Joseph's master took him and put him into the prison, the place where the king's prisoners were confined; and he was there in the prison.

At the place of the condemned, two were sent there with him. Joseph tells one of them that he will be restored to life in three days. The other was cursed to death in three days.

This was the same fate of the two criminals on either side of Jesus on the cross. One was saved when he turned to Jesus and said, "Lord, remember me in your Kingdom". Jesus turned to him and told him that he would be with him in paradise.

Genesis 40

Then Joseph said to him, "This is the interpretation of it: the three branches are three days; within three more days Pharaoh will lift up your head and restore you to your office; and you will put Pharaoh's cup into his hand as in your former practice when you were his cupbearer".

Joseph tells this condemned man that in three days he would be restored, to live and serve the king.

Three days?

That's right. Remember Jesus was raised from the dead in three days. Not only Jesus but many others were raised with him.

Psalm 105:18 tells us about Joseph, *"They shackled his feet with chains, and they bound him in irons..."*

The ancient Rabbinic source, Pesiqta Rabbati, uses phrases from Psalm 22 to characterize Messiah (the midrash on Psalm 22 makes a similar citation): *The Holy One, blessed be He, began telling him of the conditions, and said to him: "Those who are hidden with you their sins in the future will force you into an iron yoke...And because of their sins your tongue will cleave to the roof of your mouth." (161a-b)*

So, you can see that the ancient Rabbis believed Psalm 22 spoke of the Messiah. And you saw how they used Psalm 105, about Joseph being chained in an iron yoke to explain the Messianic Psalm.

So, Joseph is down in this dark pit; he was innocent yet here he is paying a price he did not owe. Jesus paid the price he did not owe.

The chief prison keeper noticed Joseph and gave him authority over it all. He did not supervise anything under Joseph's authority, because the LORD was with him; and the LORD made whatever he did prosper.

In that same way, Jesus descended into the place of the condemned and he oversaw it all. This is what was happening after Jesus died on the cross.

In the book of Revelation, you can see Jesus holding the keys of Hades and death. He has been given all authority over the place of the condemned.

Psalm 105:18-22, connects Joseph to Messiah:

"They shackled his feet with chains, and they bound him in irons; until the time when his word proved true, God's utterance kept testing him. The king sent and had him released, the ruler of peoples set him free; he made him lord of his household, in charge of all he owned correcting his officers as he saw fit and teaching his counselors wisdom."

Genesis 41:14
Then Pharaoh sent and called Joseph, and they quickly brought him out of the pit..."

He was raised out of that place of the condemned, which was the dungeon, and he was brought up before the throne.

The king, who sat on the throne, had dreams that no one could interpret. So he sent for Joseph.

As he stood before the throne, he was the only one found worthy in all the land, to reveal the secrets of God's future plan. The scripture in Genesis says *"...there is no one who can interpret it..."*

This speaks of what you can see in the book of Revelation. John has this powerful vision in Heaven, and he sees the throne.

Revelation 5:1-5

Then I saw in the right hand of him who was seated on the throne a scroll written within and on the back, sealed with seven seals. And I saw a mighty angel proclaiming with a loud voice, "Who is worthy to open the scroll and break its seals?" And no one in heaven or on earth or under the earth was able to open the scroll or to look into it, and I began to weep loudly because no one was found worthy to open the scroll or to look into it. And one of the elders said to me, "Weep no more; behold, the Lion of the tribe of Judah, the Root of David, has conquered, so that he can open the scroll and its seven seals"

Just like Jesus was the only one found worthy to take the scroll, Joseph was the only one found to reveal the plan of God to save many including all of Israel. Also, the scroll in Revelation has seven seals and Pharoah's dream had repeated mentions of seven.

You can clearly see how you can use the whole Bible to understand the Bible. This is the better way. It is better than reading a commentary or a book. Yes, this is just a book you are reading now; however, this book is designed to turn you toward the Bible.

Some will say that this is made up. That you cannot stretch scripture into saying that Joseph was a picture and a type of Christ.

You can see in the New Testament book of Acts, that Stephen connected both Joseph and Moses as foreshadowing's of Jesus. He did this as he was referencing the Old testament scriptures just like you and I are doing right now.

Now back to Joseph.

He was despised and rejected by his own and they conspired to kill him. He was sold for pieces of silver, handed over to the Gentiles, falsely accused, sent to the place of the condemned, where he tells the fate of two who were condemned with him.

He was raised up out of that place and brought before the throne. He was the only one in all of the land who was found worthy to reveal the future plan of God which was a time of great harvest and then a seven-year time of great trouble.

Now you can see Jesus standing in front of the throne of Heaven through the life and story of Joseph.

Right after he reveals the prophetic dreams of this king who sat on the throne, he is highly exalted. He was honored and placed at the right hand of the throne as all bow the knee to him except for he who sat on the throne.

Genesis 41

"Can we find a man like this, in whom is the Spirit of God?" Then Pharaoh said to Joseph, "Since God has shown you all this, there is none so discerning and wise as you are. You shall be over my house, and all my people shall order themselves as you command.

Only as regards the throne will I be greater than you." And Pharaoh said to Joseph, "See, I have set you over all the land of Egypt."

You can see this same scene in Heaven after Jesus took the scroll out of the right hand of, he who sat on the throne. He was glorified and honored as they praised him and shouted out, *"Worthy is the Lamb who was slain, to receive power and wealth and wisdom and might and honor and glory and blessing!" (Revelation 5:11 NASB)*

You can see the same picture with Joseph as he was standing before the throne, *"...they called out before him, "Bow the knee!" Thus he set him over all the land of Egypt. (Genesis 41:43 NASB)*

The New Testament book of Philippians shows us that every knee shall bow to Jesus:

"...God highly exalted Him, and bestowed on Him the name which is above every name, so that at the name of Jesus EVERY KNEE WILL BOW, of those who are in heaven and on earth and under the earth, and that every tongue will confess that Jesus Christ is Lord, to the glory of God the Father". (Philippians 2:9-11 NASB)

At this point you must be amazed at how much Joseph looks like Jesus. I know that I am. But there's more because the story continues:

Genesis 41:42

"Then Pharoah clothed him in garments of fine linen

and put a gold chain about his neck."

Above: you can see the gold chains and the fine linen that the high Egyptian officials would wear.

SEE JESUS IN THE OLD TESTAMENT

Again, look at how Revelation is revealed in Joseph's story. John sees the same picture of Jesus with gold and a new tunic:

Revelation 1

"...one like a son of man, clothed with a long robe and with a golden sash around his chest"

Above: Jesus' new tunic with a golden sash

Then Joseph was given a new name:

And Pharaoh called Joseph's name Zaphenath-paneah. (Genesis 41:45)

This new name means: "God speaks, and he lives" and "Savior of the Age". Those are clear descriptions of Jesus.

In Revelation you can see Jesus with his new name:

Revelation 3

"...'The one who overcomes, I will make him a pillar in the temple of My God, and he will not go out from it anymore; and I will write on him the name of My God, and the name of the city of My God, the new Jerusalem, which comes down out of heaven from My God, and My new name."

Joseph was before the throne, all had to bow the knee to him except he who sat on the throne. He was given new garments of fine linen, a gold chain, and now he receives his new name which means God speaks and he lives.

See how Revelation compares?

It is like God wants you to use stories like Joseph, Moses, and Joshua, as types to understand the last book of the Bible, Revelation.

We left off seeing Joseph with a new name. Jesus has a new name as well, *"...and my own new name." (Revelation 3 NASB)*

Present

The next scene in Joseph's story explains so much to you, me and the whole church. This is huge. This will help you understand how God has not replaced Israel with the church, but that he has received a Gentile bride until the time of the harvest of the Gentiles is over, and then all of Israel will be saved.

Now back to Joseph's story.

He was given a Gentile bride.

Genesis 41:45

"And he gave him in marriage Asenath."

The king on the throne just gave Joseph a bride named Asenath. Joseph must have been overwhelmed at this point. He surely saw how God was in control and how he restored him. Joseph knew that this was all part of God's amazing plan to save as many as possible.

Joseph began an intimate relationship with his Gentile bride. She bore him two sons, and these two sons will become legit tribes of Israel through the house of Joseph. It was like they were grafted in.

If you are a Gentile believer in Jesus, you should be very thankful that God has this same plan for you. If Israel did not reject Jesus the first time, then this would not have been possible. But God, in his great wisdom, brilliantly weaved this story together for you and me.

Paul understood this at the end of Romans chapter eleven.

Romans 11

In relation to the gospel they are enemies on your account, but in relation to God's choice they are beloved on account of the fathers; for the gifts and the calling of God are irrevocable. For just as you once were disobedient to God, but now have been shown mercy because of their disobedience, so these also now have been disobedient, that because of the mercy shown to you they also may now be shown mercy. For God has shut up all in disobedience, so that He may show mercy to all.

Oh, the depth of the riches, both of the wisdom and knowledge of God! How unsearchable are His judgments and unfathomable His ways!

So, thank God for his mercy and grace upon you.

Joseph was given his Gentile bride, and Jesus has his mostly Gentile bride.

You can see the same scene in the book of Revelation. Jesus talks to his Gentile Churches in Revelation chapters two and three.

Joseph collects a great harvest before the great famine.

This speaks of what Paul wrote in Romans chapter eleven.

Romans 11

Some of the people of Israel have hard hearts, but this will last only until the full number of Gentiles comes to Christ. And so all Israel will be saved.
As the Scriptures say,
"The one who rescues will come from Jerusalem,
and he will turn Israel away from ungodliness.
And this is my covenant with them,
that I will take away their sins."

*Many of the people of Israel are now enemies of the Good News, and this benefits you Gentiles. Yet they are still the people he loves because he chose their ancestors Abraham, Isaac, and Jacob. For God's gifts and his call can **never** be withdrawn.*

According to that passage God will collect a great harvest of Gentiles and when the last one has come in, then all of Israel, at one moment in time, will be saved.

This is just like Joseph collecting a great harvest in the Gentile land, and when that last piece of grain was brought into his storehouse, the seven-year period of famine came.

The scriptures say this famine was over the whole face of the earth and it was for seven years.

It was during this time of great trouble, or you could say Jacob's trouble, that Israel was saved.

Paul backs this up by saying, *"As the Scripture say..."*

He was referencing an Old Testament prophecy about Israel, from Isaiah and he connected it to the people of Israel not the church.

Future

In Joseph's story, during the seven-year period of famine, he was the world's only hope. If anyone was starving and needed bread to live, they had to go to him during this world famine.

Genesis 41:53-55

The seven-years of plenty that occurred in the land of Egypt came to an end, and the seven-years of famine began to come, as Joseph had said. There was famine in all lands, but in all the land of Egypt there was bread. When all the land of Egypt was famished, the people cried to Pharaoh for bread. Pharaoh said to all the Egyptians, "Go to Joseph. What he says to you, do."

During this time of great trouble all must go through Joseph to live.

In that same way, all have to go through Jesus to live.

Many pray to God when great trouble comes their way. But God the Father points them to Jesus.

The people were going to the king who sat on the throne in Egypt, and he re-directed them to his right-hand man Joseph.

The Holy Spirit points you to Jesus. The Father points you to Jesus.

Jesus said, *"I am the way, and the truth, and the life. No one comes to the Father except through me. (John 14;6)*

Jesus also said that he is the bread of life.

This was the greatest need during this time, bread.

Now you are going to see something amazing.

Jacob or Israel was troubled, and he realizes that they were going to die. He tells his sons to go down to Egypt and buy food. They all knew this famine was severe. The sons of Israel had no idea that they were about to see their long-lost brother Joseph. They figured he was dead, out of their lives long ago. But God had a plan.

After the great harvest, during the time of the great seven-year famine or great trouble, Israel is saved.

How were they saved?

They came bowed down to their own brother, who they had rejected many years ago and then he reveals to them that he is alive.

Genesis 45:4-5

"I am your brother, Joseph, whom you sold into Egypt.
And now do not be distressed or angry with yourselves because you sold me here, for God sent me before you to preserve life."

Previously, Joseph was speaking the Egyptian language and now he speaks to them in their own Hebrew and says to them, "Ani Yosef" – I am Joseph.

Someday Israel will bow the knee to their long-lost brother, Yeshua. Perhaps he will say to them in Hebrew, "Ani Yeshua"

Then Joseph tells them not to be angry with themselves because God sent him down to Egypt to save lives.

Many blame the Jewish people for the death of Jesus on the cross. But the scriptures make it very clear that it was God's plan from the beginning. It was his masterful plan to save as many as possible.

The Father wanted his son Jesus to go to that cross and die. This was the only way to save many people. It was the only way to preserve life.

Joseph said they meant it for evil, but God sent him to preserve life. He was a clear foreshadowing of Jesus. He understood God's hand in it all.

The Jewish people are Joseph's brothers. They are also Jesus' brothers, and they will see him at the right hand of the Power.

"I want you to understand this mystery, dear brothers and sisters, so that you will not feel proud about yourselves. Some of the people of Israel have hard hearts, but this will last only until the full number of Gentiles comes to Christ. And so all Israel will be saved. As the Scriptures say..." (Romans 11:25 NLT)

When all of Israel is saved they will see him for who he is. They will be shocked, and they will weep together.

Right after Joseph made himself known to his brothers, he wept with each one of them individually. They were the fathers of the twelve tribes of Israel, and they each wept with their brother.

Genesis 45

Then he fell on his brother Benjamin's neck and wept, and Benjamin wept on his neck. And he kissed all his brothers and wept on them, and afterward his brothers talked with him

They looked upon him whom they had left for dead years ago and they wept together.

Zechariah 12

"And I will pour out on the house of David and on the inhabitants of Jerusalem the Spirit of grace and of pleading, so that they will look at Me whom they pierced; and they will mourn for Him, like one mourning for an only son, and they will weep bitterly over Him like the bitter weeping over a firstborn.

After they realized he was alive they went to their father Israel and gave him the good news, "He's alive".

"...the spirit of their father Jacob revived. And Israel said, "It is enough; Joseph my son is still alive..." (Genesis 45:27-28)

Jacob was revived. Israel finally saw that he was alive, and when he did he was revived. This speaks of life from the dead.

This is exactly how Israel will be saved. When they finally believe that Yeshua is alive, they will be revived. This is so beautiful.

This is Romans chapter eleven being fulfilled.

For all those years Israel thought that his most favored son, the son he loved the most, was devoured by a wild animal, like a lion.

But now it is a new day. It is life from the dead.

It reminds you of that Prodigal Son story in Luke chapter fifteen. Remember the son left his father after he received his inheritance early, while his father was still alive. He left him and went to a land far away.

After his money ran out, his so-called friends ran out on him. They abandoned him (Like the countries of the world abandon Israel during and after the Holocaust).

Then a great famine arose. This speaks right into Joseph's story and the coming Great Tribulation.

It was during the famine that Joseph's brothers come back to him, and it was the severe famine that drove the Prodigal son back to his father's land.

When Israel was finally united to Yosef or Joseph they were saved. They were not going to die anymore.

In the Prodigal son story, the father tells the other son, who had never left him and was angry about the great celebration of his returned son, to try and understand. He told him that we had to celebrate because his brother was dead and is now alive again.

The other brother was angry and even bitter toward his long-lost brother who was now received by the father. Many churches are like that of the other brother. They hate Israel. They hate that God is already blessing the returning sons of Israel even before they have fully come back.

In Romans chapter eleven you can see the same thing: *For if their rejection proves to be the reconciliation of the world, what will their acceptance be but **life from the dead**...*"

Then he continues and illustrates how Israel is the Olive Tree and that the Gentiles have been grafted into that tree, but God will graft the natural branches, Israel back in again:

Romans 11

If the first piece of dough is holy, the lump is also; and if the root is holy, the branches are as well.

*But if some of the branches were broken off, and you, being a wild olive, were grafted in among them and became partaker with them of the rich root of the olive tree, **do not be arrogant** toward the branches; but if you are arrogant, remember that it is not you who supports the root, but the root supports you. You will say then, "Branches were broken off so that I might be grafted in." Quite right, they were broken off for their unbelief, but you stand by your faith. Do not be conceited, but fear; for if God did not spare the natural branches, He will not spare you, either. See then the kindness and severity of God: to those who fell, severity, but to you, God's kindness, if you continue in His kindness; for otherwise you too will be cut off. And they also, if they do not continue in their unbelief, will be grafted in; for God is able to graft them in again.*

For if you were cut off from what is by nature a wild olive tree, and contrary to nature were grafted into a cultivated olive tree, **how much more will these who are the natural branches be grafted into their own olive tree?**

Paul started this beautiful chapter eleven, of the book of Romans with this: *I say then, God has not rejected His people, has He? Far from it! For I too am an Israelite, a descendant of Abraham, of the tribe of Benjamin.*

God has not rejected his people Israel as some churches and Christians claim. Paul makes it clear here and you do not need a theologian to interpret that for you.

Paul also identified himself as a member of the tribe of Benjamin.

Benjamin was the last-born son of Israel. He shared the same full bloodline as Joseph. Paul was the last of apostles - those who saw Jesus, who spent time with him.

Remember, it was twelve apostles and then Judas betrayed Jesus and died and so there was eleven. But when Paul, who was of the tribe of Benjamin joined them, they were complete as twelve.

It is interesting that Joseph was the eleventh born son and Benjamin was the twelfth. There is something special about that because if you look at each brother as a timeline, or as Israeli history, you can see that Joseph arrived on the scene and then Benjamin.

Joseph was thought to be dead for a long time, but then he was discovered to be alive.

When they came back the second time and were reunited with their long-forgotten brother. He gave them new clothing and food for their families. Joseph took great care of them even though he had his Gentile wife with him.

His new family (Gentile bride) and his old family (Israel) were then united as one family forever.

Remember Jacob or Israel received both of Joseph's sons as his own and they became legitimate tribes of Israel.

So, you can clearly see that Joseph's story was meant to show you Jesus. You can use his story to understand God's plan with the mostly Gentile Church and with Israel.

You can understand the book of Revelation more clearly. God meant for this, and it is marvelous.

Joseph's story takes up 1/4 or 25% of the book of Genesis. That is like majoring in History and spending your whole final year studying one man.

Why did God do this?

Because God purposefully wanted us to see His plan through the life of Joseph who was a portrait of the greater than Joseph, God the Son, Jesus.

There are two more amazing gems God placed in the scriptures to honor his servant Joseph:

Near the end of the book of Ezekiel you can see Joseph's name on the East Gate of the New Temple. You will see more about this in the Ezekiel chapter in this book.

Ezekiel describes walking out of the north gate of the Temple complex and then around to the Gate that faces East. He sees a river flowing out of the south side of the gate.

Earlier he described the names of the sons of Israel on all of the gates. Then on that most glorious gate, the East Gate, you see the name Joseph.

Secondly, Jesus had an earthly stepdad with the name of Joseph. He was there when baby Jesus was wrapped in cloth and was born from a womb that was not defiled by man. At Jesus death, there was another man named Joseph who wrapped his dead body in cloth and placed him in a tomb, just like the womb that was not defiled by any dead man. Then in three days Jesus burst forth out of that tomb, like the womb. He was the first fruit to God, and made it possible for us to live.

It is amazing how God did this! God is so good!

If this book is a blessing to you, would you please consider leaving a positive review from wherever you purchased it? This will help spread this message to the world, that Jesus is indeed in the Old Testament.

CHAPTER TEN: GENESIS 49 – TWO MESSIANIC PROPHECIES

Judah was prophesied as being the tribe through which the Messiah would come. But did you know that Joseph had a Messianic prophecy as well? Jacob has been living in Egypt, and he is old. He tells all twelve of his sons to gather around him so he can tell them the future of each one of their tribes. This becomes prophetic and two of these prophecies point to the future Messiah.

Look for yourself:

Judah

"The scepter will not depart from Judah,
Nor the ruler's staff from between his feet,
Until Shiloh comes,
And to him shall be *the obedience of the peoples..."*

Joseph

"Joseph is a fruitful branch,
A fruitful branch by a spring;
Its branches hang over a wall.
"The archers provoked him,
And shot at him and were hostile toward him;
But his bow remained firm,
And his arms were agile,
From the hands of the Mighty One of Jacob
(From there is the Shepherd, the Stone of Israel),
From the God of your father who helps you,
And by the Almighty who blesses you
With blessings of heaven above,
Blessings of the deep that lies beneath,
Blessings of the breasts and of the womb.
"The blessings of your father

Have surpassed the blessings of my ancestors
Up to the furthest boundary of the everlasting hills;
May they be on the head of Joseph,
And on the top of the head of the one distinguished among his
brothers."

You can clearly see that both Judah and Joseph have prophecies pointing to Messiah.

Judah was shown as the Lion and having the Scepter to rule.

The Roman historian Josephus recorded that the term "Scepter" refers to their tribal identity and to perform the judicial punishment on capital offenses such as murder.

Even during the captivity in Babylon the tribe of Judah kept their judges.

Furthermore, the word "Shiloh" was taught by the early Rabbis and Talmudic authorities as referring to the Messiah.

But the scepter had departed around 6-7 A.D.

King Herod's son, Herod Archelaus, was dethroned and sent to Vienna. He was the second son of Herod the Great.

The older son, Herod Antipater, was murdered by his own father, Herod the not so Great. There was a saying during that time that said it was safer to be a dog in that household that a member of that family.

Herod Archelaus was placed over Judea as "Entharch" by Caesar Augustus and he was broadly rejected, and so he was removed from the throne around 6-7 A.D.

He was replaced by a Roman procurator named Caponius.

The legal, judicial power of the Sanhedrin was immediately restricted and the right to perform adjudication over the capital cases was lost. This was the standard Roman policy when they ruled a foreign land.

This right to Judicate in capital matters would have meant the "Scepter Departed from Judah." This meant that the Messiah should have come according to the scripture. This troubled the Jewish leadership, the Sanhedrin.

What they did not realize is this, the Messiah was there. He was a young man who was born in Bethlehem, had already taught in the Temple, and was about to change the world. He had arrived right on time and the prophecy was indeed fulfilled.

So, you can see that the prophecy in Genesis 49 was about the Messiah being born of the lineage of Judah.

Now, let us look at Joseph's prophecy:

Joseph

From there is the Shepherd, the Stone of Israel

From there is the Shepherd the Stone of Israel? That is Messianic through and through. The Shepherd is none other than the Lord Jesus Christ.

Jesus himself referenced the Stone that the builders rejected has become the Chief Cornerstone and he pained that as himself. He is the Good Shepherd and the Stone or Rock.

The archers provoked him,
And shot at him and were hostile toward him;
But his bow remained firm,
And his arms were agile
From the hands of the Mighty One of Jacob

The archers provoked him, they were hostile toward him. you know that speaks of his own brothers who were hostile toward him even to death.

The archers provoked him, or you could say that they pierced him. But his arms were agile from the hands of the mighty one of Jacob. This Mighty One of Jacob speaks of Yahweh.

Messiah ben Joseph

Throughout Jewish history there was a Messianic figure called Messiah ben Joseph, or Messiah the son of Joseph.

Yes, there was Messiah ben David, in other words Messiah the Son of David. Jesus himself was called the Son of David. Yet he was more than David's son, he was God the Son.

In that same way he was called Messiah the Son of Joseph. He was called the Son of Joseph as his earthly stepdad was named Joseph and that is part of the pattern but there was an ancient, prophetic lineage as well as a foreshadowing of Jesus in the line of Joseph.

As you may recall, Joseph was a huge picture of Christ. We went into the details of this in the last chapter. But here is a summary of his life and how it looks a lot like Jesus:

He had a miraculous birth; he was the father's most favored son – the most favored son of Israel. He was despised and rejected by his own, he was sent out of fellowship with his father to visit with his brothers.

His own brothers conspired to murder him, and Judah produced the plan to sell him for pieces of silver (the name Judas derives from the name Judah).

He was handed over to the Gentiles and later he was falsely accused and sent down into the place of the condemned. It was there that he tells the fate of the two condemned with him. One lives, and the other was cursed to death.

Then Joseph was raised up out of that place of the condemned and brought before the throne. It was there that he was the only one found worthy to reveal the future through the dreams of Pharaoh.

He was then exalted and made the right-hand man to the throne. Every knee had to bow down to him except for he who sat on the throne.

At that point he was given his Gentile bride.

There was a great harvest and when that last piece of grain was collected and put into his storehouse, the seven-year time of Great Trouble came. This was a seven-year period of great famine, and it covered the whole face of the earth. But Josephs bride was safe in the palace with Joseph.

During this time of great trouble, or Jacob's trouble, his own brothers, his bloodline brothers come back to him bowed down in fulfilment of his own God-given dreams.

He recognizes them and weeps.

He reveals who he is to them, saying "Ani Yosef" – Hebrew for, "I am Joseph."

His brothers were shocked and afraid.

But he gently tells them to come closer, do not be afraid, I am Joseph whom you sold as a slave.

He forgives them and weeps over each of them – each of his eleven brothers.

He blesses them and gives them new clothing and food for their families. He sends them out to gather all of Israel's family to come live with him in the best of the land.

He unites or grafts-in his new Gentile family to the family of Israel forever.

You see, Joseph was clearly a picture, a masterpiece painting of Jesus the Messiah. Joseph's story took place two thousand years before the birth of Christ.

There was an ancient expectation among the Jewish people because they were waiting for Messiah bar Joseph. In Hebrew this would be pronounced Mashiach bar Yosef, or Mashiach bar Ephraim. Mashiach means Messiah.

Bar means son.

Yosef is Joseph.

So why did they also call him Mashiach bar Ephraim?

Ephraim was the second son of Joseph. He received the firstborn blessing instead of Manasseh who was the actual firstborn of Joseph.

Joshua is Yeshua in Hebrew, Jesus in the Greek, and he was of the tribe of Ephraim. Joshua was a huge type, a picture, and a portrait of the Messiah Jesus. Not only does he share the same name, but he was the one who could lead the people into the Promised Land.

Moses, who represented the Law, could not bring the people into that promised land but Joshua, or Yeshua did. Remember it was both, Joshua of the tribe of Ephraim, of the House of Joseph, and Caleb of the tribe of Judah, who had the courage to take the land the first time, but the people of Israel rejected their report.

You can see the Messiah in Zechariah 12.

Remember, the Joseph's brother Judah came up with the plan to sell him for pieces of silver. Judas sold Jesus for pieces of silver, and his name derives from the name Judah.

In Zechariah you can see the Messiah, and just like Joseph, he too is sold for pieces of silver.

Zechariah 11

So they weighed out thirty shekels of silver as my wages. Then the LORD said to me, "Throw it to the potter, that magnificent price at which I was valued by them." So I took the thirty shekels of silver and threw them to the potter in the house of the LORD.

Zechariah 12

Dead Sea Scroll

I will pour on David's house, and on the inhabitants of Jerusalem, the spirit of grace and of supplication; and they will look to me whom they have pierced; and they shall mourn for him, as one mourns for his only son, and will grieve bitterly for him, as one grieves for his firstborn.

Like Joseph, he is mourned as a slain firstborn. Jacob mourned over Joseph and then later, you see how Joseph and his brothers mourned together when they realize he is alive.

You can see him in some of the non-biblical texts of the Dead Sea Scrolls: 4QTestimonia is dated to before 100 BC (Before Christ), and in it you see four anticipated redeemer figures: a prophet like Moses, a king, a priest, and a Joshua hero, a son of Joseph.

He is found in another scroll from the Dead Sea collection. Joseph Apocryphon 4Q372 which dates from before 200 BC, shows one who is actually called "Joseph" by name. Similar to Zechariah's pierced king, it states that at his death, he cries out to God his father, in psalms, to deliver him, and predict his rising again in glory.

The ancient rabbi's wrote of a figure called Messiah ben Joseph. They wrote that he comes from Galilee to die, pierced by ruthless men, at the gate of Jerusalem. They also recorded that because of his death, Israel is scattered among the nations, but his death confounds satan, atones for sin, and abolishes death itself. And then he is raised to life again.

It is written in the Jewish literature, in the Targums and the Talmud, recorded in every period from Moses to the birth of Christ. It was written by the Jewish people for the Jewish people and was passed down from generation to generation in Hebrew, Aramaic, Arabic, and Persian.

If we step back and look at this simply, you can see the pattern of Messiah Son of Joseph.

Jesus was born into the house of Joseph. He had a stepdad named Joseph who had a father named Jacob. He was called the son of Joseph and so he was the son of Joseph on many levels. He was of the house of Joseph. This is interesting because both Ephriam and Manasseh are the two tribes of Israel, from Joseph's bloodline, and are also included as the House of Joseph.

Messiah's Bloodline

He had the bloodline of both Joseph and David through Mary's genealogy.

Matthew traces the line of Mary's royal bloodline from Solomon and Luke traces the line of genetic descent from Nathan, to bypass the curses on Josiah's sons.

Mary's mother, Anna or Hannah, was descended from the high-priestly stock. Jesus is called our Great High Priest, and his bloodline shows this as well.

Mary was also a descendant from Joseph. Omri king of Ephraim, from the house of Joseph, begat Ahab. Ahab begat Athaliah who married Jehoram of the house of David. Through their son, Ahaziah, the seed of Omri entered the Solomonic lineage of David.

This continued through ten generations to Josiah. Then it passed through Josiah's daughter Tamar to Shealtiel and Pedaiah, whom Tamar bore to Neri. Then Pedaiah (in the name of Shealtiel) begat Zerubbabel who begat Rhesa. From Rhesa, the seed of Omri descended fifteen generations to Levi, and thence to Panther, Joakim, and Mary.

That was Jesus' bloodline descent.

But what about his stepdad, Joseph the carpenter?

You can see that the Ephraimite royal status passed by the same route to Zerubbabel, then to Abiud and Rhesa, and converged in Joseph, begotten by Jacob, according to the law, for his brother Heli.

And so, Jesus, received the royal title to David's throne from Joseph of Nazareth who was the foremost claimant to David's throne in his time.

This is amazing stuff. Not only do you see types and pictures of Jesus in the tribe of Joseph, and Levi, but you see the shared bloodline.

Joshua was a type of Jesus as he shares the same name and was of the tribe of Ephriam of the House of Joseph.

Both Caleb and Joshua were the courageous warriors who were ready to take the land of Israel the first time.

Caleb was of the tribe of Judah and Joshua of the tribe of Joseph.

In Ezekiel chapter 37, God tells him to take two sticks. He tells him to write Judah on one and Joseph on the other. Then he tells him to hold them as one stick in his hand.

Ezekiel 37

The word of the LORD came again to me, saying,
"Now you, son of man, take for yourself one stick and write on it, 'For Judah and for the sons of Israel, his companions'; then take another stick and write on it, 'For Joseph, the stick of Ephraim and all the house of Israel, his companions.' Then put them together for yourself one to another into one stick, so that they may become one in your hand.

This looks like the cross because you see two sticks.

Remember, Israel was expecting two different Messiahs: One from the tribe of Judah, and one from the tribe of Joseph. But they did not realize scripture spoke of the One Messiah with two vastly different arrivals with two very different missions.

The first visit was the suffering servant, who would come and bear the sins of the world.

The second coming speaks of the catching up of his bride and then God's wrath poured out on this world. And it is during this seven-year period Israel is saved – just like you can see it in both Joseph and Moses stories. Jesus will then come back to this earth as a mighty King and warrior. He will have the antichrist and his false prophet thrown into the lake of fire and he has satan chained up for one-thousand years, just as the scriptures say.

So, both Judah and Joseph show us attributes of the Messiah and the scripture backs this up.

It is no wonder that God selected a righteous man named Joseph to be the husband of the Messiah's mother, Mary.

CHAPTER ELEVEN: MOSES – TYPE OF CHRIST

1566-1406 BC Before Christ

Stephen, a man full of the power of the Holy Spirit, is in front of the council of the religious leaders in Jerusalem. He gives a teaching that cut to their heart and soul. In it he declares both Joseph and Moses as types, and foreshadowing's of Jesus.

Look at what Stephen said by the power of the Spirit:

Acts 7:35-37

"This Moses whom they disowned, saying, 'WHO MADE YOU A RULER AND A JUDGE?' is the one whom God sent to be both a ruler and a deliverer with the help of the angel who appeared to him in the thorn bush. This man led them out, performing wonders and signs in the land of Egypt and in the Red Sea, and in the wilderness for forty years. This is the Moses who said to the sons of Israel, 'GOD WILL RAISE UP FOR YOU A PROPHET LIKE ME FROM YOUR COUNTRYMEN.'

So, this New Testament book of Acts makes it very clear that Moses was a type of and a foreshadowing of Jesus.

Moses was rejected by his own the first time, just like Joseph was.

Then he moved to the Gentile land and received his Gentile bride. Was that the end of the story?

No.

Moses was shepherding the father's flock in the land of Midian and suddenly and unexpectedly God calls him to go back to save all of Israel during a time of great trouble.

This is like Joseph's story because he too was given a Gentile bride in the Gentile land, and he saved all of Israel during a great time of trouble.

God did not make a mistake here.

This is a prophetic pattern that must not be missed. This is God's plan revealed through both, Joseph, and Moses.

Take a closer look at Moses' story.

After Joseph died, the children of Israel lived in and became numerous in the land of Egypt.

Before this, way back in Abraham's time, God told him of a time of oppression for Israel: *Then God said to Abram, "Know for certain that your descendants will be strangers in a land that is not theirs, where they will be enslaved and oppressed for four hundred years. (Genesis 15:13 NASB)*

They were in Egypt for four-hundred years.

Now compare the story of Jesus.

There was a 400-year gap between the time of prophet Malachi and the time of Christ. These are what is called the silent years where no new prophet arose, or scripture was recorded.

In Exodus you can see the story of Moses. His birth looks a lot like Jesus' birth:

Exodus 1
Now a new king arose over Egypt, who did not know Joseph... Then Pharaoh commanded all his people, saying, "Every son who is born, you are to throw into the Nile, but every daughter, you are to keep alive."

That evil king, who did not know Joseph, was like Harod the Great. He wanted all of the male Hebrew baby boys murdered.

Remember how Harod heard that a new King of Israel had been born in Bethlehem?

What did he do?

He commanded that all the male Hebrew baby boys to be killed, two years old and under. He was attempting to murder the Messiah, even after they told him the prophecy of Malachi.

Matthew 2

"Where is He who has been born King of the Jews? For we saw His star in the east and have come to worship Him." When Herod the king heard this, he was troubled, and all Jerusalem with him. And gathering together all the chief priests and scribes of the people, he inquired of them where the Messiah was to be born. They said to him, "In Bethlehem of Judea; for this is what has been written by the prophet:
'AND YOU, BETHLEHEM, LAND OF JUDAH,
ARE BY NO MEANS LEAST AMONG THE LEADERS OF
JUDAH;
FOR FROM YOU WILL COME FORTH A RULER
WHO WILL SHEPHERD MY PEOPLE ISRAEL.'"...Then when Herod saw that he had been tricked by the magi, he became very enraged, and sent men and killed all the boys who were in Bethlehem and all its vicinity who were two years old or under

The Magi protected baby Jesus from Herod because they feared God over men. In that same way the midwives of Egypt feared God and did not harm the Hebrew baby boys.

They were both honored by God for protecting the innocent babies.

Moses was found in the water by the Egyptian princess: *And the child grew, and she brought him to Pharaoh's daughter and he became her son. And she named him Moses, and said, "Because I drew him out of the water." (Exodus 2:10 NASB)*

The Hebrew form of the name is Moshe[1]. It is of Egyptian origin from a short form of an ancient Egyptian personal name meaning 'conceived.'

Remember, God the Holy Spirit caused Jesus to be conceived in Mary. Another name for God's Spirit is 'Living Water.'

---

1.   https://www.ancestry.com/name-origin?surname=moshe

Moses had a sister, who looked after him while he was being hidden in the Basket in the Nile river. Her name was Miriam. The name Mary derives from the name Miriam.

So right away you can see the connections of the birth of Moses and Jesus.

But there is so much more.

Stephen pointed out that the people of Israel rejected Moses even though he was there to deliver them the first time: *he thought that his brothers understood that God was granting them deliverance through him; but they did not understand... But the one who was injuring his neighbor pushed him away, saying, 'WHO MADE YOU A RULER AND JUDGE OVER US?" (Acts 7)*

You can see that Israel rejected this prince, who humbled himself by leaving the Royal Palace and coming down to help his own people. Instead of receiving him, they rejected him.

So what did Moses do?

He left and went away to a Gentile land. He ended up living in this Gentile land far away from Israel for a long time.

Exodus 2

Now the priest of Midian had seven daughters; and they came to draw water and filled the troughs to water their father's flock. Then the shepherds came and drove them away, but Moses stood up and helped them and watered their flock.

Here you see Moses stood to help these women who were being harassed by the evil shepherds.

Jesus did that too. Remember the woman caught in adultery? Jesus stood up for her against those who wanted to stone her.

You can see seven Gentile women at the well. They were daughters of one father, and now Moses is there to save them and help them water the flocks.

So, how many Gentile Churches do you see in Revelation?

Yes. There are seven.

SEE JESUS IN THE OLD TESTAMENT

Revelation 1

"Write on a scroll what you see, and send it to the seven churches: to Ephesus, Smyrna, Pergamum, Thyatira, Sardis, Philadelphia, and Laodicea."

John is told to write this revelation on a scroll and give it to the seven churches. Then he sees Jesus standing up in the midst of the seven churches:

Revelation 1

Then I turned to see the voice that was speaking with me. And after turning I saw seven golden lampstands; and in the middle of the lampstands I saw one like a son of man, clothed in a robe reaching to the feet, and wrapped around the chest with a golden sash. His head and His hair were white like white wool, like snow; and His eyes were like a flame of fire. His feet were like burnished bronze when it has been heated to a glow in a furnace, and His voice was like the sound of many waters. In His right hand He held seven stars, and out of His mouth came a sharp two-edged sword; and His face was like the sun shining in its strength.

When I saw Him, I fell at His feet like a dead man. And He placed His right hand on me, saying, "Do not be afraid; I am the first and the last, and the living One; and I was dead, and behold, I am alive forevermore, and I have the keys of death and of Hades. Therefore write the things which you have seen, and the things which are, and the things which will take place after these things. As for the mystery of the seven stars which you saw in My right hand, and the seven golden lampstands: the seven stars are the angels of the seven churches, and the seven lampstands are the seven churches.

Jesus is standing up next to the seven golden lampstands. This speaks of the High Priest because his job was to keep the Menorah, or seven golden lampstands lit and shining bright.

How did he do that?

He kept it burning by making sure the olive oil continued to fill each of those seven lamp cups.

This speaks of how Jesus pours the Holy Spirit into his people, the church. The olive oil was always symbolic of the Holy Spirit, and we need to be filled and powered by him. We cannot shine on our own, we need the High Priest to keep pouring that precious oil into us.

Remember, over the heart of the Priest, was the twelve precious stones of Israel. They remained over his heart while he took care of the seven golden lampstands.

In that same way Moses kept his own people Israel over his heart as he took care of these seven Gentile daughters.

The church should reflect the heart of our Great High Priest, Jesus. We should have those twelve precious stones over our hearts too.

When there is a revival, a real revival, the church loves Israel. You can see that with Isaac Newton in the 1700's, C.H. Spurgeon in the 1800's, Billy Graham, Martin Luther King Jr, Chuck Smith in the 1900's, Franklin Graham, and Greg Laurie in the 2000's.

So we see Moses standing up for the seven Gentile daughters against the evil shepherds, and watering the father's flock.

Then Moses ends up marrying one of those daughters. This speaks of the church being one body, unified and married to one Bridegroom: *And he gave his daughter Zipporah to Moses. Then she gave birth to a son, and he named him Gershom, for he said, "I have been a stranger in a foreign land."(Exodus 2)*

Moses being a type of Christ is in a foreign land.

Why?

Because he was Jewish, through and through. He was never a Midianite; he was an Israelite.

This is the same with Jesus, he was Jewish, and an Israeli. He still is and he is the King of Israel.

Exodus 2
Now it came about in the course of those many days that the king of Egypt died. And the sons of Israel groaned because of the bondage, and they cried out; and their cry for help because of their bondage ascended to God. So God heard their groaning; and God remembered His covenant with Abraham, Isaac, and Jacob. And God saw the sons of Israel, and God took notice of them.

Now you can see Israel crying out to God. This is what Israel has been doing since October 7th, 2023. They have been hurt and oppressed by this crazy world with nowhere to turn but to God.

All that Israel wants is for their own hostages to be set free just like they wanted to be free from Pharoah.

The world has shown no pity toward Israel. The world is a picture of Egypt, and they show no compassion for Israel even though they have fought a good fight. They have fought hard to keep innocent civilians alive like no other country has in the history of warfare.

Even though Israel is doing that, the International Criminal Court has called the Prime Minister of Israel a War Criminal.

The colleges and Universities around the world are protesting Israel and giving their allegiance to Hamas. This is insane.

The only people who have shown support and love to the people of Israel are the true Christians.

If you see Jesus in Moses story, you can see that we are in the Church Age, the time of the Gentiles. But that time will come to an end and the spotlight will turn toward the great rescue mission for Israel.

So, at this point Moses has been shepherding the father's flock in this Gentile land, and his Gentile bride was safe with him, but now God has heard the cries of Israel.

Exodus 3

Now Moses was pasturing the flock of his father-in-law Jethro, the priest of Midian; and he led the flock to the west side of the wilderness and came to Horeb, the mountain of God.
Then the angel of the LORD appeared to him in a blazing fire from the midst of a bush; and he looked, and behold, the bush was burning with fire, yet the bush was not being consumed. So Moses said, "I must turn aside and see this marvelous sight, why the bush is not burning up!"

Moses had his bride living with him and he was pastoring the flock when suddenly and unexpectedly, God calls on him: *And the LORD said, "I have certainly seen the oppression of My people who are in Egypt, and have heard their outcry because of their taskmasters, for I am aware of their sufferings. So I have come down to rescue them from the power of the Egyptians…"*

God still wants to rescue Israel just like you see in that scripture. He will accomplish it, and it will be during Jacob's trouble which is another name for the seven-year tribulation period.

When Moses returns to rescue his people, God uses him to bring judgments down upon Israel's enemies. These plagues or judgments are the same as you see in the book of Revelation.

So far this scene in Moses story shows Jesus with his bride and then called back to save Israel during a time of great trouble.

You saw this in Joseph's story as well.

So, now you can see the tribulation period in Moses' story. God has him pour out judgments. You can see an antichrist type in this Pharaoh and his army going against God and his people.

Exodus 7

Then the LORD said to Moses, "See, I have made you as God to Pharaoh, and your brother Aaron shall be your prophet.

God just declared typology is real. He said to Moses that he would be a type of God to this evil antichrist type, the Pharoah.

God continued and told Moses this: *"When Pharaoh does not listen to you, I will lay My hand on Egypt and bring out My armies, My people the sons of Israel, from the land of Egypt by great judgments. Then the Egyptians shall know that I am the LORD, when I extend My hand over Egypt and bring out the sons of Israel from their midst."*

God said that this will all happen by great judgments. That speaks directly into Revelation chapters six through nineteen, which is the tribulation period where you see great judgments poured out upon this world.

Remember, Revelation chapters one through five, spoke of Jesus and his church. Just before the tribulation period, which starts in chapter six, you see the churches in chapters two through three, and then God tells John to write down the things he see after these things.

What things?

The church age.

And it all happens before chapter six, which is the beginning of the tribulation. Interestingly, the church is not mentioned again, in Revelation until after the seven-year tribulation period.

In chapter four through five, you see John, and he hears a voice like the trumpet that tells him to come up here, and then sees an open door to heaven. He is then caught up into heaven and sees the throne of God and in his hand the scroll, then the Lamb of God who takes the scroll, and that starts the seals being broken open. That is what starts that tribulation period in chapter six.

Now back to Moses' story. Next you see God telling this evil ruler to let his people go.

Exodus 7

"Let My people go, so that they may serve Me in the wilderness. But behold, you have not listened up to now."

So, who is this Pharoah that God is talking to?

You can know who he is because the Bible gives us the exact date.

1 Kings 6:1
*Now it came about in the **four hundred and eightieth year after the sons of Israel came out of the land of Egypt**, in the fourth year of Solomon's reign over Israel, in the month of Ziv, that is, the second month, that he began to build the house of the LORD.*

From that scripture you can go back 480 years and determine the date of the Exodus.

Solomon's Temple was complete in 967 BCE or BC (Before Christ), and so if you add the 480 years, you get 1447 BC.

Amenhotep II was the Pharoah who's reign started in 1453 B.C.E., and you can see the Exodus date of 1447 B.C.

Remember the B.C. dates count down, unlike today where we count up. By the way, how amazing that dates and times have pointed to the birth of Christ.

This date means one thing: Amenhotep II was indeed the Pharaoh of the Exodus.

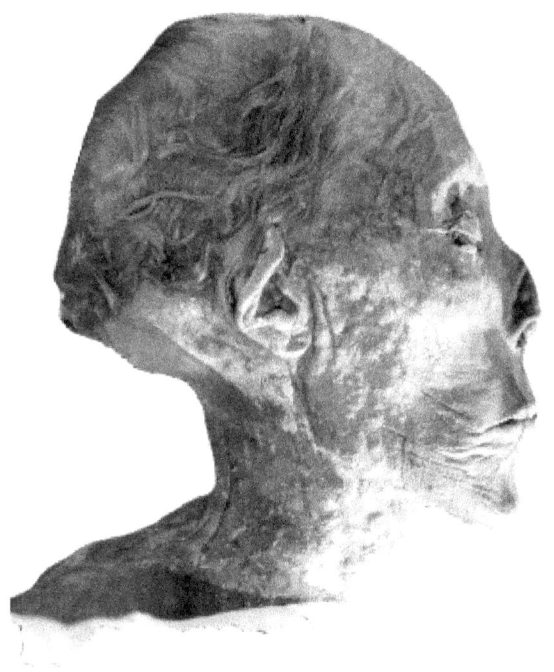

Above is an actual picture of Amenhotep II

In fact, when archeologists discovered his tomb and opened it up, they saw a preserved body with boils or tumors all over it.

They also found an ornament belonging to him and it is a carving of this beast-looking creature with boils all over it and it was a statue of Amenhotep II.

He is like the antichrist who is also called the Beast in the book of Revelation. It is also interesting that one of the future Judgements in Revelation is boils.

How amazing is that? Today you can see what this evil Pharoah looked like.

The reason these archeologists figured it out is because they used the Bible. The best of them do that, they use the Bible to find places, dates, people, and structures. This is more proof that the Bible is the greatest book, document, historical record of all time.

Did you know that the Bible makes it to #1 on the New York Times Best Sellers list since it was started. They stopped listing it because of that.

Now let's head back to Moses story and how it shows us Jesus. In it you can see God's great plan in the future. We are now seeing the tribulation period shown in his story.

Exodus 7

This is what the LORD says: "By this you shall know that I am the LORD: behold, I am going to strike the water that is in the Nile with the staff that is in my hand, and it will be turned into blood.
Then the fish that are in the Nile will die, the Nile will stink, and the Egyptians will no longer be able to drink water from the Nile.

Now you can compare one of the Judgements in Revelation and see the same thing in one of the Trumpet Judgements.

Revelation 8

"The second angel sounded...and a third of the sea became blood, and a third of the creatures which were in the sea and had life, died..."

Can you imagine the stench if one third of all sea life died?

I lived along the Pacific Ocean in beautiful Santa Cruz California and occasionally, the Anchovies would come in close to shore so thick that they would consume all of the oxygen in the water. This would cause every fish in that area to die. The result was that millions of fish washed up along the beach, and the stench filled the air.

It didn't matter if you were four miles inland, when that typical late morning, onshore breeze picked up, you would nearly gag from the smell of rotting fish.

In that Great Tribulation period everything progressively increases in intensity and pain.

Why does God do that?

Because he is doing everything in his power to save as many as possible. People turn to him when things get tough.

Later in Revelation you can see that everything in the sea dies. Before it was one third, but now the heat has turned up and the stench is beyond imagination.

Revelation 16

The second angel poured out his bowl into the sea, and it became blood like that of a dead man; and every living thing in the sea died.
Then the third angel poured out his bowl into the rivers and the springs of waters; and they became blood.
And I heard the angel of the waters saying, "Righteous are You, the One who is and who was, O Holy One, because You judged these things; for they poured out the blood of saints and prophets, and You have given them blood to drink. They deserve it."

You can see that in both Exodus and Revelation, God is giving them the blood that they shed to drink. Egypt killed the Hebrew baby boys by throwing them into the Nile river and now God is giving them that same water with a reminder of what they did.

For many decades now, the world has been aborting millions of babies through abortion. Their blood has traveled down the drains and eventually into the sea. May God have mercy on us.

Exodus 7

Then the fish that are in the Nile will die, the Nile will stink, and the Egyptians will no longer be able to drink water from the Nile."'" Then the LORD said to Moses, "Say to Aaron, 'Take your staff and extend your hand over the waters of Egypt, over their rivers, over their streams, over their pools, and over all their reservoirs of water, so that they may become blood; and there will be blood through all the land of Egypt, both in containers of wood and in containers of stone.'"

...So all the Egyptians dug around the Nile for water to drink, because they could not drink from the water of the Nile.

The next plague or judgement you see in Moses' story is also seen in Revelation. This time it has to do with something they worshipped, the frog.

So, again, God is giving them what they wanted but in large amounts. This is how God works.

He ultimately gives everyone what they really want. This is how it works when the rapture or catching up of his bride to heaven happens. Some say that is cruel of God to take away his believers and bring hell on earth to the rest.

But this is how he works.

At one moment in time, God gives everyone exactly what they want: those who want Jesus and love being around his people will get exactly that. And that speaks of Heaven, of paradise with Jesus because that is where he dwells.

But to those who want a world without God, without Jesus, without the true Bible believing Church, they will get exactly that. They hate God and love the demonic influence of this world and the ruler of this world, satan.

This is what it will be like during the seven-year tribulation period, and God in his great mercy still provides the way to be saved even during that time. But this will be their last chance.

So, now you will see God give the Egyptians large amounts of what they worshiped – the frogs.

Exodus 8

"Behold, I am going to strike your entire territory with frogs..."

The above images are of actual idols from ancient Egypt

They made frogs to be god's, and they received their god in full.

In Revelation you can see frogs as demonic forces

Revelation 16

And I saw coming out of the mouth of the dragon, and out of the mouth of the beast, and out of the mouth of the false prophet, three unclean spirits like frogs; for they are spirits of demons, performing signs, which go out to the kings of the entire world, to gather them together for the war of the great day of God, the Almighty.

The demonic trinity was just displayed in the book of Revelation. You saw the evil spirits that looked like frogs coming out of the Dragon – satan; the Beast – Antichrist; the False Prophet – who is the fake Jesus.

Exodus 9

Then the LORD said to Moses and Aaron, "Take for yourselves handfuls of soot from a kiln, and Moses shall toss it toward the sky in the sight of Pharaoh. Then it will become fine dust over all the land of Egypt, and will turn into boils breaking out with sores on every person and animal through all the land of Egypt."

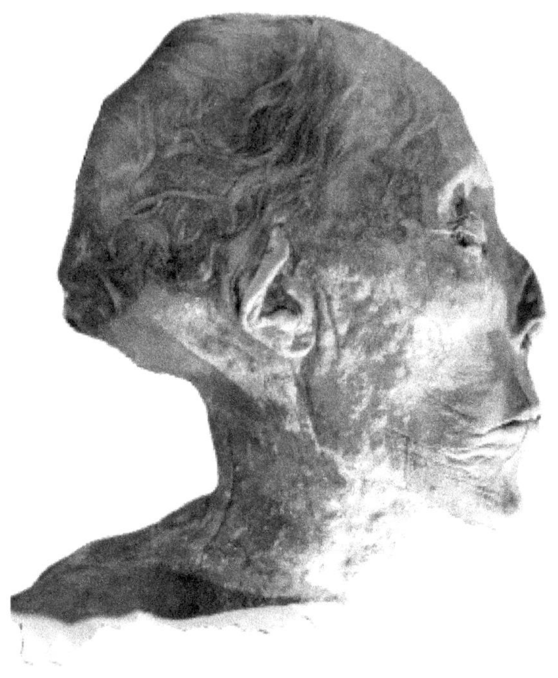

Above: the Pharaoh of the Exodus, Amenhotep II

Remember the sores, boils or tumors on the face of the Pharoah of the Exodus. This is evidence of what really happened, and it will happen again in the Great Tribulation period.

Revelation 16

So the first angel went and poured out his bowl on the earth; and a harmful and painful sore afflicted the people who had the mark of the beast and who worshiped his image.

In the Exodus account, the children of Israel did not receive this plague of these sores or boils, but the Egyptians did.

In that same way those who took the mark of the beast and who had worshipped his image, will receive these harmful and painful sores on themselves.

It is interesting that God uses the past tense in Revelation and in other prophecies. The reason for this is because it is as good as done when God declares it.

Exodus 9

So Moses reached out with his staff toward the sky, and the LORD sent thunder and hail, and fire ran down to the earth. And the LORD rained hail on the land of Egypt. So there was hail, and fire flashing intermittently in the midst of the hail, which was very heavy, such as had not occurred in all the land of Egypt since it became a nation.

This was intense hail, and fire like nothing these people had ever seen.

God warned them ahead of time and the Egyptians who feared God brought their livestock into their homes. Those who did this were safe, both themselves and their livestock.

In the area where Israel was located there was no hail, no judgement: *The hail struck everything that was in the field through all the land of Egypt, from people to animals; the hail also struck every plant of the field, and shattered every tree of the field. Only in the land of Goshen, where the sons of Israel were, was there no hail.*

This type of hail happens from time to time in history. Rostov, India, 1939, 23 people and even more cattle were killed by hailstones weighing up to 2 pounds each, and it fell on a 30-square-mile area

You can see the same type of judgement in Revelation.

Revelation 8

...there was hail and fire mixed with blood, and it was hurled to the earth and a third of the earth was burned up, and a third of the trees were burned up, and all the green grass was burned up.

Revelation 16

*And huge hailstones, weighing about a talent each, *came down from heaven upon people;*
*(*about 100 lb. or 45 kg)*

The God of Abraham, Isaac, and Jacob is protecting Israel from these judgements, but Pharaoh and his followers are suffering. This is so similar to the antichrist and his followers in Revelation.

During that time the beast or antichrist and his false prophet will hate the Jewish people of Israel. They will want to try and keep Israel under the control of the world system that satan has been ruling up to this point.

So, just like this antichrist type Pharaoh, he will not let the children of Israel go free. He will try to keep them under his thumb much like the world elites do today. They hate Israel because they hate God.

Exodus 10

Let My people go, so that they may serve Me. For if you refuse to let My people go, behold, tomorrow I will bring locusts into your territory. And they will cover the surface of the land...”

Again, the same type of Judgment is seen in the tribulation period in the book of Revelation.

Revelation 9

He opened the shaft of the abyss, and smoke ascended out of the shaft like the smoke of a great furnace; out of the smoke came locusts upon the earth, and power was given them, as the scorpions of the earth have power. They were told not to hurt the grass of the earth, nor any green thing, nor any tree, but only the people who do not have the seal of God on their foreheads.
And their torment was like the torment of a scorpion when it stings a person.

This is like the plague in Exodus only much worse. These demonic locust-scorpion-like creatures are stinging people on earth.

Again, God protects his own. You can see that those who have the seal of God on their foreheads are not harmed by these vile creatures.

This is why Jesus described this time like no other since the beginning.

You may be wondering, "I thought this book was about Jesus in the Old Testament".

It is. It is about his first coming and his second coming. It is all in their and so it must be taught.

The awesome thing about this is that you can learn to use the Old Testament as a commentary to understand the New Testament. Especially books like Revelation.

Exodus 10

Then the LORD said to Moses, "Reach out with your hand toward the sky, so that there may be darkness over the land of Egypt, even a darkness which may be felt."

There was thick darkness in all the land of Egypt for three days. They did not see one another, nor did anyone rise from his place for three days, but all the sons of Israel had light in their dwellings.

Again, God protects Israel. This darkness is different, it is so thick you could feel it.

When Jesus died on the cross there was darkness for three hours. Even secular historians recorded a darkness in that region so thick they said you could feel it.

Now you can see this same judgement in the book of Revelation, and it affects the beast and his kingdom.

Revelation 16

And the fifth angel poured out his bowl on the throne of the beast, and his kingdom became darkened; and they gnawed their tongues because of pain, and they blasphemed the God of heaven because of their pain and their sores; and they did not repent of their deeds.

In that same way, this antichrist type Pharoah and his followers refuse to repent to God. This is exactly how it will be during the Great Tribulation period, even toward the end of it. They will have experienced hell on earth, yet they refuse to yield to God. They will do it their way. They are getting exactly what they want.

When the end of time comes, Jesus returns in Revelation chapter nine-teen, and the beast and his false prophet are destroyed forever. They end up in the lake of fire.

Then that dragon, who is satan is bound up for one-thousand years and there is finally peace on earth as Jesus rules and reigns from Jerusalem. This is described in Revelation chapter twenty, and it was written six times in seven verses.

The earth will repopulate just as it did after Adam and Eve. Those who are born during this perfect time will have the best environment, government, and prosperity. People will live long lives just like the time of Adam, Eve and Noah. The scripture says that a child will be one-hundred years old.

Then just like in the Garden of Eden, God gives everyone a choice. Satan will be released after the one-thousand years have ended and he will be the choice, just like there was in the Garden. You can see this sequence of events clearly in the end of Revelation. From chapters nineteen to the end at chapter twenty-two.

God never violates people's choice. Real love is always a choice. Jesus wins in the end!

CHAPTER TWELVE: PASSOVER LAMB – TYPE OF CHRIST

1447 BC Before Christ

Passover is a sign to Israel and the nations. God used it to illustrate what he would do to save Israel and anyone who receives Jesus, the Lamb of God.

You see, John the Baptizer proclaimed this when he saw Jesus: "Behold the Lamb of God, who takes away the sin of the world."

John was clearly referencing the Passover lamb.

In Jewish homes today, Passover celebration is a meal, called a "Seder", with different elements that help remind them of the miraculous exodus from Egypt.

The earliest mentions of this Passover Seder is not found in the Mishna or the Germara, but in the New Testament (The Mishna is a collection of original oral laws supplementing scriptural laws. The Gemara is a collection of commentaries on and elaborations of the Mishna).

Recently, Professor Israel J. Yuval of the Hebrew University, said, "the current Passover Seder tradition, includes many ceremonies and stages that have been adopted by the ancient Jewish Disciples of Yeshua, the Messianic Jews of old".

He stated that after the destruction of the Jewish Temple by the Romans in 70AD, the Jewish people were wondering what to do with the Sader and the Passover Holiday. They were left with two competing narratives.

He said that the oldest one was the Messianic, the celebration of Jesus' last supper. The newer one was the response to it, the Rabbinic Sader which came later.

The first mention of the Sader meal since the Exodus, is found in the New Testament with Jesus' last supper.

God commanded his people Israel, to celebrate the Passover "permanently," a constant reminder of his salvation. It is not only an Old Testament command, or a holiday just for Jews because Paul encourages Christians to celebrate it with the updated understanding of Jesus Christ as the Passover Lamb.

Today the Jewish people celebrate this meal by having the cup of wine, the bread and the lamb.

They will take the Matza, the unleavened bread, and place three of them into cloth, a covering or back. The middle compartment of it is where you find the middle bread, and it is taken out and broken in half. This speaks of Jesus' body which has been broken for you. And he was the one on the middle cross.

Then that second half is hidden away for the children of that family to look for and find it later. The child who finds it gets a reward, a prize.

In that same way, Jesus is waiting to be discovered by the future generation of the children of Israel. He has been buried, but is alive today and when they discover him, there will be a great celebration.

Passover is not just a Jewish celebration. Passover is about the Lamb, Jesus. Passover is about being saved. Passover is about the blood of the Lamb Jesus who saves us from our sins.

Passover is mentioned twenty-nine times in 27 verses in the New Testament. Jesus celebrated the Passover throughout his own life.

You can see that the Gospels especially focus on His last Supper, that Passover meal, the night before He was crucified.

If you look at the original Passover story, in Exodus you can gain more insight into what Jesus did with the ultimate Passover, at the cross.

In Moses story, this final judgement of God, was what set Israel free from the grip of that evil king, that antichrist type of ruler in Egypt.

Exodus 12

"This month shall be the beginning of months for you; it is to be the first month of the year for you. Speak to all the congregation of Israel, saying, 'On the tenth of this month they are, each one, to take a lamb for themselves, according to the fathers' households, a lamb for each household...

...Your lamb shall be an unblemished male a year old; you may take it from the sheep or from the goats.

You shall keep it until the fourteenth day of the same month, then the whole assembly of the congregation of Israel is to slaughter it at twilight. Moreover, they shall take some of the blood and put it on the two doorposts and on the lintel of the houses in which they eat it. They shall eat the flesh that same night, roasted with fire, and they shall eat it with unleavened bread and bitter herbs.

They were to kill this lamb or goat on the fourteenth day of this First Month – this is the day Jesus was crucified.

It was by the blood, of the lamb or goat without blemish, which marked the doorpost of each home, which spared them from the Death Angel. The mark was the blood.

The blood of this animal was symbolic of the blood of Jesus and is all that was required for you to be saved by God.

Back in the days of the Tabernacle and then later, in the Temple, this was the only requirement for the Jewish people.

If you were to go to the Temple of God, and worship him, you were to bring this unblemished animal with you. If you could not afford the lamb or goat, then you could sacrifice turtle doves. But it all came down to the blood. The blood of Jesus is precious in God's site.

When the priest would meet with you and inspect your offering, he was not there to inspect you, but to look at the lamb, goat or doves. He would inspect – usually the lamb – and look for any fault in it. He would examine it and cross-examine it.

Finally, he would say, "I find no fault in him", and you were freed to go in and worship God guilt free.

When Jesus was being examined and cross examined by the rulers, it was Pontius Pilate who said, "I find no fault in him".

Jesus was the faultless Lamb of God.

It was by the shedding of his own blood that you and I are found faultless in God's eyes.

When you hear others accuse you as a believer, you can say yes I am still a sinner, but the one who was faultless stands before me always and makes me faultless before God.

When satan or his minions accuse you of sinning, you can say thanks for the reminder of what a sinner I am, I love Jesus all the more because he is the spotless, unblemished Lamb of God, who takes away my sins by his blood.

It is nothing you did except for believing and receiving him, but it is everything he did.

Did you know that the Temple priests would purchase the lambs from the hills of Bethlehem during the time of Jesus?

Yes.

Five miles south from Jerusalem these lambs were carefully selected and taken care of by the shepherds so that they would be selected by the religious leaders for the Temple sacrifice.

Jesus was born in that same place of Bethlehem. He was wrapped in swaddling cloth by Joseph at his birth.

History says that the shepherds of Bethlehem would wrap these newborn lambs in cloth to keep them unblemished for the Temple sacrifice.

Bethlehem was also a source for the finest flour from the wheat grown there. It was where the olive oil, the grapes for wine and other fruitful crops were grown. This is why the name Bethlehem means "House of Bread".

The soil was rich here and the hill country was perfect for raising sheep. Jesus was born in a place of good soil. He spoke much about how our hearts are like the place where the seed is sown.

It is no wonder that the religious leaders headed to Bethlehem for a one stop shopping experience for the needs of the Temple.

The lambs were the big draw.

Jesus is the Lamb of God who takes away the sin of the world. He was born in Bethlehem fulfilling the scriptures.

When God sees a believer in Christ, he sees his precious son Jesus. He sees the blood of his own son, and he has no judgement against anyone who has the blood of his own son. This is the sign on the doorpost of your heart, it is the blood of Jesus Christ.

The blood shall be a sign for you on the houses where you live; and when I see the blood I will pass over you, and no plague will come upon you to destroy you when I strike the land of Egypt. (Exodus 12:13 NASB)

There was darkness over all the land and then the Passover came.

Exodus 10

Then the LORD said to Moses, "Reach out with your hand toward the sky, so that there may be darkness over the land of Egypt, even a darkness which may be felt."

Jesus was on that cross which is like the doorpost, with the blood stained upon it, and there was also darkness over the land. The Bible records that the darkness was three hours long while Jesus was on the cross.

Even secular historians recorded a darkness, so dark you could feel it, in that region from that very time of the cross.

After Jesus died there was a spiritual darkness it seems. His followers were in great sorrow and distress for three days. But they also had the protection and hope of Jesus.

Exodus 10

"...there was thick darkness in all the land of Egypt for three days. They did not see one another, nor did anyone rise from his place for three days, but all the sons of Israel had light in their dwellings"

The sons of Israel had light. Jesus is the Light. He called himself the Light of the World.

Hank Williams senior wrote that song, "I saw the Light":

I wandered so aimless; life filled with sin

I wouldn't let my dear savior in

Then Jesus came like a stranger in the night

Praise the Lord, I saw the light

I saw the light, I saw the light

No more darkness, no more night

Now I'm so happy no sorrow in sight

Praise the Lord, I saw the light

That song is so powerful, and it displays how Jesus is the Light.

God was shining his light on his people while everywhere else it was so dark you could feel it.

SEE JESUS IN THE OLD TESTAMENT

When you come to Jesus it is like walking toward a campfire. As you leave the outer darkness, you are attracted to the warm, beautiful light. As you walk closer and closer, your heart warms up and at the same time you see what you really look like.

In the darkness you could not see the stains, scars, and dirt. But as you draw closer to the fire, you begin to realize that you are unclean. This is only true when you are facing the light of that blaze. When you turn away from the light, you are in the shadows and can no longer see your own faults. You will see other people's stains as they are turned toward the light, and you will point out their stains. But in this state, you will not see your own sin.

But when you turn around and draw toward the light again, you see your need again. It is humbling to turn toward the light.

As you draw closer and closer to this brilliant light, you realize much more how dirty and in need you really are. This happens while in the presence of his warm light.

Those who saw the light but turned away went back out into the outer darkness where the light becomes less and less visible. Some return and enter into the camp. Others decide they hate the light and want no part of it. This is why they end up in a place that is so far from the light that they cannot see the way around anymore. It is so dark they can feel it.

Stay in the light my friend. Jesus' love and healing is always there in his presence. The blood of the Lamb who is the Light of the World, will clean you from all unrighteousness. All of it.

Passover is so amazing in that it points you to Jesus.

Look at the timing of this Passover event:

"In the first month, on the fourteenth day of the month at twilight is the LORD'S Passover." (Leviticus 23:5)

This is the same day of the year that Jesus was crucified. It was the 14th day of the month of Nisan.

It was three days later, on the 17th day, of that same month that Jesus was raised from the dead.

It was the same day that Noah's Ark rested on that mountain called Ararat. You know that Ararat means the "Curse is reversed," and you know that Noah's name means "Rest".

That 17th day speaks of a new day, a new day of hope, a new beginning.

So the Passover is always the 14th day of Nisan according to the Jewish calendar. Three days later marks a special day, a day of hope and restoration.

Some say that it was three days after the Passover, after the Exodus or exit out of Egypt that the children of Israel walked on dry ground to the other side of the Red Sea.

They were being followed by the evil army of that antichrist type of king. His army was destroyed at the dawn of that new day when the walls of water collapsed upon their enemies and destroyed them. Israel witnessed it from the other side. They were safe and secure that early morning on the 17th day of Nisan.

They sang a new song of joy and thankfulness to God.

Exodus 15

The song of Moses

Then Moses and the sons of Israel sang this song to the LORD, saying:

"I will sing to the LORD, for He is highly exalted;
The horse and its rider He has hurled into the sea.
"The LORD is my strength and song,
And He has become my salvation;
This is my God, and I will praise Him;
My father's God, and I will exalt Him.
"The LORD is a warrior;
The LORD is His name.

"Pharaoh's chariots and his army He has thrown into the sea;
And the choicest of his officers are drowned in the Red Sea.
"The waters cover them;
They went down into the depths like a stone.
"Your right hand, LORD, is majestic in power;
Your right hand, LORD, destroys the enemy.
"And in the greatness of Your excellence You overthrow those who rise
up against You;
You send out Your burning anger, and it consumes them like chaff.
"At the blast of Your nostrils the waters were piled up,
The flowing waters stood up like a heap;
The depths were congealed in the heart of the sea.
"The enemy said, 'I will pursue, I will overtake, I will divide the spoils;
I shall be satisfied against them;
I will draw my sword, my hand will destroy them.'
"You blew with Your wind, the sea covered them;
They sank like lead in the mighty waters.
11 "Who is like You among the gods, LORD?
Who is like You, majestic in holiness,
Awesome in praises, working wonders?
"You reached out with Your right hand,
The earth swallowed them.
"In Your faithfulness You have led the people whom You have
redeemed;
In Your strength You have guided them to Your holy habitation.
"The peoples have heard, they tremble;
Anguish has gripped the inhabitants of Philistia.
"Then the chiefs of Edom were terrified;
The leaders of Moab, trembling grips them;
All the inhabitants of Canaan have despaired.
"Terror and dread fall upon them;
By the greatness of Your arm they are motionless as stone,

Until Your people pass over, LORD,
Until the people pass over whom You have purchased.
"You will bring them and plant them in the mountain of Your
inheritance,
The place, LORD, which You have made as Your dwelling,
The sanctuary, Lord, which Your hands have established.
"The LORD shall reign forever and ever."
For the horses of Pharaoh with his chariots and his horsemen went into
the sea, and the LORD brought back the waters of the sea on them, but
the sons of Israel walked on dry land through the midst of the sea.

Then Miriam who was Moses sister, leads the women of Israel in this amazing worship:

Miriam the prophetess, Aaron's sister, took the tambourine in her
hand, and all the women went out after her with tambourines and
with dancing.
And Miriam answered them,
"Sing to the LORD, for He is highly exalted;
The horse and his rider He has hurled into the sea."

Did you know that this song of Moses is sung again near the end of the tribulation period in the book of Revelation?

Yes it is.

Look at how you can see Israel and a remnant of Gentiles being saved once again but this time at the end of the world.

Revelation 15

Then I saw another sign in heaven, great and marvelous, seven angels
who had seven plagues, which are the last, because in them the wrath
of God is finished.
And I saw something like a sea of glass mixed with fire, and those who
were victorious over the beast and his image and the number of his
name, standing on the sea of glass, holding harps of God.
And they sang the song of Moses, the bond-servant of God, and the
song of the Lamb, saying,

SEE JESUS IN THE OLD TESTAMENT

"Great and marvelous are Your works,
Lord God, the Almighty;
Righteous and true are Your ways,
King of the nations!
"Who will not fear You, Lord, and glorify Your name?
For You alone are holy;
For ALL THE NATIONS WILL COME AND WORSHIP
BEFORE YOU,
For Your righteous acts have been revealed."

Did you catch that?

This final song of victory is called the song of Moses and the Lamb.

Again, the New Testament connects Moses to the Lamb of God, Jesus.

CHAPTER THIRTEEN: TABERNACLE – MODEL OF CHRIST

The Tabernacle was a portable worship center in ancient Israel. This was where the LORD would meet with Moses as he sat on the Mercy Seat of the Ark, in the Holy of Holy place.

Later, around four-hundred years later, King Solomon built the first Temple which was modeled off the Tabernacle, but he made it seven times what it was. For instance, instead of one seven golden lamp stand known as the Menorah, there were seven of them. It was magnificent and even the paver stones outside were made of solid silver.

But the Tabernacle was much smaller, and it was made specifically from God's specifications. God designed it himself and it was made to be light so they could pack it up and move. The burden was to be light.

Each item, each furnishing of the Tabernacle illustrates the Messiah Jesus.

Even the fabrics tell his story.

The crimson-red dye they used for the tent coverings, the veil of curtain that separated the Holy Place from the Holy of Holies, the Priest garments, the Yarn tied to the scape goat, all of these tell the story of Jesus.

You see, even the red dye comes from the Scarlet worm, or Crimson worm. It looks more like a grub than a worm and it was harvested off trees by the ancient Israelis to make the red dye.

They collected them, dried them, and then crushed them. This would become a fine powder, like crimson dust. Hot water was added to make the red liquid dye used for the Tabernacle fabrics.

They would collect these off the Acacia trees (Also called the Thorn Tree). The Acacia wood was used to make the furniture of the Tabernacle, and they are common to the area of the desert wilderness, where Moses led the children of Israel, and they are harvested even to this day from those places.

Later they collected them off the Kermes Oak trees common in the land of Israel. This is where the name "Kermes Worm" came from and where we got the name for that red color.

So, this little creature used for the red dye in the Tabernacle tells the story of Jesus.

This little creature, called the Tola'at Shani, Scarlet worm, or Crimson worm. It would climb up a tree one time in its life to give birth to its offspring and it would die on that tree.

The Tola would attach itself firmly to that wood of the tree and as it did, it would swell up and turn a dark crimson red. Then it would die and burst open, its young would suddenly be dyed with the parent's crimson red color for the rest of their lives. Then they would feed off the body of their parent. This caused them to grow and live a life just like the one that gave them life through its death.

Then the place where the parent crimson worm died would be stained blood red for three days.

After three days, the red stained turns as white as snow and it even looks like a frost type substance. It then falls to the ground like a snowflake.

This brings you to the scripture in Psalm twenty-two, verse six. Take a look at it from the Dead Sea Scrolls: *"But I am a worm, and no man; a reproach of men, and despised by the people."*

The worm in Psalm 22 is the Tola'at Shani.

You can also see it in Isaiah chapter one, verse eighteen from the Dead Sea Scrolls:

"Come now, and let's reason together," says Yahweh:
"Though your sins be as scarlet, they shall be as white as snow.

Though they be red like crimson, they shall be as wool".

You see in that passage God saying let's reason together. Though your sins be as scarlet (Shani in Hebrew), they shall be as white as snow. Then he says though they be red like crimson (Tola'at in Hebrew) they shall be as wool (White like lamb's wool).

Isn't that amazing?

There are so many hidden treasures in the Old Testament for you to find.

Now let us unpack the Tabernacle and how God designed it to show you Jesus. He even tells Moses to construct it exactly as he tells him:

Exodus 25

Then the LORD spoke to Moses, saying,
"Tell the sons of Israel to take a contribution for Me; from everyone whose heart moves him you shall take My contribution. This is the contribution which you are to take from them: gold, silver, and bronze, violet, purple, and scarlet material, fine linen, goat hair, rams' skins dyed red, fine leather, acacia wood, oil for lighting, balsam oil for the anointing oil and for the fragrant incense, onyx stones and setting stones for the ephod and for the breastpiece. Have them construct a sanctuary for Me, so that I may dwell among them. According to all that I am going to show you as the pattern of the tabernacle and the pattern of all its furniture, so you shall construct it.

All these materials come together to form the pattern or model of Jesus Christ. God repeats it over and over from Exodus chapter twenty-five all the way through to chapter forty.

Most read this part of the Old Testament and get bored. It is hard to read something that repeats over and over. However, God does not want you to be bored but to find the treasure.

It is like he buried, or hid treasure and he gives you a map to find it. That treasure is his Son Jesus. So, he repeatedly shows you the map, which is his word to remind you to look at it, to study it, to imagine it.

When God repeats something, it means it is very important.

He repeated the dreams in Joseph's story. He repeated the Gospels, Matthew, Mark, Luke, and John four times by these four different authors. He repeated the thousand-year reign in Revelation chapter twenty, six times in seven verses.

These repeated things are treasures from God and vital to you and me. It is like having a map showing where to find water, food, and shelter when you have been shipwrecked onto a deserted Island.

Now let us unpack the treasure of the Tabernacle.

The whole area was one-hundred and fifty feet by seventy-five feet, which included the outer courtyard, and the Tent of Meeting.

The entrance was always on the east side, and as you walked in you would be greeted by the priests. These men were there to examine and then take your offering to the Lord. They would then bring it to be prepared and then cooked on the Bronze Altar, which was like a giant barbeque. You could feel the warmth of the flames and hear the crackling of the fire as the meat sizzled. So this place smelled good, and you wanted to enter and smell the barbequed meat.

In fact, when you offered this meat to the Lord, you gave it to the Lord, but you also ate of it too. It was like having a meal with God.

You would also hear the sweet melody of the priest choir singing worship songs to the Lord, including the Song of Moses.

Then there was the Bronze Laver or wash basin filled with precious water.

After those things, you see the entrance into the Tent of Meeting.

The tent had its entrance facing east and it had a colorfully decorated curtain that you would walk through.

Upon entering the tent you would smell the fresh baked loaves of bread, the fragrant aroma of incense, and the bright light from the solid gold Lampstands with its flames reflecting off the precious stones on the golden Breast Plate of the High Priest, the golden Table of Showbread, the gold Altar of Incense, the acacia wood beams overlaid with gold, and the white, purple, blue, crimson tapestries on the ceiling and sides.

So, this first room of the Tabernacle, called the Holy Place, would fill your sense of smell with sweet fragrance of bread, cinnamon, frankincense. You could see the brilliance of the colors in the tapestry, and the curtains as the gold reflected the light all around. Your sense of smell, taste and sight would be satisfied, and then you would hear the peaceful harmony of worship music and the prayers from the priests.

That first room was called the Holy Place, and the next and final chamber was called the Holy of Holy Place or the Holy of Holies.

To enter this most Holy part of the Tabernacle required you to bow down to the floor, and crawl under the beautifully decorated Curtain or Veil that separated it from the Holy Place.

When you entered, there was no source of light except for the glory of the presence of the Lord. This is where Moses would meet with the Lord. The only furnishing in this room was the Ark of the Covenant. Inside of the Ark was the stone tablets that God himself wrote, the Ten Commandments. You also see the Rod of Aaron, and the Bowl of Manna inside of this Ark.

The lid of the Ark was called the Mercy Seat. This was made of solid gold and had two angels on both ends, and the wings touched in the middle. This is where the Lord would visit with Moses and would sit on the Mercy Seat.

So, this room had one light source, the brilliant glow of the Lord himself.

The Tabernacle was the principal place of the camp of Israel. All the tents or homes of the Israelis were camped around this main place.

Why was Yahweh the Lord God so concerned about what this place looked like?

Because it was a picture of Christ.

John 1

And the Word became flesh, and dwelt among us; and we saw His glory, glory as of the only Son from the Father, full of grace and truth.

Did you know that word, *"dwelt"* literally means tabernacled. It means he tabernacled among us.

The New Testament was written in the Greek language. It was not by accident that the Greek word John used to describe Jesus is, tabernacled. This word means: to fix one's tabernacle, have one's tabernacle, abide (or live) in a tabernacle (or tent), to tabernacle.

This word was only used by John in the New Testament and there is one other place where he used it.

In Revelation you can see John using this same Greek word, to describe how the Tabernacle speaks of God.

Revelation 7

*"These are the ones who come out of the great tribulation, and they have washed their robes and made them white in the blood of the Lamb. For this reason they are before the throne of God, and they serve Him day and night in His temple; and He who sits on the throne will spread **His tabernacle** over them. They will no longer hunger nor thirst, nor will the sun beat down on them, nor any scorching heat; for the Lamb in the center of the throne will be their shepherd, and will guide them to springs of the water of life; and God will wipe every tear from their eyes."*

He spreads his Tabernacle over those who are saved. This speaks of being covered in his righteousness.

It is no wonder that Jesus told us to abide in Him. That word abide in the Greek also means dwell. You dwell or tabernacle in Jesus because if you are one of his you are in Christ.

What was the main reason for the Tabernacle?

The scripture gives you the answer: *"Have them construct a sanctuary for Me, so that I may dwell among them." (Exodus 25:8)*

That is what God wants. He wants to dwell among us, so that we can dwell with him. It is about God with us.

Remember Matthew wrote and quoted from Isaiah 7, *"BEHOLD, THE VIRGIN WILL CONCEIVE AND GIVE BIRTH TO A SON, AND THEY SHALL NAME HIM IMMANUEL," which translated means, "GOD WITH US." (Matthew 1:23 NASB)*

Now you can see each element of this Tabernacle and how it shows Christ.

The East Entrance

The Eastern entrance is the only way into the Tabernacle. Jesus is the only way to Heaven. He said, *"I am the way, and the truth, and the life; no one comes to the Father except through Me."*

The East Gate was where Jesus entered Jerusalem on Palm Sunday as he rode the donkey.

The Acacia tree

It was used for all the wood framework for the posts, the beams, the furnishings and so forth. This Acacia tree is the only tree in the world that thrives in the dryest of the desert wilderness places.

The Acacia tree is also known as the Thorn tree. It has extremely large thorns just under the green leaves.

You know that thorns were a result of the fall of man in the Garden of Eden. So this tree could very well be called the cursed tree.

Some have concluded that it was from the Acacia tree that the crown of thorns was made and place onto Jesus head.

The Altar

It was made of solid bronze. It was about seven and a half feet in length and width. It was about four and a half feet tall.

What happened on the inside of the tent was not visible to the public. However, what happened on the Altar was visible by all. And this was the place where the sacrificial deaths took place. This is where the blood was shed for all to see. Jesus was crucified publicly for all to see.

The burning coals from the Altar were used to light the incense located inside the Holy Place. The Bible tells us our prayers are like the smoke of the incense going up into Heaven and to God and it is a sweet smell to him. Keep in mind that those coals from the outside, from the publicly seen altar, had the blood of the sacrifice dripped upon them.

It is by the blood of Jesus, form his sacrifice, that the Father directly hears our prayers.

The Bronze Laver

The wash basin or laver was made of solid bronze, and was used for the washing.

Scripture specifically tells us it was made from the mirrors of the Egyptian women. The Israelites received these valuable items just before they left that land and headed out for the Promised Land. This was a higher quality bronze that was shiny and beautiful and as you washed you may have seen what you really looked like.

It was used for cleansing and washing. Ephesians 5:26 speaks of Christ and his bride the church: *"...that He might sanctify her, having cleansed her by the washing of water with the word."*

The Tent Coverings

There were four separate coverings. Three were skins and the inner one was a tapestry of white, lined artistically and dyed in colorful patterns of purple, scarlet, and blue.

The tent was about forty-five feet long and fifteen feet wide.

The inside of the Tabernacle tent was full of light, warmth, brilliance, fire, gold, sweet smelling incense, tapestries, bread, and wine, and it was all beautiful on the inside.

However, the outside was not attractive. There was nothing beautiful or majestic about the outside appearance. Jesus was described in Isaiah 53 in that same way, yet he was God the Son. Jesus was beautiful on the inside, and he talked about the importance of being good inside and not just the outside appearance.

If a local shepherd of that wilderness area would have seen the Tabernacle tent from the outside, he would not have thought it was anything special. The outer covering was made of a tough waterproof skin, likely from a Manatees type of a sea creature.

Each layer of the coverings become increasingly beautiful from the outside to the inside.

The next layer under the outer layer was the Rams skin. You saw the Ram in Genesis chapter twenty-two, when Abraham and Isaac were on that mountain and a Ram was caught in the thicket by its horns. This was a huge symbolic sacrifice to God on the same Mountain where Jesus would be sacrificed over two-thousand years later.

This Ram skin was dyed red. It was dyed with that Scarlet or Crimson worm, the Tola'at Shani, to achieve this blood red color. It was over the Goat skin layer which speaks of the blood of Jesus covering our sin.

The next layer was Goat skin. Goats often represent sin. Remember the Scapegoat was representing the sins of the nation of Israel and on Yom Kipper it was released far away from the camp to show how God takes our sin away.

So this layer is like a sin bearing cover which speaks of Jesus because he became sin who knew no sin so that we might be free to enter. This layer was between the inner layer which speaks of Heaven. Jesus took that sin upon himself so that we can enter into that inner place of Heaven.

The final layer, the inner layer was the pure white linen that was artistically dyed with the crimson red, purple and blue. It was what you saw as you stood inside the Holy Place.

It displays Heaven with all its beauty and light. The light of the golden lampstands shined brightly upon this inner layer.

The Holy Place

This was the room where the High Priest did his work.

This room was the home of the Seven Golden Lampstands, the Tabel of Showbread, and the Altar of Incense.

The lampstands represents the church, the table with the bread and wine together represents communion, and the incense represents our prayers to God.

The Table of Showbread

It was made of Acacia wood and overlaid with gold. On top of it you can see a cup of wine and twelve loaves of fresh baked bread. This speaks of the Sader meal of Passover, and that last supper where Jesus performed the first communion with his twelve disciples.

Seven Golden Lampstands

Revelation chapter one tells you that the Seven Golden Lampstands represents the church.

Also known as the Menorah, this golden lampstand was to be kept filled with olive oil and always lit by the High Priest. It was made of solid gold. As you may know, gold is the only element in the world that does not corrode. It lasts forever and you can see in scripture that the streets are paved with gold in Heaven and the foundations are made of pure gold.

Exodus 37

Then he made the lampstands of pure gold. He made the lampstands of hammered work, its base and its shaft; its cups, its bulbs, and its flowers were of one piece with it. There were six branches going out of its sides; three branches of the lampstands from the one side of it and three branches of the lampstands from the other side of it; three cups shaped like almond blossoms, a bulb and a flower on one branch, and three cups shaped like almond blossoms, a bulb and a flower on the other branch—so for the six branches going out of the lampstands.

The Lamp was fashioned like the almond tree.

The Almond trees blossom in late winter before any other tree.

Also the High Priest Aaron had a rod that blossomed almonds. This speaks of the dead wood coming to life again. It speaks of revival.

So this is why God had it fashioned this way.

Jesus referenced the seven golden lampstands as the Seven Churches in Revelation. The church is to be a light on a hill and shine brightly. How does it shine brightly? By the Great High Priest Jesus, who pours the oil, the Holy Spirit into us. As he pours in, our hearts burn with the anointing of God, and we shine brighter for Jesus.

In Revelation, Jesus himself calls the seven golden lampstands, the seven churches. He was using typology here to show us his church is foreshadowed in the Old Testament.

Revelation 1

"...the seven lampstands are the seven churches."

Altar of Incense

God gave specific instructions for this precious furnishing for how it was to be made.

"Now you shall make an altar as a place for burning incense; you shall make it of acacia wood.

Its length shall be a cubit, and its width a cubit; it shall be square, and its height shall be two cubits; its horns shall be of one piece with it. You shall overlay it with pure gold, its top and its sides all around, and its horns; and you shall make a gold molding all around for it...”(Exodus 30 NASB)

It was square and almost two feet tall and wide.

Where was it located? Scripture tells you:

You shall put this altar in front of the veil that is near the ark of the testimony, in front of the atoning cover that is over the ark of the testimony, where I will meet with you.

Who took care of it? The following scripture explains:

Aaron shall burn fragrant incense on it; he shall burn it every morning when he trims the lamps. And when Aaron sets up the lamps at twilight, he shall burn incense. There shall be perpetual incense before the LORD throughout your generations.

The High priest took care of it as he took care of the golden lampstands. Aaron was the first of them other than Melchizedek.

...Aaron shall make atonement on its horns once a year; he shall make atonement on it with the blood of the sin offering of atonement once a year throughout your generations. It is most holy to the LORD.”

With the blood of the sin offering, Aaron made atonement, and it was holy to the Lord.

Then the LORD said to Moses, “Take for yourself spices—stacte, onycha, and galbanum, spices and pure frankincense; there shall be an equal part of each.

You shall make incense from it all, a skillful mixture, the work of a perfumer, salted, pure, and holy. And you shall crush some of it very fine, and put part of it in front of the testimony in the tent of meeting where I will meet with you; it shall be most holy to you.

David gave you a connection of our prayers and the incense in Psalm 141:

“...LORD, I call upon You; hurry to me!

Listen to my voice when I call to You!
May my prayer be counted as incense before You;
The raising of my hands as the evening offering.
Set a guard, LORD, over my mouth;
Keep watch over the door of my lips..."

The incense was a covering and a pleasing aroma to God, and there was an atonement that had to be made for the Altar itself once a year. Aaron was to go with the blood of the sin offering and put it on the horns of the altar and this pleased the Lord.

The Altar of Incense was burning constantly, and the Bible tells you it is the prayers of the saints and that it is a sweet aroma to God. He delights in our prayers, and we are to pray continuously.

Revelation 5

When He had taken the scroll, the four living creatures and the twenty-four elders fell down before the Lamb, each one holding a harp and golden bowls full of incense, which are the prayers of the saints.

The Curtain or Veil

This specially made curtain was to separate the two rooms inside the tent of the Tabernacle.

Exodus 26:31-33

"You shall also make a veil of violet, purple, and scarlet material, and fine twisted linen; it shall be made with cherubim, the work of a skilled embroiderer.

Then you shall hang it on four pillars of acacia overlaid with gold, their hooks also of gold, on four bases of silver. You shall hang up the veil under the clasps, and bring in the ark of the testimony there within the veil; and the veil shall serve as a partition for you between the Holy Place and the Most Holy Place."

This veil was used to cover the Ark when Aaron and the other priests packed everything up to move to another location.

It was made of the most beautiful fabric as it was embroidered with violet, purple, and the scarlet thread made of the crimson material.

On it you would see the cherubim which were the special angels who worshiped God.

Later it became the Veil of the Temple. This was much larger in size. Some say up to thirty feet tall and it was thick, around three and a half inches thick.

When Jesus died on that cross, there was a massive earthquake, and the Veil of the Temple was torn from top to bottom. This opened up the Holy of Holy place for all to have direct access to God, through the sacrifice of his Son Jesus. Remember, Jesus was also called the Great High Priest.

Hebrews 10

Therefore, brothers and sisters, since we have confidence to enter the holy place by the blood of Jesus,
by a new and living way which He inaugurated for us through the veil, that is, through His flesh, and since we have a great priest over the house of God, let's approach God with a sincere heart in full assurance of faith, having our hearts sprinkled clean from an evil conscience and our bodies washed with pure water.

By the blood of Jesus we have confidence to go through the Veil which represented his own flesh, so that we could enter the Holiest place with God.

The Holy of Holy Place

This was the place where only the High Priest of the line of Aaron was allowed to go into once a year to offer the incense and the sprinkling of the blood of the sacrifice for the sins of the people.

John the Baptist had a father named Zechariah, and just before John was born he was selected for that duty by the casting of lots.

At that time, this was a frightening duty because this specially selected priest would sometimes die behind the curtain. Some say this was the reason for the golden bells on the High Priest garments. They also say that a rope was tied around the ancle of the priest so that it the bells stopped ringing the people could retrieve the dead body of the man.

Luke 1

In the days of Herod, king of Judea, there was a priest named Zechariah, of the division of Abijah; and he had a wife from the daughters of Aaron, and her name was Elizabeth.
They were both righteous in the sight of God, walking blamelessly in all the commandments and requirements of the Lord. And yet they had no child, because Elizabeth was infertile, and they were both advanced in years.
Now it happened that while he was performing his priestly service before God in the appointed order of his division, according to the custom of the priestly office, he was chosen by lot to enter the temple of the Lord and burn incense. And the whole multitude of the people were in prayer outside at the hour of the incense offering. Now an angel of the Lord appeared to him, standing to the right of the altar of incense. Zechariah was troubled when he saw the angel, and fear gripped him. But the angel said to him, "Do not be afraid, Zechariah, for your prayer has been heard, and your wife Elizabeth will bear you a son, and you shall name him John..."

John the Baptist's father Zechariah was troubled when he saw the angel Gabriel. He thought he was going to die in the Holiest place of the Temple.

But the angel shared great news for him and his wife. It was the greatest of all the prophets, who would be born by his wife Elizabeth, who was too old to have a child. She was also related to Mary. Her baby John leaped inside of her womb when Mary, who was pregnant with Jesus walked into her presence for a visit.

The Ark of the Covenant

This box was made of Acacia wood, overlaid with gold and it carried key elements inside of it including the stone tablets with the Ten Commandments written by the finger of God, the staff of Aaron that budded, and the golden bowl of Manna.

It stood two feet high and three feet long.

The lid was called the Mercy Seat and was made of solid gold.

The elements inside are all symbolic of what God did and what Jesus would do.

The Ten Commandments

The ten commandments represent the holy life that only Jesus fulfilled. Remember, Jesus said, *"Do not presume that I came to abolish the Law or the Prophets; I did not come to abolish, but to fulfill. For truly I say to you, until heaven and earth pass away, not the smallest letter or stroke of a letter shall pass from the Law, until all is accomplished!*

Jesus lived the perfect life and completed the fulfillment of the law. You and I are incapable of that. We try but we fail again, and again.

It is good to teach the law of God, and in America our Judicial system was based on the Ten Commandments. However, the antichrist elites of the globalist groups have fought hard to remove it. Just looking at the results of their work today, it is obviously rotten fruit.

But Jesus fulfilled it, every bit of it, and he is marvelous to us who believe and follow him. Jesus is our great hope.

Aaron's Rod

The next item in the Ark is Aaron's Rod that budded, and that represents Jesus death and resurrection.

The rod that Aaron carried represented his authority.

In the book of Numbers, chapter seventeen, you can see a rebellion against Moses and Aaron. These evil men wanted to take that authority away for themselves. Then God himself said he will take care of this matter for them.

God had each of the leaders, bring their twelve staffs or rods, and then Aaron was told to bring his one rod, and put them together. God was about to show something amazing to Israel.

Exodus 17

And it will come about that the staff of the man whom I choose will sprout. So I will relieve Myself of the grumblings of the sons of Israel, who are grumbling against you." So Moses spoke to the sons of Israel, and all their leaders gave him a staff, one for each leader, for their fathers' households, twelve staffs in all, with the staff of Aaron among their staffs. Then Moses left the staffs before the LORD in the tent of the testimony.

Now on the next day Moses went into the tent of the testimony; and behold, Aaron's staff for the house of Levi had sprouted and produced buds and bloomed with blossoms, and it yielded ripe almonds.

Exodus 37

Then he made the lampstands of pure gold...shaped like almond blossoms, a bulb and a flower on the other branch—so for the six branches going out of the lampstands.

Here you can see a direct connection of the almond blossoms on the Seven Golden Lampstands and Aaron's rod.

What is interesting is that Aaron's rod was a dead piece of wood. God miraculously caused it to come back to life. It was life from the dead.

Also it showed that this was the man who God chose. Not only that but Aaron and his son's would be the priests who would bear the iniquity or guilt connected with the priesthood.

Numbers 18

So the LORD said to Aaron, "You, your sons, and your father's household with you shall bear the guilt in connection with the sanctuary, and you and your sons with you shall bear the guilt in connection with your priesthood.

Acts 17

He has set a day on which He will judge the world in righteousness through a Man whom He has appointed, having furnished proof to all people by raising Him from the dead."

He was God's selection, appointed to be judged, to bear the guilt that had to be dealt with.

The Manna

The Manna is symbolic of Jesus being the Bread of Heaven.

John 6

Jesus then said to them, "Truly, truly, I say to you, it is not Moses who has given you the bread out of heaven, but it is My Father who gives you the true bread out of heaven. For the bread of God is that which comes down out of heaven and gives life to the world."

This special bread kept the people of Israel strong and young looking for forty years. This was all they needed for nutrition, but it also spoke of Jesus himself.

Then they said to Him, "Lord, always give us this bread."

Jesus said to them, "I am the bread of life; the one who comes to Me will not be hungry, and the one who believes in Me will never be thirsty...

Your fathers ate the manna in the wilderness, and they died. This is the bread that comes down out of heaven, so that anyone may eat from it and not die. I am the living bread that came down out of heaven; if anyone eats from this bread, he will live forever; and the bread which I will give for the life of the world also is My flesh."

Jesus directly links this manna to himself. He just used typology from the Old Testament and showed how it spoke of him. This Manna, this bread from Heaven, was something the children of Israel did not know. It was clearly a picture of the one that they would say, "Who are you?"

The Mercy Seat

The whole Ark, this whole box represents the very place where Jesus body was laid in the Tomb of Joseph of Arimathea.

Remember Mary Magdeline came to the tomb early in the morning, three days after Jesus died on the cross and discovered something symbolic.

John 20

Mary was standing outside the tomb, weeping; so as she wept, she stooped to look into the tomb; and she saw two angels in white sitting, one at the head and one at the feet, where the body of Jesus had been lying.

The Mercy Seat was to be kept empty. The only things you could have seen on it were the two Cherubim or Angels on either side of the seat with their wings touching. You would also see the sprinkles of blood from the sin atoning sacrifice.

In that same way Mary Magdalene saw two angels, one at the head and one at the foot of where Jesus body had been. But she found it empty.

Jesus fulfilled everything that was under that seat. He fulfilled the law, Aaron's Rod that came back to life, and the Manna, the Bread of Heaven. And his resurrection is shown by the empty space on that seat.

This truly is the place of mercy. It was purchased by the blood of the Lamb.

The Great High Priest

The Great High Priest is mentioned in the New Testament book of Hebrews, as a foreshadow, a type of Christ throughout the book. Fifteen times Jesus is called our High Priest.

The Levites were the tribe of the priests; however, Aaron and his sons were the only ones other than Moses who were allowed to go into the Tabernacle.

The garments that were made for the High Priest were glorious. Aaron was just a man but the special clothing he wore is what made him glorious.

He wore pure white linen shorts under the white linen coat or robe, with a white sash that functioned like a belt. These garments covered his whole body, it was a long-sleeved coat, and this speaks of the purity or holiness of Christ. This also reminds you of the coat that Joseph wore, and he was the father's most favored son.

The next piece of clothing was a blue robe. Along the hem of this robe was blue, purple and scarlet yarn shaped into the form of pomegranates, and there were also golden bells. The pattern was a pomegranate, then a bell, then a pomegranate and so on.

On top of the blue robe you could see the Ephod. It was made of blue, purple and scarlet yarn, with gold thread woven in as well.

The shoulder pieces had Onyx stones, on one side, and one on the other. The names of the tribes of Israel were engraved on these stones.

Then you would see the Breast plate. This piece was worn over the chest, or heart of the High Priest and it had twelve polished, precious stones set in pure gold. Each of these had the engraved name of one of the tribes of Israel. Twelve tribes, twelve precious stones.

So, Jesus, who is our Great High Priest is in that Holy Place, he is filling the Seven Golden Lampstands with the olive oil so that the fire could burn bright.

When he did that, those twelve precious stones over his heart would glow more beautifully. They would reflect that light and sparkle brilliantly.

In that same way, as Jesus takes care of his Church, and he pours the Holy Spirit into it, it becomes on fire for God. This speaks of revival. And when this happens, Israel becomes more beautiful.

Israel should always be beautiful to the revived Church.

Finally, you see the Holy Crown. It was made of solid gold, and it speaks of royalty. In Revelation nine-teen you see Jesus returning and he wears a golden crown.

The book of Hebrews mentions the connection of Jesus and the High Priest repeatedly. Take a look:

Hebrews 4

Therefore, since we have a great high priest who has passed through the heavens, Jesus the Son of God, let's hold firmly to our confession. For we do not have a high priest who cannot sympathize with our weaknesses, but One who has been tempted in all things just as we are, yet without sin. Therefore let's approach the throne of grace with confidence, so that we may receive mercy and find grace for help at the time of our need.

You too can find grace in him who is our covering, our Tabernacle, our Great High Priest, Jesus.

CHAPTER FOURTEEN: THE PROPHETS

The Prophets throughout ancient Israel told of Jesus. You see Isaiah, Ezekiel, Micah, and more. But we are focused on teaching it the way Yeshua (Jesus) did on that resurrection day. He took them through the Tanakh, in the same order that it is to this day: the Torah, the Prophets, and the Psalms.

Joshua is the first of the listed Prophets in the Tanakh.

However, we know that Noah, Abraham, Jacob, Joseph, Moses, David, and others also prophesied. Moses was called a prophet.

We know that Moses was a Prophet, but this is how the Tanakh, the original Jewish Bible is divided.

Remember in Luke 24, Jesus himself put the Bible in that order: "These are My words which I spoke to you while I was still with you, that all the things that are written about Me in the Law of **Moses** and the **Prophets** and the **Psalms** must be fulfilled." (Luke 24:44 NASB)

So, the first prophet in the Tanakh is Joshua - the Joshua scroll.

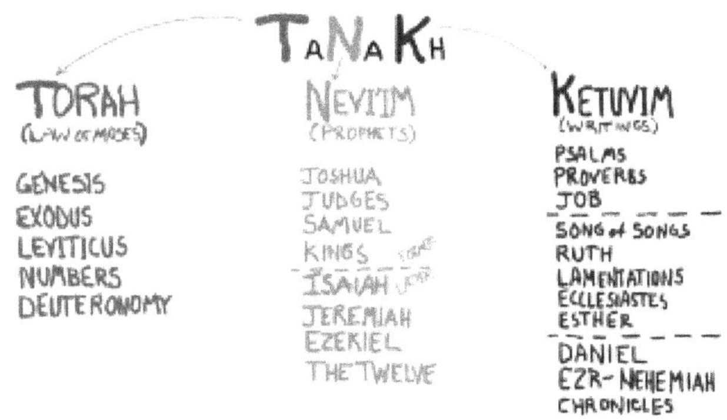

After Joshua the prophet you see Judges, Samuel, and Kings – you will see Jesus in all of these. In fact, Joshua's name alone is the same as Jesus. You will see more about that in the next chapter.

These first four books of the Prophets were called the "Former".

The rest of them were considered the "Latter".

In the latter you see Isaiah, Jeremiah, Ezekiel, and then the "Twelve" which are all the rest.

Interestingly Daniel was listed in the Ketuvim (Writings or Psalms) which is the last section of the Tanakh. You would think he would be at the top of the list with Isaiah, but you see him later in the last part.

However, it makes no difference because all the Tanakh is considered scripture which is the inspired word of God. David was a mighty prophet of God as well as the greatest king – other than Jesus of course.

Book of Joshua (Yeshua)

You can see Jesus in Joshua because Moses, who represented the Law, could not bring the people into the promised land but Joshua could. It is amazing how you can see Jesus in Joshua's story.

You will see more details about how Joshua was a picture and foreshadowing of Jesus in the next chapter, titled, "Joshua – Type of Christ".

Book of Judges

Judges is an amazing account of Israel's journey through a cycle of rebellion, oppression, then returning to the Lord, and the Lord delivering them out of harm and back to him.

The book focuses on the judges that were appointed and raised to lead his people. You can also see the types and foreshadowing's of Jesus Messiah.

You can see Jesus throughout the Book of Judges, pointing to Jesus' saving work as the Supreme Judge of judges, the King of kings and Lord of lords.

These judges served as temporary saviors, but Jesus would be the Supreme and eternal Savior who would bring salvation to all who believe in Him.

Gideon

You can see how Jesus is displayed in the story of Gideon.

In the book of Judges, the second book of the Prophets in the Torah, you can see how humble Gideon was at first and how he becomes a great warrior through the power of God.

He brought revival to God's people, Israel by turning them away from the false gods and toward the God of Abraham, Isaac, and Jacob. God has him downsize his Army from 32,000 men down to just 300 men to fight against an army of 135,000. God brilliantly has them surround the enemy camp at the Valley of Jezreel, at night and break clay jars with torches of fire in them, sound the trumpets, and yell.

The evil forces who were camping at Jezreel or Armageddon, panicked and turned on each other. God's plan was brilliant.

This is how you can see Jesus's first and second coming.

Christ is shown in Gideon's story because he was humble, the first time and then he saves all of Israel as a valiant warrior.

Jesus will come and defeat the enemies of Israel in that same valley, the valley of Armageddon.

Tola

He was a man who rose up to save Israel.

Now after Abimelech died, *Tola the son of Puah, the son of Dodo, a man of Issachar, rose up to save Israel; and he lived in Shamir in the hill country of Ephraim.*

(Judges 10:1 NASB)

His grandfather's name, Puah means, 'splendid', and his father's name, 'Dodo' means, 'his beloved'.

So, he was the son of splendid and the son of his beloved father. Jesus' Father is splendid, and he is the son of his beloved Father.

That passage also said he rose up to save Israel.

Jesus rose from the dead to save Israel and those Gentiles who would be grafted into Israel.

His own name, Tola means, "Crimson worm", or "Scarlet Worm". This is the same worm of Psalm 22, "I am a worm (Tola or Tola'at) and no man".

This little creature was more of a grub than a worm.

It was used in ancient Israel, and even in modern Israel, to get the crimson-red dye for fabrics of the tabernacle and the Temple. This scarlet thread was sewn into the curtain that separated the Holy place from the Holy of Holy place. It was used in the tapestries, the priestly garments, and the yarn tied around the scapegoat.

They would collect these tiny Tola'at from the trees and dry them out. After they were dehydrated, they would then crush them into a powder. That powder was used for making the dye by adding boiling hot water. It was also used in the incense for the Tabernacle.

This little creature has a life that displays the good news of Jesus. It climbs up a tree, one time in its life, to give life to its offspring and dies. It turns crimson-red, and sticks itself to the tree, dies and bursts open.

That spot on the tree is stained with that blood-red dye for three days and then turns as white as snow, and has a flakey like texture. It then falls to the ground like a snowflake. This is reminiscent of the Manna, that bread of Heaven that fed the Israelites for 40 years. Jesus also called himself the Bread of Heaven.

You will see much more about this Tola'at, this crimson worm when we explore Psalm 22.

Samson

Samson is in the Book of Judges. In many ways, he parallels the life of Jesus. Like Jesus, he was a chosen deliverer and set apart from birth for a special purpose. Samson's supernatural strength illustrates Jesus' miraculous power, while his betrayal by Delilah draws similarities to Jesus' betrayal by Judas Iscariot. At the end, Samson's sacrificial death where he destroyed the Philistine temple mirrors Jesus' selfless sacrifice for the redemption of humanity.

"Joseph, son of David, do not be afraid to take Mary as your wife; for the Child who has been conceived in her is of the Holy Spirit. She will give birth to a Son; and you shall name Him Jesus, for He will save His people from their sins." (Matthew 1:20-21 NASB)

The angel's message to Joseph, explained the purpose and significance of the birth of Jesus - that Jesus has come into the world with the mission of saving his people from their sins.

Like Jesus, an angel foretold Samson's birth. An angel appeared to Samson's mother and announced that she would conceive and bear a son. Jesus and Samson were born with a divine purpose, a mission ordained by God.

Samson was raised up by God to begin delivering the Israelites from the oppression of the Philistines. Jesus came as the Deliverer, sent by God to save humanity from the bondage of sin and provide salvation to all who believe in Him.

Samson and Jesus experienced betrayal and sacrifice. Samson was betrayed by his wife, Delilah, who was like Judas Iscariot. Delilah revealed the secret of his strength to the Philistines. In a similar manner, Jesus was betrayed by one of His disciples, Judas Iscariot, who handed Him over to the authorities. Both Samson and Jesus willingly sacrificed themselves for the greater purpose of fulfilling God's plan.

Both offered themselves as living sacrifices to save others. Samson sacrificed himself to defeat the Philistines and destroy their temple dedicated to a false god. Jesus sacrificed himself to defeat Satan and destroy his earthly kingdom.

Book of Samuel
1070-1012 BC Before Christ

1st and 2nd Samuel were written by the Prophet Samuel and took place during his lifetime.

The first book covers Samuel the Prophet. The second book of Samuel is about David as King of Israel.

The books cover Saul and David's reigns and describe Israel's history right after the last Judge, who was Samuel.

1st Samuel

Israel had fallen into moral and political corruption, and it was so bad that even the priests were corrupt and did not know the Lord. Then comes Samuel.

He shared the office of a prophet, priest, and judge, like Christ.

He was the last Judge of Israel and Christ is the final Judge.

Both Samuel and Jesus were born miraculously. Samuel's mother, Hannah, was barren. She prayed to God for a son, promising that if God would answer her prayer and give her a son, her son's life would be devoted to God's service. Miraculously she conceived Samuel, and just as she promised, she devoted her son, Samuel, to God.

Through prayer, both, Hannah, and Mary praised God for their sons. Hannah thanked God, making several prophetic references to Christ. She praised God as her rock, a title we know is identified with Christ. Hannah also declares that the Lord will judge the ends of the earth and give strength to his King. This reference is the first time the Bible mentions the Messiah as also a king. Similarly, Mary praises God with a heartfelt prayer.

Both Samuel and Jesus minister in the Temple as children. The two grow in wisdom and stature and gain favor with God and among men.

Long periods of silence proceeded the dedication of Samuel and Jesus to the nation Israel. Before Samuel, people were not listening. God was not speaking, but then he spoke to Samuel, and by faith, Samuel gave a voice to God's Word to Israel. In that same way, before Jesus, there were 400 years of complete silence. There were no prophetic revelations. Jesus not only gave voice to God's Word; Jesus was, and is the Word.

"In the beginning was the Word, and the Word was with God, and the Word was God…And the Word became flesh, and dwelt among us; and we saw His glory, glory as of the only Son *from the Father, full of grace and truth."*

(John 1 NASB)

2nd Samuel
David as King of Israel
1000 BC Before Christ

Both David and Jesus were Good Shepherds born in Bethlehem.

Samuel anointed David as the King of Israel, and this happened many years before he became the King. In that same way, Jesus was anointed as the King of Israel, as a child when the wise men from the east came to Bethlehem.

While Saul was still King, Samuel anointed David. The king did not know he was the true anointed, but the prophet did. In that same way, the prophets knew Jesus was God's anointed King, but the king did not know. This speaks of Herod being the evil king before Jesus was born. God chose David to be King of Israel just like Jesus was born the King of Israel.

Both David and Jesus were the great-grandsons of Ruth and Boaz from the tribe of Judah.

While David and Jesus were being rejected by their own, they gathered the weak, poor, and unimportant. Jesus also gathered those who were outcasts, the common people, and burdened, to give them rest.

The brothers of both David and Jesus criticized them. When David showed up at the fight between the Philistines and Israelites, David's brother accused him of pride. Jesus brothers didn't believe in him and even thought he was mad before the resurrection.

As you can see, the redemptive story of Jesus is in the pages of the books of Samuel.

In the last days, you will see Jesus, the Rock. He will arrive and impact that giant, destroy that image of the world system as seen by Daniel, and that image will fall to ground as dust. Just like David ran to the giant Goliath and the Stone not cut out by human hands destroyed the enemy of the God of Israel.

Book of Kings

Yes, originally one book, the book of Kings has three major types of Christ: Solomon, Elijah, and Elisha.

You can see Jesus' in Solomon's wisdom, in Elijah's faith, and in Elisha's faithfulness.

Solomon
1013-931 BC Before Christ

The Bible says that Solomon was the wisest man who ever lived.

Jesus referenced Solomon as a type of himself when he said, "*The Queen of the South will rise up with this generation at the judgment and will condemn it, because she came from the ends of the earth to hear the wisdom of Solomon; and behold, something greater than Solomon is here.*" *(Matthew 12:42 NASB)*

Jesus was full of wisdom and truth and he himself said he is the greater than Solomon. The type, picture, or foreshadow is never greater than the original.

Is your shadow greater than you or does it show a lesser image of you? Of course, it shows a lesser, but it definitely has your image.

Is a replica painting worth more than the original? Of course not.

King Solomon or "Solomon the Wise" ruled Israel at its greatest time of peace and prosperity. Solomon means 'Peace'. He reigned in peace, and he is a picture of the Prince of Peace.

The footprint of the land of Israel during Solomon's reign was at its largest in history, even to this day.

Take a look at the footprint of Israel today. It is barely the size of New Jersey, and it is not even as close to being the size it was during the reign of King Solomon. This will change when Jesus returns to rule and reign from Jerusalem.

Israel's footprint today, in 2024.

Now look at Israel during the reign of Solomon, it is much larger than it is today. But it still is not all of the land that God promised Abraham, Isaac, and Jacob.

The footprint of Israel during King Solomons reign, 967 BC

But it was not all the land that God had promised, because the full promised land goes east, all the way to the Euphrates River, then north to the boarder of Turkey, all the way down the coast to the Nile River, and down the Nile hundreds of miles, then straight across to the mouth of the Euphrates.

This full promised land speaks of the time of peace, when the Prince of Peace, Jesus comes back to establish his kingdom on earth. He will rule and reign from Jerusalem, in the new Temple that Ezekiel saw in his prophetic vision.

All the land that God promised to Israel.

Solomons Temple
The Chief Corner Stone, 967 BC Before Christ

Jesus said to them, "Did you never read in the Scriptures, 'A STONE WHICH THE BUILDERS REJECTED, THIS HAS BECOME THE CHIEF CORNERSTONE; THIS CAME ABOUT FROM THE LORD, AND IT IS MARVELOUS IN OUR EYES'..." (Matthew 21:42 NASB)

Solomons Temple was amazing, and it was one of the seven wonders of the world. Kings and rulers would travel from the far reaches of the world, to make the trip of their lifetime to see it.

The ancient buildings were built with a special cornerstone, and it would support the entire foundation of the building.

Jewish history tells the story of the building of Solomon's Temple, a project that took years. The massive stones for the Temple were quarried a good distance away from the Temple site and delivered to the builders.

As they were laying the foundation, a very oddly shaped stone that did not seem to fit, arrived.

It was different and was not what they were expecting. The lead worker thought the stone quarry made a mistake by sending it. So they rejected it and had it thrown away, pushed down the hill.

After much time the rejected stone was almost forgotten, and it was caught in the thicket, and not noticed.

But near the end, the workers were crying out to the stone quarry for the chief corner stone, so they could complete the Temple.

The quarry sent back a message saying it had already been delivered to them a long time ago.

The lead worker of the Temple argued that he had never received the stone, but someone reminded him of the oddly shaped stone, the one that did not seem to fit his plans, that he had rejected a long time ago.

They were shocked that it was the stone that would support the whole building. With significant effort, they raised the stone, and continued erecting what would become a building which would bring glory to God and salvation to the world.

When Jesus referred to himself as the Stone the builders rejected, the Jewish people of his time knew exactly what he was talking about.

Even today, in Jerusalem you can see those same large rectangle shaped stones in the ancient walls from Solomon's time.

On the Temple Mount, many have said that the Dome of the Rock is where the Temple was located. Some say that it was to the north of that where the Dome of the Spirits or Tablets is located. They say this because there is chisel marks inside the Dome of the Rock, where there is a rectangular shaped flat spot carved into the rock.

But the Dome of the Spirits, to the north has a perfectly flat spot in the bedrock, the very mountain with no chisel marks. This would make perfect sense because David purchased the threshing floor, for building the first Temple. This would have been a smooth, flat spot on that rock mountain for separating the chaff from the grain.

The Ark sat in both spots at two different Temples from two different era's.

The first Temple, known as Solomon's Temple, was likely where you see the Dome of the Spirits or Tablets. The name itself gives it away, because this would have been the Holiest site, the Holy of Holies where the Ark of the covenant sat inside of that Temple.

If you look at the Golden Gate, or the East Gate, it lines up perfectly with the Dome of the Tablets. In fact two archeologists discovered some Solomon era pillars underneath where you see the Golden Gate today.

At that time, Solomons Palace was built to the south of the Temple, and it had been built on a solid foundation too.

Herod's Temple (The Second Temple) was built over that site. There is biblical evidence to prove that.

In the book of Acts, Peter and John entered through the Beautiful gate, located directly in front of Herod's Temple, a paralyzed man was healed. The scripture says that the man was filled with joy and then later he finds Peter and John at Solomons Porch. That porch would be located directly in front of where Solomons Temple was located. But it was not in front of Herod's Temple, and it did not line up with the Beautiful gate.

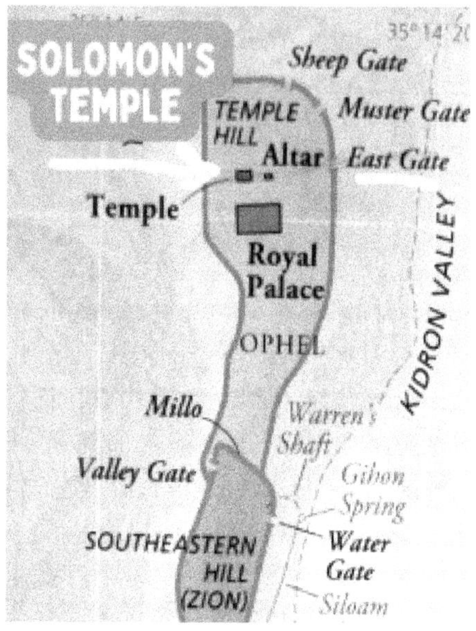

Map of where Solomon's Temple was in Jerusalem

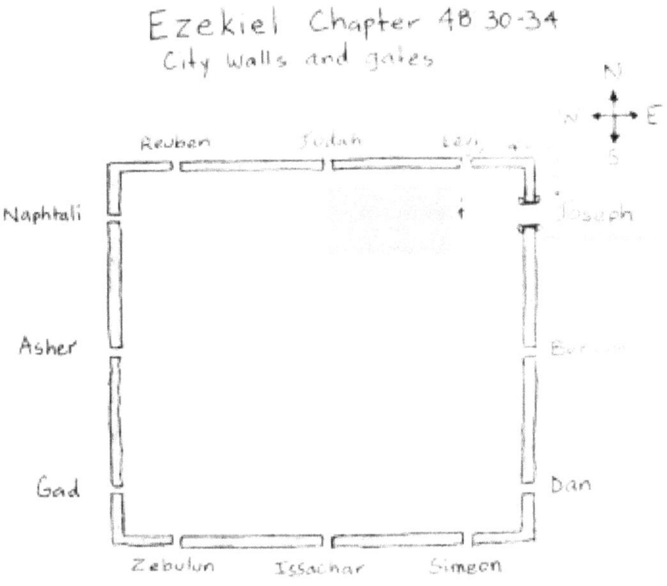

Ezekiel's vision of the New Temple, in the New Jerusalem with the outer gates named after the sons of Israel.

Elijah

Who was the first person in the Bible to raise the dead?

Yes, it was the great prophet Elijah.

He also ascended into Heaven when his mission was complete here on Earth.

When Elijah stood against the hundreds of prophets of Baal, he prayed and God accepted his sacrifice, his burnt offering but rejected the religious false prophets. Fire came down from Heaven and consumed the offering, the wood, the water, and the stones.

Then Elijah approached all the people and said, "How long are you going to struggle with the two choices? If the LORD is God, follow Him; but if Baal, follow him." But the people did not answer him so much as a word. Then Elijah said to the people, "I alone am left as a prophet of the LORD, while Baal's prophets are 450 men. Now have them give us two oxen; and have them choose the one ox for themselves and cut it up, and place it on the wood, but put no fire under it; and I will prepare the other ox and lay it on the wood, and I will not put a fire under it. Then you call on the name of your god, and I will call on the name of the LORD; and the God who answers by fire, He is God." And all the people replied, "That is a good idea." (1 Kings 21-24 NASB)

Elijah was so fearless and confident in God. He even makes fun of these false prophets by mocking their god. Watch this:

"...they called on the name of Baal from morning until noon, saying, "O Baal, answer us!" But there was no voice and no one answered. And they limped about the altar which they had made. And at noon Elijah ridiculed them and said, "Call out with a loud voice, since he is a god; undoubtedly he is attending to business, or is on the way, or is on a journey. Perhaps he is asleep, and will awaken." (1 Kings 26-27 NASB)

Nothing happened as they prayed for hours and hours, even cutting themselves as they prayed. By the evening sacrifice (3 PM), Elijah had enough. Now you are about to see God's power displayed through the faith, the trust that the true Prophet of God had:

Then Elijah said to all the people, "Come forward to me." So all the people came forward to him. And he repaired the altar of the LORD which had been torn down. Then Elijah took twelve stones, corresponding to the number of the tribes of the sons of Jacob, to whom the word of the LORD had come, saying, "Israel shall be your name." And with the stones he built an altar in the name of the LORD; and he made a trench around the altar, large enough to hold two measures of seed. Then he laid out the wood, and he cut the ox in pieces and placed it *on the wood. And he said, "Fill four large jars with water and pour it on the burnt offering and on the wood." And he said, "Do it a second time," so they did it a second time. Then he said, "Do it a third time," so they did it a third time. The water flowed around the altar, and he also filled the trench with water.*

Elijah's Prayer

Then at the time of the offering of the evening *sacrifice, Elijah the prophet approached and said, "LORD, God of Abraham, Isaac, and Israel, today let it be known that You are God in Israel and that I am Your servant, and* that *I have done all these things at Your word. 37 Answer me, LORD, answer me, so that this people may know that You, LORD, are God, and* that *You have turned their heart back."*

Then the fire of the LORD fell and consumed the burnt offering and the wood, and the stones and the dust; and it licked up the water that was in the trench. When all the people saw this, *they fell on their faces; and they said, "The LORD, He is God; the LORD, He is God!"* (1 Kings 30-39 NASB)

Nine centuries later, God accepted a far greater sacrifice for sin and delivered His Son, by raising Him from the dead.

What I love about Elijah's prayer is that it was no more than 10 seconds and God did a mighty work. Often people pray for a long time, using many, many words and it's as if they think that God will listen because of their hard work in prayer.

Jesus himself said not to pray like that.

He said, "And when you are praying, do not use thoughtless repetition as the Gentiles do, for they think that they will be heard because of their many words. (Matthew 6:7 NASB)

I personally have said short prayers and seen many miracles from those.

One time an old friend of mine named Fritz invited my family to his church.

His face looked pale and grey before church started. As usual the pastor ended his message with the song, "How great is our God", and as we sang, I looked to my right at Fritz, and his head was tilted back, his eyes rolled far back toward his eyebrows.

He looked dead. His face had that grey and white look, it looked cold and lifeless. I remember that same look on my great grandfathers face when he was dead.

I called his name, and he did not respond. The lady sitting in the pew in front of him, turned around and put her hands on his jaw to keep his head straight and kept loudly saying, "Are you okay".

There was no response, he just looked lifeless.

At that moment I said a short prayer, in my head, to God, "God pleas help Fritz. What should I do?"

I knew that God told me to take hold of his hand. I say knew because when he speaks to me it is not an audible voice, but it is his voice speaking in a supernatural way, to my spirit and I just know it. It is hard to explain.

I took a hold of my friend's hand, and it felt cold and lifeless as did his face and eyes.

Suddenly I felt the warmness of God rush through me and suddenly his hand became warm, and it squeezed my hand. He gripped my hand, and his face became warm, and his cheeks filled with color.

He turned his head toward me and looked at me with a big smile and said, "Hey Buckshot". He called me buckshot all the time and I like that nickname.

He smiled and reached into his inside coat pocket, pulled out a snickers chocolate candy bar and said, "How about a snickers" as he handed it over to me.

He acted like his usual joy filled self.

I asked him how he was feeling, and he said he never felt better and that he felt the Holy Spirit.

Then the paramedics came down the aisle with the ambulance cart and said, "Fritz, how are you?'

He was annoyed and said, "What are you guys doing here?"

They said, "Your wife called 911 and we are here to take you to the hospital and get you some help".

He responded to them, "I am fine, I don't need you guys or the hospital. You guys can go now".

His wife wasn't having that and told him sternly, "Fritz, you go with them now".

He lived well into his 90's. He is in heaven now and I can't wait to hear him say, "Hey buckshot" to me when I get to Heaven.

God does not always do miracles like this but sometimes he does. He usually does not do this on the stage or up front of a large church.

Another one of the many miracles I have seen was when my son had a bunch of major surgeries on his leg, and as a result, it was stuck at 40 degrees at the knee.

The doctor was very concerned and had him go into the operating room where they put him under anesthesia so that a team of the strongest nurses and doctors could pry his leg loose.

After hours of this, the doctor came to my wife and I and said, "I have bad news for you. Your son's leg is going to be stuck at 40 degrees from his knee for the rest of his life. There is nothing we can do about it. It is science and you will just have to live with it. I am sorry."

My wife was in tears, and we were both depressed.

Though I did not feel like praying and my wife certainly did not either, I looked at her while tears flowed down her face and said, "Honey lets pray for him".

She said, "What's the use?"

I did it anyway and it was only a 5 second prayer and I did not feel like doing it.

At the end of the prayer, I just knew that God healed him.

I said to my wife, "Honey, Jesus healed him, I just know it".

She was still very sad.

We went downstairs and walked into the Physical Therapy room and the lady working with him said, "Louis has something to tell you".

Our son yelled out, "Yeah, mom, dad, it just went, it just went, my leg just moved".

The lady said, "Yes it was amazing, his knee bent way back to almost 80 degrees."

I asked her when this happened, and she said about five minutes ago.

I looked at my wife and she was filled with joy. I said, "Honey, that was when we prayed to Jesus for him".

It was a blessing from Jesus, and we thanked him.

But these miracles pale in comparison to the miracle of salvation. What Jesus has done for you and me on the cross, shedding his own blood for you and me, all the way to death for three days, then coming back to life, so that you and I can be considered righteous before God and go to Heaven.

That is the greatest miracle ever.

CHAPTER FIFTEEN: JOSHUA – TYPE OF CHRIST

1486-1376 BC Before Christ

As promised, you will see Jesus in Joshua's life. In fact, you will see Jesus in his very name, "Joshua".

Joshua is the English name for the Hebrew name Yeshua. This was Jesus original name because he was Jewish through and through.

Yeshua means, "Salvation".

Salvation means being saved, being rescued by a great deliverance.

That is exactly what Jesus did when he came down from heaven, was born of a virgin Jewish mother who had the lineage of David and Joseph.

He taught, healed the sick, opened the eyes of the blind and then he was betrayed and sold for silver. He was falsely accused, scourged, sentenced to die on the cross, and he died that horrible death.

But in three days, he was raised from the dead.

His work on the cross, and life from the dead was for you and me because we who believe and trust him, receive what he earned for us.

This was the greatest rescue mission of all time.

That is why his very name means "Salvation".

Joshua was Moses' assistant for 40 years and then it was time to enter into the Promised Land. This was the whole goal as Israel wandered in the wilderness, one of the dryest places on earth. They had a hope of one day entering the land of milk and honey.

Moses represented the Law.

We know that in the book of Romans and other places in the Bible, God made it clear that the Law in and of itself cannot save you. It was never meant to save you. In fact, it was meant to show you that you are in need to be saved.

195

The law is perfect, and those ten commandments are broken by us daily if you are honest. We fail over and over and if we think we don't, we are deceiving ourselves and living in the shadows.

God is light and that light shines onto us to reveal how we need him.

"This is the message we have heard from Him and announce to you, that God is Light, and in Him there is no darkness at all. If we say that we have fellowship with Him and yet walk in the darkness, we lie and do not practice the truth; but if we walk in the Light as He Himself is in the Light, we have fellowship with one another, and the blood of Jesus His Son cleanses us from all sin. If we say that we have no sin, we are deceiving ourselves and the truth is not in us. If we confess our sins, He is faithful and righteous, so that He will forgive us our sins and cleanse us from all unrighteousness. If we say that we have not sinned, we make Him a liar and His word is not in us. (1 John 1:6-10 NASB)

Jesus, Yeshua, or Joshua the Messiah is the fulfillment of that Law. He was the only one who passed the test of the Law. He was sinless like no one else in history.

Moses was a mighty prophet of the Lord and yet he sinned. One example is that he had an anger outburst when the people were complaining because they were thirsty. God told him to speak to the rock, but he struck it out of anger.

"Take the staff; and you and your brother Aaron assemble the congregation and speak to the rock before their eyes, that it shall yield its water. So you shall bring water for them out of the rock, and have the congregation and their livestock drink...Listen now, you rebels; shall we bring water for you out of this rock?" Then Moses raised his hand and

struck the rock twice with his staff; and water came out abundantly, and the congregation and their livestock drank. But the LORD said to Moses and Aaron, "Since you did not trust in Me, to treat Me as holy in the sight of the sons of Israel, for that reason you shall not bring this assembly into the land which I have given them." (Numbers 20 NASB)

God just told Moses that he would not be the one to lead the people into the promised land.

But the one who led the people after Moses could. He was a mighty prophet, a warrior.

Jesus is the Mightiest Warrior. But he is not just a warrior, but God the Son, the King of Israel, the promised One, the King of kings, the Lord of lords, the Way, the Truth and the Life!

You also see a Christophany in Joshua's story.

What is a Christophany? You might be asking.

These are appearances of the Lord Jesus Christ before he was born in the flesh through the Holy Spirit and Mary.

Also called Pre-Incarnate which simply means before Christ was born in the flesh. Jesus came down from heaven and was born in the flesh through the virgin Mary. Carnate is simply flesh or meat. Like a Carne meal at a Mexican food restaurant, it is meat.

You can see him with Abraham. Remember the Lord came to Abraham with two angels.

You saw him with Jacob. Remember how Jacob wrestled with the Lord all night? Yes that was the Lord.

You saw him with Moses. The Lord met with Moses, face to face at the Tabernacle and other places.

Now, in Joshua's story you see him as the Commander of the Lord's army:

"Now it came about when Joshua was by Jericho, he raised his eyes and looked, and behold, a man was standing opposite him with his sword drawn in his hand, and Joshua went to him and said to him, "Are you for us or for our enemies?" He said, "No; rather I have come now as captain of the army of the LORD." And Joshua fell on his face to the ground, and bowed down, and said to him, "What has my lord to say to his servant?" And the captain of the LORD'S army said to Joshua, "Remove your sandals from your feet, for the place where you are standing is holy." And Joshua did so." (Joshua 5:13-15)

Did you catch that?

Joshua asks him, "Are you for us or for our enemies?"

This mysterious warrior answers, "No".

I love that answer.

Then Joshua fell on his face to the ground and bowed down and then called him Lord.

If that were an angel – as some of your translations say, then the angel would have immediately told him not to bow down to them. Remember that was what started the whole rebellion in Heaven. It was satan or Lucifer who wanted to be worshiped and every angel saw that, and they always made sure no one bowed down to them.

You can see an example of that in Revelation with the apostle John:

"I, John, am the one who heard and saw these things. And when I heard and saw them, I fell down to worship at the feet of the angel who showed me these things. And he said to me, "Do not do that; I am a fellow servant of yours and of your brothers the prophets, and of those who keep the words of this book. Worship God!" (Revelation 22:8 NASB)

So, this is solid proof that the appearances in the Old Testament were not angels because they would have immediately said do not do that.

Only God is to be bowed down to and worshiped.

Joshua
A foreshadowing of Jesus Return

Joshua led the people into the promised land, and Jesus will do the same at the end of the seven-year tribulation period.

It is also known as the time of Jacob's Trouble.

You can see the same pattern in both Joseph and Moses.

I don't claim to know it all but just what God reveals in his word. He has laid out his plan through Joseph and Moses. Both were types and portraits of Christ. Now we are seeing that Joshua was a type as well.

This pattern repeats in the Old Testament.

Joshua and Caleb were ready to enter into the kingdom, the land of Israel the first time. They were ready to do it! Caleb of the tribe of Judah, and Joshua, of the tribe of Joseph.

But Israel rejected both Caleb and Joshua's report the first time. That whole generation had to pass away before God allowed them into the land of Milk and Honey. This speaks of what happened to Israel after Jesus was despised and rejected the first time. He was a greater than Joshua and Caleb.

But that does not mean God is finished with Israel. He has a plan to bring a remnant back and restore her completely.

As I am writing this down, the Universities, the most elite of my country, Harvard, Yale, Stanford, Columbia are protesting and chanting, "From the River to the Sea, Palestine will be free". Some are claiming to be Hamas. They hate Israel and want to see it destroyed.

They typically hate Zion or Zionism and even blame the Christian Zionists for supporting Israel.

But what does the scripture say:

The word that came to Jeremiah from the LORD, saying,

GEORGE CRABB

"This is what the LORD, the God of Israel says: 'Write all the words which I have spoken to you in a book. For behold, days are coming,' declares the LORD, 'when I will restore the fortunes of My people Israel and Judah.' The LORD says, 'I will also bring them back to the land that I gave to their forefathers, and they shall take possession of it.'"

Now these are the words which the LORD spoke concerning Israel and Judah:

> "For this is what the LORD says:
> 'I have heard a sound of terror,
> Of fear, and there is no peace.
> 'Ask now, and see
> If a male can give birth.
> Why do I see every man
> With his hands on his waist, as a woman in childbirth?
> And why have all faces turned pale?
> 'Woe, for that day is great,
> There is none like it;
> And it is the time of Jacob's distress,
> Yet he will be saved from it.

'It shall come about on that day,' declares the LORD of armies, 'that I will break his yoke from their necks and will tear to pieces their restraints; and strangers will no longer make them their slaves. But they shall serve the LORD their God and David their king, whom I will raise up for them.'

> "'For I will restore you to health
> And I will heal you of your wounds,' declares the LORD,
> 'Because they have called you an outcast, saying:
> "It is Zion; no one cares for her."'
> "...The fierce anger of the LORD will not turn back
> Until He has performed and accomplished
> The intent of His heart.
> In the latter days you will understand this."

SEE JESUS IN THE OLD TESTAMENT

(Jeremiah 30:17,24 NASAB)

Yes, you can understand much of God's plan for the end by reading the Old Testament.

Joshua was sent out to take the land on the first visit, but the people rejected it.

Joseph was despised and rejected by the sons of Israel the first time.

Moses was rejected by his own on his first visit.

But on the second visit you can see something different. Israel is saved!

When Joshua led the people into the Promised Land, he fought against their enemies for seven years.

How long is the tribulation period?

Yes. Seven years.

How long was the great famine, over all the face of the Earth, in Joseph's story?

Yes. Seven years. And they came to him 2 years into it bowed down and he revealed who he was to them and saved them.

In Joshua you see seven trumpet blasts.

In the book of Revelation there are seven trumpet judgements. All of these judgments speak of Jesus and lead up to his final return.

CHAPTER SIXTEEN: ISAIAH

700 BC

If you have ever read Isaiah 53 to your Jewish friend, they would have asked you why you were reading the New Testament to them. Many of those same Jewish people have realized Jesus as the Messiah because someone read it to them. However, that is not the only place in Isaiah where you see Jesus.

You can see him in many other places in this powerful scroll.

Chapters seven and nine speak of his birth, of the very first Christmas. In fact, they have been said in plays, movies, and even cartoons like Charlie Brown Christmas. So, in these first places we see him in Isaiah, we see his birth.

Then it continues to the famous Isaiah 53 where we see the cross.

After that you will see Isaiah 61 and you know that Jesus read part of that passage in his hometown Synagogue in Nazareth. He stopped mid-sentence and said, "Today these scriptures are fulfilled". But if you read the rest of it, it speaks of his return in vengeance to protect and comfort Zion which is another name for Israel.

Isaiah 7
Dead Sea Scroll

Therefore, Yahweh himself will give you a sign. Behold, the virgin will conceive, and bear a son, and shall call his name Immanuel

There is no need for you or anyone else to worry about interpreting Isaiah 7 properly because the New Testament writer Matthew has documented it. God made sure to have it recorded that his son Jesus is the fulfillment of this amazing prophecy. It is why Christmas is so special.

Matthew 1

"Joseph, son of David, do not be afraid to take Mary as your wife; for the Child who has been conceived in her is of the Holy Spirit.

Jesus was the Messiah; the son of Joseph and he was born in the house of Joseph.

You might say, no, because he was born through Mary and God the Holy Spirit. He was in the House of Joseph his stepdad, but he was also the Messiah Son of Joseph, yes the Joseph of the Old Testament.

He was called the Son of David because we know that he was of the Tribe of Judah, of the root of Jessie and David. But did you know that some of the names in the genealogy of Mary show a lineage of the line of Joseph through Ephriam?

Yes.

So, he fulfilled, both the Son of David and Son of Joseph.

She will give birth to a Son; and you shall name Him Jesus, for He will save His people from their sins."

Here you can see that Joseph, named him Jesus. It is the name Yeshua in Hebrew or Joshua in English. The name means: Salvation, and Matthew recorded how the Angel said to Joseph, "...*name Him Jesus, for He will save His people from their sins".*

Now all this took place so that what was spoken by the Lord through the prophet would be fulfilled: "BEHOLD, THE VIRGIN WILL CONCEIVE AND GIVE BIRTH TO A SON, AND THEY SHALL NAME HIM IMMANUEL," which translated means, "GOD WITH US." (Matthew 1:20-23 NASB)

This Isaiah 7 prophecy has been debated by many who contend with Jesus. They claim that the original Hebrew word for virgin means, "Young Woman". It makes no difference because a young, unmarried Jewish woman at the time of Jesus, would have been a virgin anyway and I will go with the oldest interpretation of that text from the very Jewish Matthew.

Not only was Matthew spot on, but you can see that the Dead Sea Scroll of Isaiah shows the same translation which is dated to at least 150 years before Christ: "*Therefore Yahweh himself will give you a sign. Behold, the virgin will conceive, and bear a son, and shall call his name Immanuel*".

A big take away from that Isaiah passage is the name "Immanuel" which Matthew tells you means, "God with us".

That is huge!

That ancient prophecy, from the Prophet Isaiah, written around 700 years before Christ, says that this boy child, born of the young woman, who was a virgin, gave birth to a son who was literally God with us.

This is what makes Christmas so special. You may have seen, "A Charlie Brown Christmas", where this passage is read, and you experienced the warmth of God's love.

The very Jewish New Testament writer named Matthew confirms this passage is speaking about the one and only Messiah and that the Messiah is God with us.

While I was typing this manuscript, just minutes ago, a Jewish friend of mine from Israel, commented on my YouTube video (The Whole Bible with George Crabb).

She commented on Isaiah chapter seven. She and I have been discussing these ancient scriptures for years. As of right now, she does not believe Jesus as Messiah. But I continue to love and pray for her, her family, and for Israel.

It was October 7th, 2023, when she and I were having a strong debate about the scriptures through my YouTube channel, when suddenly she commented, "Please pray, we are under attack by Hamas".

I immediately commented back that I am praying for her, her family and Israel. I also mentioned that I wish I was there to fight for them and protect them.

She responded by thanking me for those prayers.

This was huge. Before this she rejected my prayers and asked me not to pray for her.

So today, as I am writing this on July 7th, 2024, my Israeli friend is commenting to me about the Isaiah seven teaching video. Here is our conversation.

Her: "Explain how this is a prophecy about Jesus when Isaiah tells us this woman is already pregnant !! Hara הרה means pregnant - present tense. Your answer.

My response: ...It is good to see you comment again. I am keeping you and all of Israel in my prayers.

First, let's look at the oldest manuscript of Isaiah 7 - the Dead Sea Scroll:

"Listen now, house of David. Is it not enough for you to try the patience of men, that you will try the patience of my God also? Therefore Yahweh himself will give you a sign. Behold, the virgin will conceive, and bear a son, and shall call his name Immanuel..." Yes, she was a virgin who was also pregnant with the child.

You and I know that no other woman in Biblical history was a virgin with child.

Is this even possible? What about today?

We are actually seeing that humankind has figured out a way to accomplish this today.

Does this mean that man is greater than Yahweh?

Does it mean that God cannot do something that even humankind can do?

Not at all. Yahweh is greater than his creation, and he can do anything. It was a great miracle that this most beautiful Israeli Jewish woman was both with child and a virgin.

Yeshua himself was a great and mighty miracle. He was the Ancient of Days, God the Son (Proverbs 30), and now a tiny baby boy in this undefiled womb.

There is also no instance where it can be proved that alma designates a young woman who is not a virgin. The fact of virginity is obvious in Genesis chapter 24, verse 43[1] where alma is used of one who was being sought as a bride for Isaac.

I love Israel and I love you. Only God could put that love into my heart. Yeshua loves Israel. He always has, and always will, even to the end.

Her response: "Why are you lying?? The Dead Sea Scroll has the two same words: Almah, which derives from Alumim = youth, and hara which means pregnant at this very moment!! The Hebrew is the same in this verse now as it was then."

My response to her: "This is what I was just saying that she was pregnant and a virgin at the same time. Yahweh is capable of doing what humans can do today."

As you can see, I have had some heavy discussions with my Jewish friends from Israel.

At the end of these discussions, we remain friends. It is important to be patient and not lose hope. Keep reaching out in prayer and in friendship. The Jewish people are the best debaters in the world. Just watch Ben Shapiro. But God is greater than the highest I.Q. and intellect that he gave them.

I strongly believe that believers and followers of Jesus, those who have been born again in him, should have received a special love in their hearts toward Israel.

This Isaiah seven prophecy is what makes Christmas so special. It is the hope of life that is found in the birth of God with us who came down from Heaven to save us.

---

1.   https://www.youtube.com/watch?v=v1rlhjodr_I&t=1483s

Without a doubt God put a special anointing on Christmas. Every child around the world loves Christmas when they get to celebrate it. Little ones have a sense of what is good, what is meant to be and what gives them life and love. They sense that Christmas is good.

This next Isaiah prophecy also speaks of Christmas. It works right alongside Isaiah seven, and is often quoted around the celebration of Jesus' birth.

Remember the book of Isaiah was one continuous scroll with no chapter numbers or verse numbers. Those were added later for study and reference, but they missed the context in many cases.

One example is Isaiah 53, if you read the latter half of chapter 52 you can already see Jesus illustrated as the "Suffering Servant" and it naturally takes you right into chapter 53.

Now, look at Isaiah nine, the last part of it relates to Isaiah 7 and the announcement of Jesus' birth.

Isaiah 9

But there will be no more gloom for her who was in anguish. In earlier times He treated the land of Zebulun and the land of Naphtali with contempt, but later on He will make it *glorious, by the way of the sea, on the other side of the Jordan, Galilee of the Gentiles.*
The people who walk in darkness
Will see a great light;
Those who live in a dark land,
The light will shine on them.

This shows how Jesus was raised in Nazareth because Zebulun and Naphtali intersected at Nazareth, and you know Jesus was born in Bethlehem but raised in Nazareth.

He is that great light. People saw the Light of the world when they met Jesus. He himself said, "I am the Light of the world". His light can see right into your heart and soul. He, and only he can do that.

Isaiah 9 continues:

> *You will multiply the nation,*
> *You will increase their joy;*
> *They will rejoice in Your presence*
> *As with the joy of harvest,*
> *As* people *rejoice when they divide the spoils.*
> *For You will break the yoke of their burden and the staff on their*
> *shoulders,*
> *The rod of their oppressor, as at the battle of Midian.*
> *For every boot of the marching warrior in the roar* of battle,
> *And cloak rolled in blood, will be for burning, fuel for the fire.*

This passage looks a lot like Ezekiel 38-39 when the Lord will destroy the enemies who come down against Israel in the latter days.

God will fulfill what has not yet been fulfilled in that Ezekiel prophecy. In fact, as I am writing this book you can see the stage being set for this. For the first time in history, Iran which is Persia, and Russia which is the region of Magog, are in alliance against Israel. And now Turkey is joining in this evil army. These regions are all mentioned in that Ezekiel prophecy.

The next part of this prophecy is about the very first Christmas. Time itself has been centered around this moment. 0 Common Era or 0 AD is measured from this magnanimous moment in world history.

Isaiah 9

> *For a Child will be born to us, a Son will be given to us;*
> *And the government will rest on His shoulders;*
> *And His name will be called Wonderful Counselor, Mighty God,*
> *Eternal Father, Prince of Peace.*
> *There will be no end to the increase of* His *government or of peace*
> *On the throne of David and over his kingdom,*
> *To establish it and to uphold it with justice and righteousness*
> *From then on and forevermore.*

When you read, "For a child will be born to us, a son will be given to us", it should fill your heart with love, hope and peace. This is life everlasting born into your life if you receive him. This is the true Christmas spirit.

The zeal of the LORD of armies will accomplish this.

Jesus is the LORD of Heaven's Armies. Remember Jesus rebuked Peter after he tried to retaliate against those who came to arrest him in the Garden of Gethsemane: *"...do you think that I cannot appeal to My Father, and He will at once put at My disposal more than twelve legions of angels? How then would the Scriptures be fulfilled,* which say *that it must happen this way?" (Matthew 26:53-54 NASB)*

Jesus could have blinked his eyes and destroyed all of his enemies in an instant if he wanted to. Instead of that, he decided to give his own life over to save me and you by his brutal death on the cross, and his miraculous resurrection from the grave three days later.

Isaiah 11

Then a shoot will spring from the stem of Jesse,
And a Branch from his roots will bear fruit.

A shoot is a newborn branch that springs up from the trunk of a tree. The shoot of Jesse is the Messiah because all good biblical students know that he is of the line of Jessie and David.

The Spirit of the LORD will rest on Him,
The spirit of wisdom and understanding,
The spirit of counsel and strength,
The spirit of knowledge and the fear of the LORD.

When John the Baptist saw Jesus, he saw the Spirit of God come down and rest upon him like a dove.

This Isaiah 11 passage looks just like what Jesus read in his hometown Synagogue, from Isaiah 61, "The Spirit of the Lord is upon me, for he has anointed me..."

We will look deeper into that chapter later my friend, and you will be amazed because it speaks of his first coming where Jesus stopped reading and said, "Today these scriptures are fulfilled", but the rest of that passage speaks of him returning in vengeance and to save Israel.

It all ties together as one story, one tapestry telling his story or history.

> *And He will delight in the fear of the LORD,*
> *And He will not judge by what His eyes see,*
> *Nor make decisions by what His ears hear;*
> *But with righteousness He will judge the poor,*
> *And decide with fairness for the humble of the earth;*

Jesus is the righteous Judge and he only Judges in righteousness. God is a just God, and a loving and good God. He does not judge like we humans do. He does not judge off of appearance, or what he heard. Jesus sees the heart of humankind; he knows our motivation.

> *And He will strike the earth with the rod of His mouth,*
> *And with the breath of His lips He will slay the wicked.*

This part of the passage reveals the rule and reign of Messiah Jesus. He will rule physically from Jerusalem. He is the Word, and his word is powerful.

Remember when the soldiers came to the Garden of Gethsemane to arrest Jesus, and they asked him if he was Jesus? When he said, "I AM", all 200 of those elite soldiers fell backwards.

In Revelation chapter one and nineteen it speaks of his word as a two-edged sword and how just by his word the evil nations of the world are destroyed: *In His right hand He held seven stars, and out of His mouth came a sharp two-edged sword; and His face was like the sun shining in its strength...His name is called The Word of God. And the armies which are in heaven, clothed in fine linen, white* and *clean, were following Him on white horses. From His mouth comes a sharp sword, so that with it He may strike down the nations, and He will rule them with a rod of iron.*

Isaiah 11 continues with amazing insights into Jesus' rule and reign:

> *Also righteousness will be the belt* around *His hips,*
> *And faithfulness the belt* around *His waist.*
> *And the wolf will dwell with the lamb,*
> *And the leopard will lie down with the young goat,*
> *And the calf and the young lion and the fattened steer* will be *together;*
> *And a little boy will lead them.*
> *Also the cow and the bear will graze,*
> *Their young will lie down together,*
> *And the lion will eat straw like the ox.*
> *The nursing child will play by the hole of the cobra,*
> *And the weaned child will put his hand on the viper's den.*
> *They will not hurt or destroy in all My holy mountain,*
> *For the earth will be full of the knowledge of the LORD*
> *As the waters cover the sea.*
> *Then on that day*
> *The nations will resort to the root of Jesse,*
> *Who will stand as a signal flag for the peoples;*
> *And His resting place will be glorious.*

What you just saw in that scripture above was a beautiful painting of the restored earth and creation as it was meant to be. A boy leads the Lion, Leopard, Bear, Lamb, and is not harmed by the Cobra.

You also saw how the Lord's resting place will be glorious.

Imagine it, the beauty of his holy mountain with trees, streams, waterfalls, precious gems in the walls, gold pavers to walk on, as you, your family, and your friends dwell in and around his Temple, his resting place.

The Restored Remnant is what we see next. This is the re-gathering of Israel and Judah back to their land from the nations of the world. God has already done much of this work in our time as you can watch any news channel and see Israel in the headlines.

Then it will happen on that day that the Lord
Will again recover with His hand the second time
The remnant of His people who will remain,
From Assyria, Egypt, Pathros, Cush, Elam, Shinar, Hamath,
And from the islands of the sea.
And He will lift up a flag for the nations
And assemble the banished ones of Israel,
And will gather the dispersed of Judah
From the four corners of the earth.
Then the jealousy of Ephraim will depart,
And those who harass Judah will be eliminated;
Ephraim will not be jealous of Judah,
And Judah will not harass Ephraim.
They will swoop down on the slopes of the Philistines on the west;
Together they will plunder the people of the east;
They will possess Edom and Moab,
And the sons of Ammon will be subject to them.
And the LORD will utterly destroy
The tongue of the Sea of Egypt;

And He will wave His hand over the Euphrates River
With His scorching wind;
And He will strike it into seven streams
And make people walk over in dry sandals.
And there will be a highway from Assyria
For the remnant of His people who will be left,
Just as there was for Israel
On the day that they came up out of the land of Egypt.

This will all be fulfilled when King Jesus rules and reigns from Jerusalem. He will have complete control over the land, and will grant his own people the right to rule with him.

The other countries will come and report to him. They will bring gifts and there will be paved highways from the north to the south. The Euphrates river will be changed into seven rivers, the sea of Egypt will not exist.

In Ezekiel, near the end of the scroll, you can see a glimpse of this. He sees a stream flow from the altar out through the south side of the East Gate, and it runs east down to the Dead Sea, and it becomes healed. That same healing flow of water heals all the waters of the oceans.

Isaiah 28

"Behold, I am laying a stone in Zion, a tested stone,
A precious cornerstone for the foundation, firmly placed.
The one who believes in it *will not be disturbed.*

A tested Stone, a Precious Cornerstone. Jesus referred to himself as the precious corner stone.

Not only was he shown as the Rock in Moses' story, but he was also the Chief Corner Stone in the building of Solomon's Temple.

You can also see that same Stone in Jacob's prophecy over the twelve sons of Israel. When he gave the second Messianic prophecy, for Joseph, who had a Gentile bride and had saved Israel, he mentions that "Stone":

SEE JESUS IN THE OLD TESTAMENT

From the hands of the Mighty One of Jacob
(From there is the Shepherd, the Stone of Israel)

You can see "The Shepherd, the Stone of Israel" and you know right away that is Jesus. He is the Good Shepherd, and he is the Stone of Israel. Remember the Rock in Moses story, and the Chief Corner Stone of Solomon's Temple. God had laid this plan out from ancient times, and he gave us his word to see it.

Isaiah 29

On that day those who are deaf will hear words of a book,
And out of their gloom and darkness the eyes of those who are blind
will see.
The afflicted also will increase their joy in the LORD,
And the needy of mankind will rejoice in the Holy One of Israel.

Jesus healed the deaf and when he did so they were hearing the Word. Jesus is the Word of God and as he gently, tenderly, and lovingly spoke to those he healed, not only were they able to hear, but they also heard the voice of the Creator.

Jesus healed many who were blind and the first thing they saw was the Messiah himself. They saw God the Son, just like you and me will see him face to face when we die, or he returns. The gloom and darkness of our fallen nature and this evil world melt away in the glory of his wonderful gaze.

You know how good it feels on your face when the warm sun shines upon you after a long frigid winter. You just stand there and soak it in. Jesus face will do the same for you after the winter of living in this world.

This next passage is all about the 1000-year reign of Messiah Jesus from Jerusalem. Just look at the restoration and beauty of the promised land illustrated in this prophecy.

Isaiah 35

The wilderness and the desert will rejoice,
And the desert will shout for joy and blossom;

GEORGE CRABB

Like the crocus
It will blossom profusely
And rejoice with joy and jubilation.
The glory of Lebanon will be given to it,
The majesty of Carmel and Sharon.
They will see the glory of the LORD,
The majesty of our God.
Strengthen the exhausted, and make the feeble strong.
Say to those with anxious heart,
"Take courage, fear not.
Behold, your God will come with vengeance;
The retribution of God will come,
But He will save you."
Then the eyes of those who are blind will be opened,
And the ears of those who are deaf will be unstopped.
Then those who limp will leap like a deer,
And the tongue of those who cannot speak will shout for joy.
For waters will burst forth in the wilderness,
And streams in the desert.
The scorched land will become a pool
And the thirsty ground springs of water;
In the haunt of jackals, its resting place,
Grass becomes reeds and rushes.
A highway will be there, a roadway,
And it will be called the Highway of Holiness.
The unclean will not travel on it,
But it will be for the one who walks that way,
And fools will not wander on it.
No lion will be there,
Nor will any vicious animal go up on it;
They will not be found there.
But the redeemed will walk there,

And the redeemed of the LORD will return
And come to Zion with joyful shouting,
And everlasting joy will be on their heads.
They will obtain gladness and joy,
And sorrow and sighing will flee away.

This passage gives you great hope in the future. God promises to rebuild Jerusalem and restore Israel, and you can see it in those beautiful, descriptive words. It paints the landscape fresh, new, alive and fruitful.

The first part of it speaks of the dry land blossoming like a flower. You can see the desert blossoming and it looks like Israel today. They have changed those dry, desolate places to be fruitful and lush.

Then it leads right into the tribulation period where God speaks of returning with great vengeance, to save those who belong to him. He says his retribution will come but to fear not because he himself will save them.

For waters will burst forth in the wilderness,
And streams in the desert.
The scorched land will become a pool
And the thirsty ground springs of water

Here you see the restored land after Jesus returns and destroys the enemies of Israel. This is spelled out in Revelation chapter 19 and in Ezekiel chapters 36-48. The disabled people will be healed, and the land healed as well. All of the creation is waiting and groaning for this day.

In Ezekiel 47, the prophet sees this spring of water flowing from out of the altar in front of the new Temple and through the south side of the East Gate, then down through the newly created gorge on the Mount of Olives. That chapter describes it flowing down with fruit trees on both sides, producing fruit every month and the leaves are for healing. Then he sees it flow down to the Dead Sea and make the waters fresh and heal it.

Ezekiel 47 (NASB)

Then he brought me back to the door of the house; and behold, water was flowing from under the threshold of the house toward the east, for the house faced east. And the water was flowing down from under, from the right side of the house, from south of the altar.

And he brought me out by way of the north gate and led me around on the outside to the outer gate, by the way facing east. And behold, water was spurting out from the south side.

When the man went out toward the east with a line in his hand, he measured a thousand cubits, and he led me through the water, water reaching *the ankles. Again he measured a thousand and led me through the water, water* reaching *the knees. Again he measured a thousand and led me through* the water, *water* reaching *the hips. Again he measured a thousand;* and it was *a river that I could not wade across, because the water had risen,* enough *water to swim in, a river that could not be crossed* by wading. *And he said to me, "Son of man, have you seen* this?" *Then he brought me back to the bank of the river.*

Now when I had returned, behold, on the bank of the river there were *very many trees on the one side and on the other. Then he said to me, "These waters go out toward the eastern region and go down into the Arabah; then they go toward the sea, being made to flow into the sea, and the waters* of the sea *become fresh. And it will come about that every living creature which swarms in every place where the river goes, will live. And there will be very many fish, for these waters go there and* the others *become fresh; so everything will live where the river goes...*

...And by the river on its bank, on one side and on the other, will grow all kinds of *trees for food. Their leaves will not wither and their fruit will not fail. They will bear fruit every month because their water flows from the sanctuary, and their fruit will be for food and their leaves for healing."*

What an amazing picture that prophecy paints. The beautiful thing is that it will happen. All of prophecy will happen exactly as God proclaims it. This gives you and me great hope. It is all going to be good, your future, my future is good and joyful. You can count on God. He never changes his mind.

Millions believe in a god who changes his mind. Islam teaches that Allah, their god, can change his mind about you from moment to moment. He is a god of abrogation, which means he can change his mind about you going to heaven.

That is not how our God, the God of Abraham, Isaac, and Jacob is. He is the only One and True God. The Bible says he never changes his mind. He is the God of Promises and not abrogation.

Isaiah 40

The voice of one calling out,
"Clear the way for the LORD in the wilderness;
Make straight in the desert a highway for our God.
"Let every valley be lifted up,
And every mountain and hill be made low;
And let the uneven ground become a plain,
And the rugged terrain a broad valley;
Then the glory of the LORD will be revealed,
And all flesh will see it together;
For the mouth of the LORD has spoken."

John the Baptist, in the spirit of Elijah cries out Isaiah 40 as it was being fulfilled.

The glory of the Lord, Jesus, God the Son needs to be revealed because he has been hidden, and a hidden God is a terrifying God.

Now in those days John the Baptist came, preaching in the wilderness of Judea, saying,
"Repent, for the kingdom of heaven has come near."
For this is the one referred to by Isaiah the prophet when he said,

"THE VOICE OF ONE CALLING OUT IN THE WILDERNESS,
'PREPARE THE WAY OF THE LORD,
MAKE HIS PATHS STRAIGHT!'"

So, you just saw how the New Testament makes it clear that these prophecies were fulfilled in Jesus' cousin, John the Baptist. John was preparing the way for the one and only true Messiah Jesus.

Jesus even referenced John as a type of Elijah who will come later before his return in great glory and power. He did show up to meet with Jesus on the mountain with Moses – The Transfiguration – but that was just a preview of what is to come in the end.

No one knows for sure, but these two could be the two witnesses you see in Revelation chapter eleven. The reason many believe this is because they will perform the same types of miracles, as they performed in the past. And the fact that these two met with Jesus on that mountain.

Isaiah 42 (Dead Sea Scrolls)
"Behold, my servant, whom I uphold;
my chosen, in whom my soul delights—
I have put my Spirit on him.
He will bring justice to the nations.
He will not shout,
nor raise his voice,
nor cause it to be heard in the street.
He won't break a bruised reed.
He won't quench a dimly burning wick.
He will faithfully bring justice.
And He will not fail nor be discouraged,
until he has set justice in the earth,
and the islands will wait for his law."

That was from the text of the scroll of Isaiah, found in 1947 in a clay jar, near the Dead Sea. This manuscript, or scroll, dates back at least 150 years before the birth of Christ. Also, they were found one year before Israel became a nation again after two thousand years of exile.

I love the words, *"He won't break a bruised reed. He won't quinch a dimly burning wick."* You have to love how Jesus was so gentle to women and children. Nowhere have I found a scripture where he shouted at them or told them to get in their proper place. Jesus was a perfect gentlemen, yet he was tough with the religious leaders and even his own twelve disciples.

Isaiah 52 - 53

Read this amazing chapter to your Jewish friend and ask them what they heard. They will often ask you why you read about Jesus in the New Testament to them. That is how powerful this prophecy is.

It starts in Isaiah 52 (Remember, the chapter and verse numbers were put in by the translators for reference).

I remember the day I saw the actual Isaiah scroll in a Museum in Seattle. It was as if God cracked open the door to Heaven and shined it down on that scroll and passage. Next to the scroll was this English translation:

Isaiah 52
(Dead Sea Scroll)
Behold, my servant will deal wisely.
He will be exalted and lifted up,
and will be very high.
Just as many were astonished at you
(his appearance was marred more than any man, and his form more
than the sons of men),
so he will cleanse many nations.
Kings will shut their mouths at him:
for they will see that which had not been told them;

and they will understand that which they had not heard.
Isaiah 53 (Dead Sea Scrolls)
Who has believed our message?
To whom has the arm of Yahweh been revealed?
For he grew up before him as a tender plant,
and as a root out of dry ground.
He has no good looks or majesty.
When we see him, there is no beauty that we should desire him.
He was despised,
and rejected by men,
and a man of suffering,
and acquainted with disease.
He was despised as one from whom men hide their face,
and we didn't respect him.
Surely he has borne our sickness,
and carried our suffering,
yet we considered him plagued,
struck by God, and afflicted.
But he was pierced for our transgressions.
He was crushed for our iniquities.
The punishment that brought our peace was on him,
and by his wounds we are healed.
All we like sheep have gone astray.
Everyone has turned to his own way,
and Yahweh has laid on him the iniquity of us all.
He was oppressed,
yet when he was afflicted he didn't open his mouth.
As a lamb that is led to the slaughter,
and as a sheep that before its shearers is silent,
so he didn't open his mouth.
He was taken away by oppression and judgment;
and as for his generation,

who considered that he was cut off out of the land of the living
and stricken for the disobedience of my people?
They made his grave with the wicked,
and with a rich man in his death;
although he had done no violence,
nor was any deceit in his mouth.
Yet it pleased Yahweh to bruise him.
He has caused him to suffer.
When you make his soul an offering for sin,
he will see his offspring.
He will prolong his days,
and Yahweh's pleasure will prosper in his hand.
After the suffering of his soul,
he will see the light and be satisfied.
My righteous servant will justify many by the knowledge of himself;
and he will bear their iniquities.
Therefore I will give him a portion with the great,
and he will divide the plunder with the strong;
because he poured out his soul to death,
and was counted with the transgressors;
yet he bore the sins of many,
and made intercession for their transgressions.

Thousands of the modern synagogues of today consider it the forbidden chapter and will skip it.

Rabbis used to read Isaiah 53 in synagogues, but after the chapter caused arguments and great confusion, they decided that the simplest thing would be to just take that prophecy out of the Haftarah readings in synagogues.

That is why today when they read Isaiah 52, then stop in the middle of the chapter and the week after they jump straight to Isaiah 54.

Isaiah lived and prophesied about 700 BCE or BC (Before Christ).

Isaiah put the prophecy in past tense and because he saw himself as part of the people of Israel, not above them. You can see that he used first person plural (we).

Remember, the original written scroll of Isaiah had no chapter numbers, or verse numbers. You can see the prophecy about Messiah Jesus starts in chapter 52 and then flows through chapter 53.

Let us break it down together and look at all of the eye-opening details of this most famous passage.

Isaiah 52

Behold, my servant will deal wisely.

The term "servant" is seen earlier in the scroll, and it speaks of the Messiah: "the Servant of the Lord" (seen in chapters 42, 49 and 50, where the Messiah is described as a servant that suffers).

He will be exalted and lifted up, and will be very high.

This speaks of Jesus as the Messiah who would in fact rise from the dead, and ascend to the heavens and sit next to the Father on the throne. Jesus told the High Priest Caiaphas, that he would see him at the right-hand of the Power.

Just as many were astonished at you (his appearance was marred more than any man, and his form more than the sons of men),

This suffering Messiah is seen exalted. But first he would suffer and be humiliated. His body would be abused and tortured so badly that he would be completely disfigured and unrecognizable. Imagine it. The extreme bruising and swelling, so bad that he was not even recognized.

so he will cleanse many nations. Kings will shut their mouths at him: for they will see that which had not been told them; and they will understand that which they had not heard.

The suffering Servant would one day see kings come to look to him, with reverence, because he is the King of kings, and Lord of lords.

Who has believed our message? To whom has the arm of Yahweh been revealed?

Isaiah calls the Messiah the "Arm of Yahweh." Earlier, in chapter 40 Isaiah declares that the "Arm of Yahweh" would rule for him. You can see it in verse 10: *Behold, the Lord Yahweh will come as a mighty one, and his arm will rule for him. Behold, his reward is with him, and his recompense before him. He will feed his flock like a shepherd. He will gather the lambs in his arm, and carry them in his bosom. He will gently lead those who have their young.*

In chapter 51 the Gentiles put their hope in the "Arm of Yahweh", and the "Arm of Yahweh" would redeem.

In chapter 52 the "Arm of Yahweh" brings salvation.

In Isaiah 53, the prophecy reveals to us that the "Arm of Yahweh" is in fact the Messiah.

He has no good looks or majesty. When we see him, there is no beauty that we should desire him.

He was not appealing to us. We did not want him. His appearance was not particularly glorious or impressive, and the way he showed up didn't cause people to desire him.

In contrast to what rabbinic Halacha teaches today, according to this prophecy, the Messiah would not be born to a prestigious rabbinic family or grow up in the grand residences of wealthy rabbis. You can be sure that the external appearance of Messiah was nothing extraordinary at all.

He was despised, and rejected by men, and a man of suffering, and acquainted with disease. He was despised as one from whom men hide their face, and we didn't respect him.

The life of the Messiah was characterized by pain, rejection, and suffering. He did not get the honor due to the Messiah, but was despised and rejected by the leaders of his people. We considered him some kind of social misfit – someone we might hide our faces from when we pass someone on the street that we are embarrassed to see.

We acquaint him with sickness and disease. Yet, he is the one who heals us from our diseases, weather here on earth or in Heaven.

We did not think he was the Messiah, the Savior of the World. We did not even recognize that it could be him.

Surely he has borne our sickness, and carried our suffering, yet we considered him plagued, struck by God, and afflicted.

The Messiah suffered in our place because he carried our sicknesses, our suffering, our pain, and the sins we committed, while we thought he was being punished, and that his suffering was God's punishment for sins that he himself had committed. But Jesus was sinless. So, we didn't understand that he took on our transgressions and suffered for our sin.

But he was pierced for our transgressions. He was crushed for our iniquities. The punishment that brought our peace was on him, and by his wounds we are healed.

The Hebrew says wounded, pierced. He died. Like someone who has fallen wounded, or someone perforated with a sword – not for any fault of his own, but it was our wrongdoing.

He was crushed because of our iniquities, our sins – the punishment and discipline we deserved went to him. The "stripes" are hard blows that leave marks, and by his scars we are healed. In exactly this way, hundreds of years later, the prophecy was fulfilled. Jesus went to the cross in order to take the death we deserved.

All we like sheep have gone astray. Everyone has turned to his own way, and Yahweh has laid on him the iniquity of us all.

The Hebrew talks of going astray like sheep wander off and get lost. All of us, the people of Israel, the people of the world, ignored him and went on our way, but despite this, God put all our sin and iniquity on him – on Jesus the Messiah.

He was oppressed, yet when he was afflicted he didn't open his mouth. As a lamb that is led to the slaughter, and as a sheep that before its shearers is silent, so he didn't open his mouth.

He was oppressed, abused... his dignity and right to a fair trial were taken from him. The Hebrew says he was afflicted – tortured – but he didn't open his mouth. This shows that he did not resist his unjust sentence. He didn't try to rebel or escape, and he did not take legal representation in spite of the fact he was facing a death sentence, but he was led like a sheep to the slaughter, or to be sheared without resisting the injustices being done to him.

He was taken away by oppression and judgment; and as for his generation, who considered that he was cut off out of the land of the living and stricken for the disobedience of my people?

They arrested him and took his to trial. As a result of the trial, he was "cut off from the land of the living." A death sentence. Not for his own crimes, but those of his people. In the Scriptures, "My people" always means the people of Israel. The Messiah would die not for his own sin but for the sin of his people – the people who should be taking the punishment for their own sins – but the Messiah took it upon himself. He is the one who did.

His generation would not care to bring him up in conversation, but would rather sweep his existence under the carpet. So, for the last two thousand years, Jesus the Messiah has been the best kept secret in Judaism, and this is precisely why he was labelled "Yeshu" in Judaism, which stands for "May his name and memory be blotted out".

This looks a lot like the brothers of Joseph. They wanted his name to be blotted out too. And just like Joseph said, that they meant it for evil, but God meant it for good, to save many people alive, Jesus can say the same.

They made his grave with the wicked, and with a rich man in his death; although he had done no violence, nor was any deceit in his mouth.

He was executed like a criminal, even though he did no crime, and never lied, in his death he was to be buried in the fancy tomb of a rich man. Yeshua really was killed on the cross and was buried in the grave of a rich man a member of the Sanhedrin, Joseph of Arimathea.

This has a deeper sign because at Jesus' birth, there was another Joseph who gave up the womb to God the Son. Mary's womb was untouched by sinful men. The same is true of Joseph of Arimathea, he has a tomb, like the womb that had not been defiled by dead men. In both instances Jesus burst forth out of the womb and the tomb as the "First Fruits."

Yet it pleased Yahweh to bruise him. He has caused him to suffer. When you make his soul an offering for sin, he will see his offspring. He will prolong his days, and Yahweh's pleasure will prosper in his hand.

So, who is responsible for the death of the Messiah? "The Jews"? As so many so-called Christians have made the accusations in the past. The Romans? They were the ones who crucified him, right?

No. "God was pleased to bruise him." God, Yahweh, is the only one able to forgive and bring salvation to the world and he turned himself into a sacrifice. What kind of sacrifice? A guilt offering. The death of the Messiah was no accident – God used his own stiff-necked people as priests to bring about the forgiveness of sins not only for his people Israel, but for the whole of humanity.

In contrast to the Yom Kippur sacrifice which was only valid until the following year and just 'covered over' sin, the atonement of the Messiah took away our sin finally! None of us as human beings are perfect – we are not able to be that perfect sacrifice. Only God himself could do that.

Even though he would be killed, he would also prolong his days. He would rise again from the dead and would see the "fruit of his seed," planted in his resurrection.

After the suffering of his soul, he will see the light and be satisfied. My righteous servant will justify many by the knowledge of himself; and he will bear their iniquities.

The Messiah would see and be satisfied by his own suffering, because many would be made righteous by what he endured, as a righteous man when he took on himself the sins and iniquities of many. All who recognize him as the Messiah will be justified.

Therefore I will give him a portion with the great, and he will divide the plunder with the strong; because he poured out his soul to death, and was counted with the transgressors; yet he bore the sins of many, and made intercession for their transgressions.

The Messiah was the intersession for us an advocate for us as sinners before a holy God. The Messiah took on his shoulders the sin of all who believe in him. It is an encouraging prophecy of hope and a future. God is not just interested in forgiveness expressed in words but also demonstrated in actions. That is why he took on the appearance of a servant and took the punishment that we deserve on himself.

Jewish scholars of ancient times always interpreted Isaiah 53 to be about the Messiah. In fact, the well-known term "Messiah ben Yosef" is from this very text.

In the ancient Jewish translation of Yonatan ben Uzziel (Targum Jonathan) from the first century opened the section with the words "The Anointed Servant" Ben Uzziel connected the chapter to the Messiah, the Anointed One.

Rabbi Yitzhak Abravanel who lived centuries ago admitted that "Yonatan ben Uzziel's interpretation that it was about the coming Messiah was also the opinion of the Sages (of blessed memory) as can be seen in much of their commentary."

Isaiah 55

"You there! Everyone who thirsts, come to the waters;
And you who have no money come, buy and eat.
Come, buy wine and milk
Without money and without cost.
"Why do you spend money for what is not bread,
And your wages for what does not satisfy?
Listen carefully to Me, and eat what is good,
And delight yourself in abundance.
"Incline your ear and come to Me.
Listen, that you may live;
And I will make an everlasting covenant with you,
According to the faithful mercies shown to David.

John recorded Jesus saying the same thing in the Temple:

Now on the last day, the great day *of the feast, Jesus stood and cried out, saying, "If anyone is thirsty, let him come to Me and drink. The one who believes in Me, as the Scripture said, 'From his innermost being will flow rivers of living water.'" But this He said in reference to the Spirit, whom those who believed in Him were to receive; for the Spirit was not yet given, because Jesus was not yet glorified. (John 7:37-39 NASB)*

Isaiah 61

Jesus read this passage from the scroll of Isaiah, in his hometown synagogue of Nazareth. He read it and then he said, "Today these scriptures are fulfilled."

Yahweh's Spirit is on me;
because Yahweh has anointed me to preach good news to the humble.
He has sent me to bind up the broken hearted,
to proclaim liberty to the captives,
and release to those who are bound;
to proclaim the year of Yahweh's favor, ...

He stopped mid-sentence, at that comma and declared those scriptures fulfilled during his first arrival.

And He rolled up the scroll, gave it back to the attendant, and sat down; and the eyes of all the people *in the synagogue were intently directed at Him. Now He began to say to them, "Today this Scripture has been fulfilled in your hearing."*

The rest of it speaks of the second coming, when he returns in vengeance and to rescue his people, Israel.

...and the day of vengeance of our God;
to comfort all who mourn;
to provide for those who mourn in Zion,
to give to them a garland for ashes,
the oil of joy for mourning,
the garment of praise for the spirit of heaviness;
that they may be called trees of righteousness,
the planting of Yahweh,
that he may be glorified.

Did you catch that?

God is into Zion. God loves Zion, he loves Israel. They are still the "Apple of His Eye" and he will save Israel just as it is written in the New Testament book of Romans.

Romans 11

I say then, God has not rejected His people, has He? Far from it! For I too am an Israelite, a descendant of Abraham, of the tribe of Benjamin.

God has not rejected His people whom He foreknew...For I do not want you, brothers and sisters, *to be uninformed of this mystery—so that you will not be wise in your own estimation—that a partial hardening has happened to Israel until the fullness of the Gentiles has come in; and so all Israel will be saved; just as it is written:*

"THE DELIVERER WILL COME FROM ZION,
HE WILL REMOVE UNGODLINESS FROM JACOB."
"THIS IS MY COVENANT WITH THEM,
WHEN I TAKE AWAY THEIR SINS."

In relation to the gospel they are *enemies on your account, but in relation to God's choice they* are *beloved on account of the fathers; for the gifts and the calling of God are irrevocable.*

God has an amazing plan to save Zion in the end. He always keeps his promises and never changes his mind.

Some claim that the church is now "Spiritual Israel" and that all the promises in the Old Testament were meant for the Church.

If that is true, then the Church would also have to take all the curses that were promised as well. But those who believe in this "Replacement Theology" do not like that. They only want the blessings.

Also, if the Church is now Israel, then what do you do with the book of Revelation where God speaks of the 144,000 Jewish believers sealed by God and mentions specifically by tribe? This all came about from over allegorizing the scriptures.

There is a specific warning from Jesus in Revelation. He calls out those who say they are Jews but are not, but are of the synagogue of satan. This is a heavy rebuke from God.

Did God warn those who say they are now spiritual Israel and hate Israel? You, as a believer were grafted into that tree. You should not be arrogant, but humble and remember the native branches are going to be grafted back into their won tree.

...'the slander by those who say they are Jews, and are not, but are a synagogue of Satan...' (Revelation 2:9 NASB)

Thousands will disagree with me on this. So be it. I am not afraid to tell the truth in love. These two must work together. Today you can see a lot of so-called love and kindness without any truth. This is not how Jesus talked with people. He offended many because he spoke the truth, even in love, but the truth still offended them.

CHAPTER SEVENTEEN: JEREMIAH

Jeremiah has been called, "The weeping Prophet." Jesus was weeping for Jerusalem just before he went to the cross.

Jeremiah was a mighty prophet of God and preached repentance, which means turning from evil and toward God. But he had no converts, there is no record of it, yet Jeremiah never gave up.

Daniel referenced Jeremiah's prophecy when he read that they would be in captivity for seventy years. He knew this was literal and that it was about time to plan on heading back to Jerusalem.

Jeremiah also had many prophecies that spoke of Jesus.

Some of his prophecies speak of God returning to save Israel when Jesus comes back to this earth to rule and reign from Jerusalem.

Jeremiah 11
Dead Sea Scroll

But I was like a gentle lamb that is led to the slaughter. I didn't
know that they had devised plans against me, saying,
"Let's destroy the tree with its fruit,
and let's cut him off from the land of the living,
that his name may be no more remembered."
But, Yahweh of Armies, who judges righteously,
who tests the heart and the mind,
I will see your vengeance on them;
for to you I have revealed my cause.

This speaks of the humanity of Jesus and God the Son Jesus. He pleaded with his Father for another way to pay for the sins of the world.

He sweat droplets of blood from the stress of that moment of prayer in the garden.

There is a medical term for this extreme stress related condition.

Hematohidrosis is also known as hematidrosis, hidrosis, and hematidrosis is a condition in which capillary blood vessels that feed the sweat glands rupture, causing them to exude blood; it occurs under conditions of extreme physical or emotional stress.

There are records of some men who sweat blood during the trench warfare of World War I.

But it was Jesus who had it to the most extreme: Luke 22:44 says: *"And being in agony he prayed more earnestly; and his sweat became like great drops of blood falling down to the ground."*

He was like a lamb led to the slaughter, yet when he returns it will be very different.

When he returns he will be the mighty King and will come in vengeance.

Jeremiah 23

"Behold, the days are coming," declares the LORD,
"When I will raise up for David a righteous Branch;
And He will reign as king and act wisely
And do justice and righteousness in the land.
"In His days Judah will be saved,
And Israel will live securely;
And this is His name by which He will be called,
'The LORD Our Righteousness.'

You know by now that Jesus was born through Mary who was of the tribe of Judah, of David's righteous branch.

This passage speaks of him ruling and reigning as King, saving Israel and causing them to live in security and in peace.

What I love about this passage is that you get to see one of the many glorious names of Jesus: The LORD our Righteousness.

He is our righteousness because we are clothed in Him. When the Father looks at you as a believer and follower of Jesus, he sees his Son's righteousness not yours. This is why it is called; Amazing Grace and it has a sweet sound.

Jeremiah prophesied about the time when King Herod decided an evil thought and tried to murder the newly born Messiah. The magi from the east came and asked: *"Where is He who has been born King of the Jews? For we saw His star in the east and have come to worship Him." When Herod the king heard this, he was troubled, and all Jerusalem with him..."(Matthew 2:2 NASB)*

He heard the word of God. He heard the scripture that prophesied the birth of Jesus. It was Micah chapter five, verse two and he heard it and was so evil, he decided he would try to murder the Son of God.

Matthew 2

And gathering together all the chief priests and scribes of the people, he inquired of them where the Messiah was to be born. They said to him, "In Bethlehem of Judea; for this is what has been written by the prophet:
'AND YOU, BETHLEHEM, LAND OF JUDAH,
ARE BY NO MEANS LEAST AMONG THE LEADERS OF JUDAH;
FOR FROM YOU WILL COME FORTH A RULER
WHO WILL SHEPHERD MY PEOPLE ISRAEL.'"

Herod heard the words of God through the prophet, and he still decided to murder the child. He had no respect for scripture, and I wonder if some of the false teachers told him it is all allegorical, and over spiritualized it for him.

God's word is God's word, and it is not to be written off as spiritual symbolism only. This is dangerous with books like Genesis and Revelation. Shame on the Seminary Schools, Pastors and Authors who do this. They need to repent.

Then Herod decides to play the bad guy and fulfills the prophetic scripture of Jeremiah. He is responsible for the pain and suffering of many mothers and fathers in the region of Bethlehem.

Matthew 2

Then when Herod saw that he had been tricked by the magi, he became very enraged, and sent men and killed all the boys who were in Bethlehem and all its vicinity who were two years old or under, according to the time which he had determined from the magi.

Then what had been spoken through Jeremiah the prophet was fulfilled:

"A VOICE WAS HEARD IN RAMAH,
WEEPING AND GREAT MOURNING,
RACHEL WEEPING FOR HER CHILDREN;
AND SHE REFUSED TO BE COMFORTED,
BECAUSE THEY WERE NO MORE."

Matthew made the connection of this Jeremiah prophecy and how it was fulfilled. This is what makes God's word so amazing. The Bible is the only book that dares to predict the future, and it comes to pass.

Much of what is written as prophecy has not been fulfilled even though many today try and say that all prophecy is fulfilled. They over spiritualize scriptures like Ezekiel chapter thirty-seven where you see Israel gathered back to their homeland from the four corners of the world.

Even C.H. Spurgeon taught that this was a future restoration of the Nation of Israel. He also said this is not to be spiritualized.

You would be playing the fool to write off all of the future, unfulfilled prophecies as just spiritual.

So, here you can see that Jeremiah prophesied about the day of weeping when Herod the not so Great murdered the baby boys of that region.

Jeremiah 31:15

SEE JESUS IN THE OLD TESTAMENT

This is what the LORD says:
"A voice is heard in Ramah,
Lamenting and bitter weeping.
Rachel is weeping for her children;
She refuses to be comforted for her children,
Because they are no more."

God does not forget when innocent babies are killed.

Jeremiah chapter thirty-one also speaks of a new covenant that God would establish for Israel. It is also opened to any Gentiles who will believe and put their trust in him. This started with his Son Jesus, and it changed everything. Even time and dates are today centered around this new covenant through Jesus.

Just like Joseph's story he was despised and rejected by his own the first time. But when Joseph and his brothers, the sons of Israel, met again, there was great forgiveness. They wept together just like you see in Zechariah chapter twelve.

Joseph had a Gentile bride, and she was safe with him. He was preparing to save the known world of that time, and when that last piece of grain was harvested into his storehouse, the seven-year Great Famine started.

It was two years into this time of great trouble, or Jacob's trouble that the sons of Israel came to him, bowed down. Then Joseph made himself known to them and it was beautiful.

He forgave them and showed amazing grace to them. He saved all of Israel and blessed them with the best of the land.

This day will come for Israel and that new covenant will be fulfilled completely. I can't wait for this day.

Jeremiah 31:31-33

The New Covenant with Israel

"Behold, days are coming," declares the LORD, "when I will make a new covenant with the house of Israel and the house of Judah, not like the covenant which I made with their fathers on the day I took them by the hand to bring them out of the land of Egypt, My covenant which they broke, although I was a husband to them," declares the LORD. "For this is the covenant which I will make with the house of Israel after those days," declares the LORD: "I will put My law within them and write it on their heart; and I will be their God, and they shall be My people. They will not teach again, each one his neighbor and each one his brother, saying, 'Know the LORD,' for they will all know Me, from the least of them to the greatest of them," declares the LORD, "for I will forgive their wrongdoing, and their sin I will no longer remember."

Did you see that?

God says, *"for I will forgive their wrongdoing, and their sin I will no longer remember."*

He is speaking directly to Israel here in this passage.

It is just like that major type of Jesus, Joseph, when he forgives their wrongdoing, and the sin they committed against him, he no longer remembers it.

CHAPTER EIGHTEEN: EZEKIEL

People struggle to understand Ezekiel, especially when they believe that God has replaced Israel with the church. You may have been in the Bible study like I have, the leader tries to teach the first few chapters of Ezekiel and then gives up.

I love this book of prophecy, and I know you will too.

In this book you can see Ezekiel himself as a type and picture of Christ.

My favorite part of Ezekiel are the prophecies of Israel being restored in the latter years. In Ezekiel 36-48, God gives you the insight into his plan with Israel.

What is amazing about that is it happened around our time. In 1948 Israel miraculously became a nation again after two thousand years.

We will be covering this thoroughly and it is exciting. But first we will look at Ezekiel foreshadowing Jesus.

Ezekiel as a Type of Christ

He was called, "Son of man" sharing the title that Jesus has.

Jesus was fully man and God, and that is why he is called the Son of Man, and the Son of God.

Ezekiel was also a priest.

He was one of the few who were a prophet and also a priest.

Jesus is called our Great High Priest. Jesus was also called a Prophet by Moses and others. He was not only a prophet but also the King of Israel, the Great Physician, the Good Shepherd, the Great I Am, the Alpha and Omega, the Beginning and the End.

He is called a prophet however you should be warned, Jesus is not the prophet Isa in Islam. They believe their version of Jesus or Isa as they call him was a mighty prophet but not the Son of God.

In fact, their version of Jesus looks like the false prophet, who appeared as lamb but spoke like a dragon (Revelation 13).

So, Ezekiel was the only prophet that the scriptures say bore the sins of the people. That is important!

You know full well that Jesus bore the sins of the entire world when he died on that cross. You simply must believe and receive his forgiveness, and you will be saved as the scriptures say.

Ezekiel was shunned by his own people, but they later realized he was speaking God's word. He spoke truth in love to them even when they refused to listen to him.

What you and I will focus in on now is how powerful Ezekiel's prophecies were when they pointed to Jesus and the time of his second coming.

He prophesied about Israel becoming a glorious nation once again. This time a united Israel, not the southern kingdom of Judah and the northern kingdom of Israel.

God shows him, that they will be gathered in the latter days, and that they would be united. This proves that God was not speaking of the return from exile from Ezra and Nehemiah's time to Jesus time because they were still divided.

God shows Ezekiel in a practical demonstration of two sticks how they would be a united Israel in the latter days.

Ezekiel 37

"Behold, I am going to take the stick of Joseph, which is in the hand of Ephraim, and the tribes of Israel, his companions; and I will put them with it, with the stick of Judah, and make them one stick, and they will be one in My hand...I will make them one nation in the land, on the mountains of Israel; and one king will be king for all of them; and they will no longer be two nations, and no longer be divided into two kingdoms."

Ezekiel showed that there would be a literal rebirth of the nation of Israel as well as a Millennial Kingdom where Jesus would rule and reign from Jerusalem for a thousand years.

The earliest church fathers believed this as well as men like Isaac Newton, C.H. Spurgeon, Martin Luther King Jr., Billy Graham, Franklin Graham, and Greg Laurie.

C.H. Spurgeon even spelled it out, "...we shall at once profess our attachment to the pre-millennial school of interpretation, and the literal reading of those Scriptures that predict the return of the Jews to their own land...the literal sense and meaning of this passage [Ezekiel 37:1-10]—a meaning not to be spirited or spiritualized away".

The return and rebirth of Israel has already happened in our time. Most pastors and religious leaders ignore this today. But what does the scripture say?

That is the most important thing to ask when interpreting scripture. First and foremost, look at what the text says, and then do the research if necessary.

Ezekiel 37
Vision of the Valley of Dry Bones

The hand of the LORD was upon me, and He brought me out by the Spirit of the LORD and set me down in the middle of the valley; and it was full of bones.

He had me pass among them all around, and behold, there were very many on the surface of the valley; and behold, they were very dry. Then He said to me, "Son of man, can these bones live?" And I answered, "Lord GOD, You Yourself know." Again He said to me, "Prophesy over these bones and say to them, 'You dry bones, hear the word of the LORD.' This is what the Lord GOD says to these bones: 'Behold, I am going to make breath enter you so that you may come to life. And I will attach tendons to you, make flesh grow back on you, cover you with skin, and put breath in you so that you may come to life; and you will know that I am the LORD.'"

So I prophesied as I was commanded; and as I prophesied, there was a loud noise, and behold, a rattling; and the bones came together, bone to its bone. And I looked, and behold, tendons were on them, and flesh grew and skin covered them; but there was no breath in them. Then He said to me, "Prophesy to the breath, prophesy, son of man, and say to the breath, 'The Lord GOD says this: "Come from the four winds, breath, and breathe on these slain, so that they come to life."'" So I prophesied as He commanded me, and the breath entered them, and they came to life and stood on their feet, an exceedingly great army.

You might be thinking, "Why did C.H. Spurgeon say this is literally speaking about the nation of Israel coming back to life?"

Because God says so.

Look at the next few verses in this amazing passage:

*Then He said to me, "Son of man, **these bones are the entire house of Israel**; behold, they say, 'Our bones are dried up and our hope has perished. We are completely cut off.'*

*Therefore prophesy and say to them, 'This is what the Lord GOD says: "Behold, I am going to open your graves and cause you to come up out of your graves, My people; and **I will bring you into the land of Israel**.*

You can't miss that. It was obviously not meant to be allegorized or spiritualized.

The church is not spiritual Israel as some say.

C.H. Spurgeon and the earliest church fathers did not think this was spiritual Israel.

So, you can read Ezekiel chapters thirty-six and thirty-seven and clearly see that God is accomplishing this today.

Israel is not perfect. Can you tell me which nation is perfect today? If you look carefully they are far more moral, and caring than other countries. They do everything in their power to target the terrorist without hurting civilians. They take injured terrorists and give them the best medical care and treatment. What country does that?

So, what comes after these two chapters in Ezekiel that showed the return of Israel?

What is next?

Well, after chapters thirty-six and thirty-seven, logically you would go to chapter thirty-eight.

In these next two chapters you see God say that in latter times, and then he describes a massive army, an evil alliance of many countries mostly from the north of Israel.

They come down like a cloud because there are so many of them. If you looked down from satellite imagery, it would look like a cloud. God says that they would have an evil thought, to come down against his people whom he brought back.

Today you can see this happening, there are stages of it coming together. It is like the beginnings of World War II. Has it climaxed yet to the full fulfillment of Ezekiel 38-39? Not yet, but it will.

You can see these countries spelled out individually by God.

Ezekiel 38 (Dead Sea Scroll)

Yahweh's word came to me, saying, "Son of man, set your face toward Gog, of the land of Magog, the prince of Rosh, Meshech, and Tubal, and prophesy against him, and say, 'Thus says the Lord Yahweh: "Behold, I am against you, Gog, prince of Rosh, Meshech, and Tubal.

In the latter years you will come into the land that is brought back from the sword, that is gathered out of many peoples, on the mountains of Israel, which have been a continual waste; but it is brought out of the peoples, and they will dwell securely, all of them.

God speaks of this evil alliance army led by Gog, who is the prince of Rosh. He also speaks of other areas, and one is still easily identified as Persia which has always been Iran.

Persia, Cush, and Put with them, all of them with buckler and helmet; Gomer with all its troops; Beth-togarmah from the remote parts of the north with all its troops—many peoples with you

These regions include Russia and the southern countries around it, Iran, and Turkey.

As I am typing this manuscript you can see these countries in that evil alliance. In fact, Iran and Russia have an alliance right now for the first time in history. Turkey is joining them and even threatened direct military action against Israel.

What is even more significant, is that Iran is already at war with Israel now. It started with them using Hamas to attack Israel on October 7th, 2023, and they did things so horrible even the nazi's would have been ashamed.

Before this attack, Israel was living in peace and was even helping Gaza. They provided electricity to them and even piped in free drinking water – a precious commodity in that region. You can see that Israel has been good to them.

What was Persia or Iran up to?

They orchestrated this evil plan of massacre not seen since the Nazi's concentration camps.

This demonic army even shot hundreds of missiles at Israel, drones, cruise missiles, and even ballistic missiles. They were given the global positioning system from the Russians to do this. So, here you already see the Russians (area of Magog) and Iran (historically Persia) performing these acts of war together.

What is amazing about this is that 99.99% of those missiles were shot down or missed and exploded in desolate areas. This was a miracle. Even an atheist missile expert who designed these systems said that was impossible and it was a miracle of God.

In that Ezekiel prophecy he speaks of the "Arrows" being knocked out of their hands. Arrow is another name for missiles and even the Israeli's have a missile called the Arrow.

Ezekiel 38-39 also says that God will destroy this evil alliance against Israel and many nations will know that he did it.

You will come from your place out of the remote parts of the north, you and many peoples with you, all of them riding horses, a large assembly and a mighty army; and you will come up against My people Israel like a cloud to cover the land. It shall come about in the last days that I will bring you against My land, so that the nations may know Me when I show Myself holy through you before their eyes, Gog."

Again you see that this army comes from the remote parts of the North, and many with them. What is the remote parts of the north in biblical terms? This was always measured from Jerusalem and the most remote place to the north of Jerusalem is Moscow, Russia. If you keep from Moscow, you will run into the Nort Pole.

You also see that it is huge, like a cloud. But God shows up to destroy them:

'This is what the Lord GOD says: "Are you the one of whom I spoke in former days through My servants the prophets of Israel, who prophesied in those days for many years that I would bring you against them? It will come about on that day, when Gog comes against the land of Israel," declares the Lord GOD, "that My fury will mount up in My anger. In My zeal and in My blazing wrath I declare that on that day there will certainly be a great earthquake in the land of Israel. The fish of the sea, the birds of the sky, the animals of the field, all the crawling things that crawl on the earth, and all mankind who are on the face of the earth will shake at My presence; and the mountains will be thrown down, the steep pathways will collapse, and every wall will fall to the ground. And I will call for a sword against him on all My mountains," declares the Lord GOD. "Every man's sword will be against his brother. With plague and with blood I will enter into judgment with him; and I will rain on him and on his troops, and on the many peoples who are with him, a torrential rain, hailstones, fire, and brimstone. So I will prove Myself great, show Myself holy, and make Myself known in the sight of many nations; and they will know that I am the LORD."'

When exactly this war happens, no one knows for sure. However, it is remarkable that you and I can witness these countries already at war with Israel today. The war may be direct or through their proxies, either way it is still war.

After the Ezekiel 38-39 war, you see the Lord's return as the Prince, and a special emphasis on the East Gate in Jerusalem.

Ezekiel had visions of the Messiah Jesus going through the East Gate repeatedly in chapters forty through to the end at forty-eight.

Before we go there in scripture we need to look at a bit of history regarding the East Gate in Jerusalem.

The 1st-century historian, Josephus[1], mentions an "eastern gate" in his *Antiquities of the Jews*[2], and makes note of the fact that this gate was considered within the far northeastern extremity of the inner sacred court of the Temple.

This East Gate is also known as the Golden Gate and Mercy Gate.

Let's take a journey back in time, over five hundred years ago, to Jerusalem, 1541 A.D.

The Islamic Ottoman Turks captured and controlled Jerusalem from the time of Suleiman the Magnificent, the Sultan of the Ottoman Empire.

The Ottoman's controlled Jerusalem for four-hundred years, then their occupation of the Jewish holy site ended in 1917, during World War I.

Suleiman the Magnificent had the walls built around Jerusalem that you see today.

It was a magnificent wall, and perhaps that is how he got his name. However, like many of the Muslims, he was hostile toward the Jewish people who were still living there in Jerusalem.

He finished most of the stone walls and the gates but something troubled him.

He heard that the Jewish Messiah would return and enter by this gate. Even though this was a beautifully built gate that would have been useful for travel, he decided to have it sealed shut.

He had it sealed shut just as you see it today to prevent the Messiah's return.

What this so-called magnificent man did not realize is that he was fulfilling prophecy in Ezekiel.

---

1.   https://en.wikipedia.org/wiki/Josephus

2.   https://en.wikipedia.org/wiki/Antiquities_of_the_Jews

The Ottomans also built a cemetery in front of the gate to prevent what they called a false precursor to the Anointed One. They put the graves there to try and stop Elijah[3], from passing through the gate. That is so arrogant, and it reminds me of how Herod the Great heard the prophecy read to him about the Messiah being born in Bethlehem, and then tried to have baby Jesus murdered.

So, how did Suleiman fulfill a prophecy of Ezekiel?

Look at it now:

Ezekiel 44

Then He brought me back by way of the outer gate of the sanctuary, which faces east; and it was shut.

And the LORD said to me, "This gate shall be shut; it shall not be opened, and no one shall enter by it, for the LORD God of Israel has entered by it; therefore it shall be shut. As for the prince, he shall sit in it as prince to eat bread before the LORD; he shall enter by way of the porch of the gate and shall go out by the same way."

Some say that a Jewish man read that passage to Suleiman, and it enraged him and so he immediately had it sealed shut as it is to this day.

The previous chapters speak in detail of the East Gate and how the Lord had entered by it, and it was glorious: *And the glory of the LORD entered the house by way of the gate facing east.*

As you keep reading these last few chapters in Ezekiel you begin to see the return of King Jesus, and how he will set up his New Temple in the heart of Jerusalem.

There is so much detail: measurements of the walls and gates, it is a city with lush gardens, festivals, cooking, flowing water from the south side of the altar, which becomes a beautiful river flowing down and out of the side of the East Gate, trees bearing fruit on both sides, abundant fish in the river and much more.

---

3.   https://en.wikipedia.org/wiki/Elijah

This is some of what Ezekiel sees: *"...on the bank of the river there were very many trees on the one side and on the other. Then he said to me, "These waters go out toward the eastern region and go down into the Arabah; then they go toward the sea, being made to flow into the sea, and the waters of the sea become fresh. And it will come about that every living creature which swarms in every place where the river goes, will live. And there will be very many fish, for these waters go there and the others become fresh; so everything will live where the river goes. And it will come about that fishermen will stand beside it; from Engedi to Eneglaim there will be a place for the spreading of nets. Their fish will be according to their kinds, like the fish of the Great Sea, very many..."(Ezekiel 47 NASB)*

The Temple is set up as a monument, to remind the people during the 1000-year reign of Yeshua. It is a reminder what took place when Jesus paid the ultimate price. This is just like the Monument of stones that Joshua or Yeshua built when they entered the Promised Land. God had him build it as a monument for what he had done for them. Remember Joshua was a picture, and type of Christ.

Now you will see something amazing in this book of Ezekiel.

You are going to see a name placed on the East Gate, a name of one who was a lot like Christ. He was despised and rejected by his own, he was sold for pieces of silver, he was falsely accused, he was sent down into that place of the condemned, he told the fate of the two condemned with him, he was raised up out of that place, he was the only one found worthy to reveal God's sealed plan, he was made the right hand man to the throne, he was given a Gentile bride, he gathered a great harvest, he saves all of Israel during the seven-year time of great trouble.

Who was that?

Jesus or Joseph?

It was Joseph's story but you can also say it is Jesus' story.

The greater than Joseph, Jesus will have the name of his friend's name, Joseph on that most important Gate of the New Temple

Now, are you ready to see where it is in Ezekiel?

It is in the last chapter, right at the end of this amazing, prophetic book. You will see the names of all of the sons of Jacob, the sons of Israel given, and it says their names are on each of the entrances, three gates on each side, starting on the north side and then to the east.

Ezekiel 48

"Now these are the exits of the city: on the north side, 4,500 cubits by measurement,
shall be the gates of the city, named for the tribes of Israel, three gates
toward the north: the gate of Reuben, one; the gate of Judah, one; and
the gate of Levi, one.

*On the **east side**, 4,500 cubits, shall be three gates: **the gate of Joseph**,*
one; the gate of Benjamin, one; and the gate of Dan, one. On the south
side, 4,500 cubits by measurement, shall be three gates: the gate of
Simeon, one; the gate of Issachar, one; and the gate of Zebulun, one.
On the west side, 4,500 cubits, shall be three gates: the gate of Gad,
one; the gate of Asher, one; and the gate of Naphtali, one.

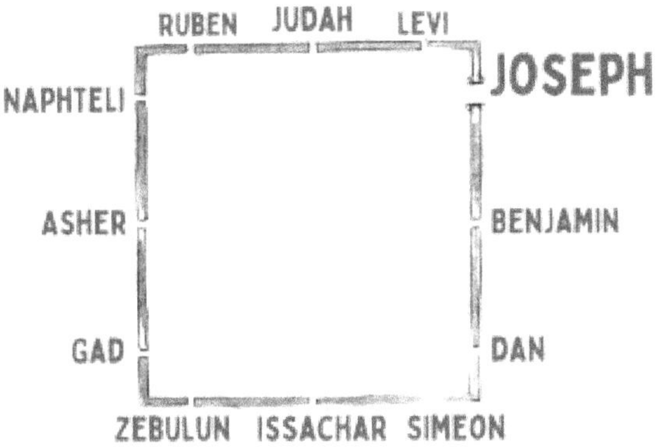

Joseph lived a life that reflected the Messiah Jesus and so God has his name placed on the most glorious gate, the East Gate of the New Jerusalem.

Prophecy is more than words. Sometimes it can be in patterns, pictures, and even a person. You and I both know that Joseph, Moses, Joshua, Boaz, David, Solomon, and Ezekiel lived lives that showed some of the greater life, of Jesus the Messiah.

This illustration of where the gates were and the names on them is a pattern type of Prophecy.

But there is more.

Ezekiel 47

Then he brought me back to the door of the house; and behold, water was flowing from under the threshold of the house toward the east, for the house faced east. And the water was flowing down from under, from the right side of the house, from south of the altar.

And he brought me out by way of the north gate and led me around on the outside to the outer gate, by the way facing east. And behold, water was spurting out from the south side.

When the man went out toward the east with a line in his hand, he measured a thousand cubits, and he led me through the water, water reaching the ankles. Again he measured a thousand and led me through the water, water reaching the knees. Again he measured a thousand and led me through the water, water reaching the hips. Again he measured a thousand; and it was a river that I could not wade across, because the water had risen, enough water to swim in, a river that could not be crossed by wading. And he said to me, "Son of man, have you seen this?" Then he brought me back to the bank of the river. Now when I had returned, behold, on the bank of the river there were very many trees on the one side and on the other. Then he said to me, "These waters go out toward the eastern region and go down into the Arabah; then they go toward the sea, being made to flow into the sea, and the waters of the sea become fresh.

So, while he is having this prophetic vision of the New Temple, he walks out of the gate just to the north and that gate is the Levi gate (See the illustration). This is fitting since Ezekiel is a priest which means he is of the tribe of Levi.

As he walks out to the north, and then heads east, he makes his way toward the front of the East Gate, the gate with Joseph's name.

He then sees the stream, flowing out from the south side of that gate, and it heals the Dead Sea, and flows out to the Seas of the world. The trees on either side produce fruit every month.

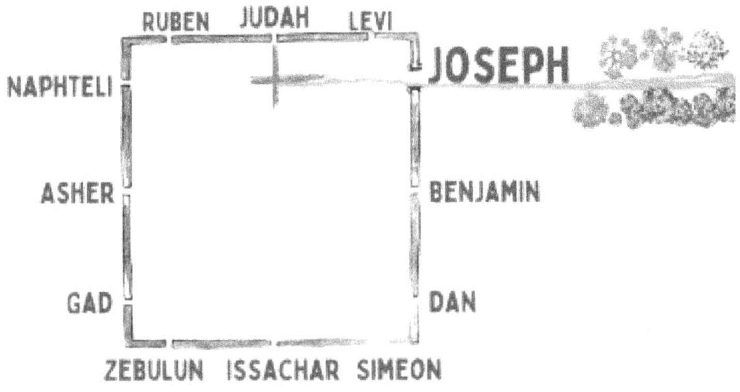

Jesus was pierced on his side and water mixed with blood poured out. This whole Temple area and its Gates show the pattern of Jesus.

If you were up on the Mount of Olives and looked out toward the East Gate and drew a straight line, you would end up at Golgotha, or Calvary, the place where Jesus was Crucified.

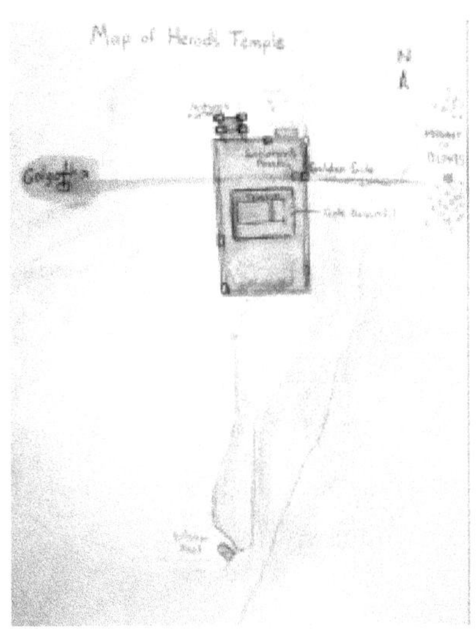

There is a pattern here. What makes it more interesting is that the original East Gate does not line up to the entrance of Herod's Temple. However, it does line up with the location of Solomon's Temple.

Jesus and his disciples did much of their work, miracles, teaching and preaching from this location called Solomon's porch or portico.

Today you can visit the Temple Mount and see a place to the north of the Dome of the Rock called the Dome of the Spirits or Dome of the Tablets. This dome is over a perfectly flat spot of the bedrock of the mountain. It would make an excellent threshing floor for separating the wheat from the chaff.

This spot is the place that King David purchased for the building of the Temple. It is large enough to fit the Ark of the Covenant.

This place is also flat, natural rock of the mountain and it shows no evidence of chisel marks.

On the other hand, the Dome of the Rock has a rocky flat spot that they say the Ark sat and it has evidence of chisel marks. This is the spot where most experts say Herod's Temple was located. I agree with them. I personally believe that Herod's Temple was built to the south of where Solomon's Temple was.

There is evidence of this in maps, and in the scriptures. Soloman's porch was located to the northeast of the beautiful gate in front of Herod's Temple.

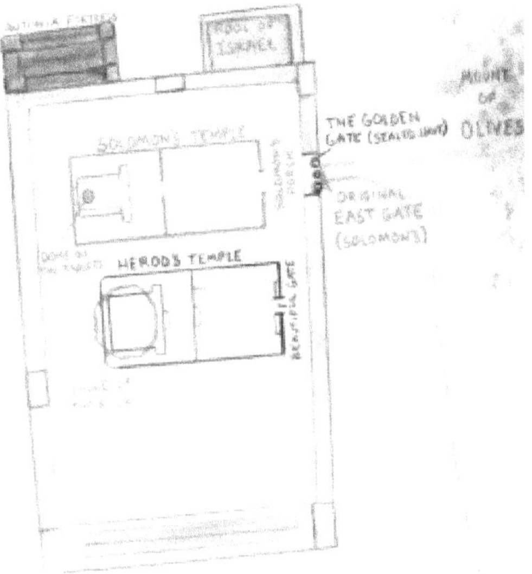

Imagine you stood on the Mount of Olives and looked out over to the Golden Gate (East Gate) and moved just enough to line up that gate with the Dome of the Spirits or Tablets.

Then you can draw a straight line from where you are on the mountain, through the East Gate and the Dome of the Tablets, and it ends up on the Traditional location of Golgotha, the very place where Jesus was crucified. This is an extraordinary discovery. You can see the pattern and it points to the cross.

Remember patterns are an important part of prophecy. You can see this even today.

Look at what Ezekiel says about this very subject:

Ezekiel 43

"As for you, son of man, inform the house of Israel of the temple, so that they will be ashamed of their wrongdoings; and have them measure the plan. And if they are ashamed of everything that they have done, make known to them the plan of the house, its layout, its exits, its entrances, all its plans, all its statutes, and all its laws..."

Someday Israel will know that Jesus or Yeshua is their Messiah. This will be a great and wonderful day. That is when Zechariah twelve will be fulfilled and they will weep together just like Joseph and his brothers did.

Let us end this chapter with the very last words of Ezekiel:
"...the name of the city from that day shall be,
'The LORD is there.'"

Hey, my friend, if you are enjoying this book please leave a favorable review because this will help spread it to the world. You can be a huge part of spreading the good news to the world, that the gospel is in fact in the Old Testament.

CHAPTER NINETEEN: JONAH

Jesus himself said Jonah was a picture and a type of him:

"...for just as JONAH WAS IN THE STOMACH OF THE SEA MONSTER FOR THREE DAYS AND THREE NIGHTS, so will the Son of Man be in the heart of the earth for three days and three nights." (Matthew 12:40 NASB)

"The men of Nineveh will stand up with this generation at the judgment and condemn it, because they repented at the preaching of Jonah; and behold, something greater than Jonah is here.
(Luke 11:32 NASB)

Jesus said something greater than Jonah is here. He was stating that Jonah was a sign of himself. And you are about to see how detailed his story really is in showing Jesus.

You can see amazing pictures of Christ in Jonah, starting with his journey on the boat.

There was a great storm, and the ship was sinking. The crew had to wake Jonah up and ask him to call upon his God: *How is it that you are sleeping? Get up, call on your god! Perhaps your god will be concerned about us so that we will not perish.*

Remember Jesus was sleeping in the boat during that great storm on the Sea of Galilee and his disciples were scared. They tried hard to row and get to land, but they could not. Now look at Jonah's story: *the men rowed desperately to return to land, but they could not, because the sea was becoming even stormier against them. Then they cried out to the LORD and said, "We earnestly pray, O LORD, do not let us perish..."*

You can see that the disciples of Jesus did the same thing during a great storm on the Sea of Galilee, they woke Jesus up and cried out to him to save them.

Remember at the scene of the cross, they cast lots for the clothing of Jesus?

In Jonah's story they cast lots to see who was causing the violent storm: *And each man said to his mate, "Come, let's cast lots so that we may find out on whose account this catastrophe has struck us." So they cast lots, and the lot fell on Jonah.*

So what did Jonah tell the crew to do? He told them to throw him overboard to ease God's anger. They did so and then the storm calmed down. In that same way Jesus was the one who had to be sacrificed to calm the raging sea of God's wrath.

Jonah 1

So they said to him, "What should we do to you so that the sea will become calm for us?"—for the sea was becoming increasingly stormy. And he said to them, "Pick me up and hurl me into the sea. Then the sea will become calm for you, because I know that on account of me this great storm has come upon you."

The storm speaks of God's wrath and the only way for this to be satisfied was by casting out one man. As far as they knew this was the sure death of this one man, Jonah.

So they picked up Jonah and hurled him into the sea, and the sea stopped its raging. Then the men became extremely afraid of the LORD, and they offered a sacrifice to the LORD and made vows.

At the cross Jesus paid the heavy price to satisfy the wrath of God. There was so much going on when Jesus died on the cross, the darkness, the massive earthquake, and it scared the Roman soldiers to the point that one of them declared that Jesus surely was the Son of God.

Jesus's death calmed the storm of God's wrath. That storm is like a raging Tsunami, and no human could stop it. Only God himself could stop it and that one man; Jesus was cast out to calm the wrath. The casting out of Jesus gave us peace with God if we follow Jesus.

Jonah 1

And the LORD designated a great fish to swallow Jonah, and Jonah was in the stomach of the fish for three days and three nights.

Jesus directly quoted this scripture when he was speaking to the religious leaders: *Then some of the scribes and Pharisees said to Him, "Teacher, we want to see a sign from You."(Matthew 12:38 NASB)*

Jesus did give them a sign but instead of a miracle he pointed them to the word of God, and to one who was a picture and a portrait of what he would do. This was their sign: *"...for just as JONAH WAS IN THE STOMACH OF THE SEA MONSTER FOR THREE DAYS AND THREE NIGHTS, so will the Son of Man be in the heart of the earth for three days and three nights."*

As you read chapter two of Jonah, it all speaks of Jesus sufferings for us. And there is a happy ending.

Jonah 2

Then Jonah prayed to the LORD his God from the stomach of the fish,
and he said,
"I called out of my distress to the LORD,
And He answered me.
I called for help from the depth of Sheol;
You heard my voice.
"For You threw me into the deep,
Into the heart of the seas,
And the current flowed around me.
All Your breakers and waves passed over me.
"So I said, 'I have been cast out of Your sight.
Nevertheless I will look again toward Your holy temple.'
"Water encompassed me to the point of death.
The deep flowed around me,
Seaweed was wrapped around my head.
"I descended to the base of the mountains.
The earth with its bars was around me forever,
But You have brought up my life from the pit, LORD my God.
"While I was fainting away,
I remembered the LORD,

And my prayer came to You,
Into Your holy temple.
"Those who are followers of worthless idols
Abandon their faithfulness,
But I will sacrifice to You
With a voice of thanksgiving.
That which I have vowed I will pay.
Salvation is from the LORD."
Then the LORD commanded the fish, and it vomited Jonah up onto
the dry land.

Now we will look at the details of this amazing chapter.

What you see in Jonah's story looks a lot like Psalm twenty-two and some of the other Psalms. You have seen the casting of lots, you see the dark storm, and you are about to see more.

Then Jonah prayed to the LORD his God from the stomach of the
fish,

and he said,
"I called out of my distress to the LORD,
And He answered me.
I called for help from the depth of Sheol;
You heard my voice.

Imagine it. He was cast out into the raging depths of the sea. It was dark and then a huge fish swallows him alive. Now he is in a thick darkness, so dark he could feel it. The acids of the stomach of that great fish would have felt like a burning pain.

He prayed, and called out to the Lord in his distress. And the Lord answered him and heard his voice.

Jonah even called this place Sheol. This was the place where the dead went to in the Old Testament.

You can imagine Jesus talking to his Father down in Sheol.

Jonah's story continues: *"So I said, 'I have been cast out of Your sight..."*

Jesus cried out from the cross and he directly quoted Psalm twenty-two: *My God, my God, why have You forsaken me"*.

I believe the greatest pain the Son of God, experienced was the separation from his Father. They were always together and now he is cast out of his sight. That is what hell is, it is the outer darkness, a place far away from God. God is light, and in him is no darkness at all. So, the opposite is true of being out of his presence.

Many say, "how could God send people to that awful dark place of suffering called hell?"

At the same time, those who say that also say, "I don't want to live in a world with God, with Jesus, his church, or his chosen nation of Israel".

God ultimately gives everyone exactly what they want.

If you desire to be with God and decide to follow Jesus his Son then you will be with him. Jesus paved the way for you at the cross.

If you want to live in a world without God, then you will get just that. However, to be absent from God is to be in the outer darkness and a place that is void of the goodness and blessing of God.

Scientist say that everything in our world, and the universe is rusting away or corroding. This is called oxidizing, and it is a form of burning. There is only one element that does not oxidize and lasts forever. It is gold. And did you know that the foundations and the streets in Heaven are made of gold? Yes, and Heaven is where the light of God is.

So, everything outside of the light of God is burning up in a place of darkness.

Now, Jonah speaks his prayer of faith that he will be raised out of that place of darkness, *Nevertheless I will look again toward Your holy temple.'*

He then speaks of the anguish and the death on the cross: *"Water encompassed me to the point of death. The deep flowed around me..."*

Psalm 22 shows the same thing: "*And You lay me in the dust of death.*"

Jonah is living out the agony of suffering and it is no wonder Jesus compares him to his mission to suffer on the cross. Now you are about to see a clear picture of the crown of thorns wrapped around the head of Jesus:

Seaweed was wrapped around my head.
(NASB)

**The weeds were wrapped around my head
(Dead Sea Scroll)**

The weeds wrapped around Jonah's head while he suffered looks a lot like Jesus' crown of thorns.

Remember, when Abraham and Isaac were on that mountain and God had provided the male Sheep, the Ram and it was caught in the thicket by its horns? That thicket speaks of weeds. That too, was a picture of Christ and the crown of thorns.

"I descended to the base of the mountains.
The earth with its bars was around me forever,
But You have brought up my life from the pit, LORD my God.
(NASB)

**I went down to the bottoms of the mountains.
The earth barred me in forever:
yet have you brought up my life from the pit, Yahweh my God.
(Dead Sea Scroll)**

I personally like the Dead Sea Scroll version the best. It is the oldest manuscript of this.

Jonah was in the dark place of the belly of this great fish, yet he speaks of descending to the base of mountains with bars around him forever. Then he speaks of being raised up out of the pit. Remember Joseph was in a pit too and that was a picture of the cross as well.

You can see more of how God listened to Jonah:

"While I was fainting away,

I remembered the LORD,
And my prayer came to You,
Into Your holy temple.

You can see similar language in Psalm 22:

Save me from the lion's mouth;
From the horns of the wild oxen You answer me.

You can see how both were prayers and Jesus was talking to his Father while he suffered on the cross. This speaks of prayer.

This next part of Jonah's suffering is amazing:

That which I have vowed I will pay.

Jesus paid it all. He vowed too, and he paid for it all. When he cried out *it is finished* from the cross, it meant that it is accomplished, the debt is paid, zero balance.

Did he have to pay for it?

No, but He loved to pay it. He loved you enough to pay this heavy price because He loved the hell out of you.

The very end of Psalm 22 says the same thing, *He has performed it.* But in Hebrew, the word is עָשָׂה, Asa. It is pronounced, "aw-saw" and it means, to accomplish.

It was fully accomplished on the cross.

Now you will see the meaning of the name Jesus, or Yeshua in Hebrew. It means "Salvation is of the Lord".

Now look at what Jonah says near the end of this time in the belly of the fish:

"...Salvation is from the LORD."

It is like Jesus signed it with his own Hebrew name, Yeshua.

The final part of this chapter shows the resurrection of Jesus as the Tomb was burst open.

Then the LORD commanded the fish, and it vomited Jonah up
onto the dry land.
(NASB)

Then Yahweh spoke to the fish, and it vomited out Jonah on the dry land.
(Dead Sea Scroll)

The earth could not keep Jesus in the tomb for more than three days.

Why?

Because Yahweh spoke this. Jesus even referenced this very story to give insight into his resurrection from the dead. He was in that place for three days and on that third day he burst out.

CHAPTER TWENTY: MICAH – JESUS' BIRTH

Herod demanded to know where the Christ was to be born, the chief priests and the scribes immediately directed him to the prophet Micah.

Micah 5
"But as for you, Bethlehem Ephrathah,
Too little to be among the clans of Judah,
From you One will come forth for Me to be ruler in Israel.
His times of coming forth are from long ago,
From the days of eternity."

Micah was a contemporary of the prophet Isaiah, and he was a prophet during the reign of Jotham, Ahaz, and Hezekiah, kings of Judah.

The small town of Bethlehem is about 5 miles, or 8 kilometers south of Jerusalem.

Bethlehem means: "house of bread".

Ephrathah means "fruitful."

It is a breadbasket, a fruitful place.

Olive groves, pomegranate fruit trees, vineyards, wheat fields, sheep grazing, this area had it all. The reason this was a blessed land for growing food was because of the fertile soil.

There was a large olive press there. So, the olive oil was produced as well as the fine wheat flower, the sweet grapes and pomegranates which were pressed into wine.

All of these elements were seen inside of the Temple, in the Holy Place.

The olive oil kept the seven-golden lampstands lit and burning bright and hot. The oil was poured into these solid gold lamps daily by the priest in the holy place.

The fine wheat flower was produced here in Bethlehem – the house of bread. The Temple authorities would come here to purchase it for the making of the twelve loaves of showbread. This bread was placed on the table of showbread in the Holy place of the Temple.

Next to the 12 loaves was the cup of sweet red wine. This was also produced in Bethlehem Ephrathah.

Already, you can see how Micah's prophecy was lining up, but there is more.

The Temple representatives came from the heart of Jerusalem to purchase these local goods: the sacks of fine flour, the sweet wine and the jars of the pure olive oil.

These same Temple officials also came here to buy the choicest lambs.

Bethlehem was well known as the perfect place to produce little lambs for the sacrifices at the Temple.

There is evidence that during Jesus time, they would wrap these lambs in cloth so that they would be protected and not become blemished.

In the hills, overlooking the tiny town of Bethlehem, there were white limestone rock caves, and they were used to secure and shelter the newborn lambs. They were also called, "Mangers."

These shelters were warm, dry, and so they gave good shelter from rain, and the cold wind. These were solid rocks like the rich man's tomb you would see in Jerusalem. There was fresh golden straw inside for the precious newborn lambs.

These were called, "Sheepfolds" and often had a rock wall with one entrance where the Shepherd would stay at the entrance. He was the door or gate for the sheep. He kept the bandits from stealing the sheep, and he kept them from the wolves and lions that would devour them.

These golden grain fields were the same fields that Boaz worked and shared with his bride Ruth.

Now imagine it!

You see that limestone cave overlooking the ancient grainfields of Boaz. You see the inside wall fluttering with light from the campfire and you see a little baby lamb laying in the straw. This lamb was born that very night, inside of this sheepfold, protected by the shepherd.

This little lamb was pure and bright and born without any spots or blemish. Surely this one was destined to be one of the Passover lambs.

Then you see, on this same night a young Jewish couple looking for shelter. The woman was in labor, she was no doubt ready to give birth at any moment.

"Joseph," she cried out to her husband, as he held her steady with his strong arms. He was protecting her, and he kept her safe on the stony path.

"Almost there, Mary" he said to his young, laboring wife.

They finally found the opening, the mouth of the manger, the opening to the rock shelter. Mary was able to lie down in the soft straw. This gave her comfort and security as she was in a shelter now, even though it was the place where animals lived. The nights in this hilly country get cold and bandits prowl about preying on the innocent.

Joseph gathered more straw and built a bed for their baby inside of a feeding trough.

She cried out in pain one last time and the baby boy was born. He was born under the bright, glowing star hovering over Bethlehem.

Warmness, and peace filled the rock shelter. Joseph was in awe as the glorious Spirit of God was filling the air. Even the animals were in awe.

Joseph cleaned the blood off, and wrapped baby Jesus in the swaddling cloth that the shepherds had for the little lambs.

Both Joseph and Mary were filled with joy and peace in their hearts. The baby warmed their hearts like the warm waves of living water.

Mary held her baby and she drifted off into a peaceful sleep. Joseph held the child and a he gazed into his eyes; he couldn't help but smile.

He then swaddled the divine baby boy into the clean cloth and laid him in the straw.

Thirty-three years later, another Joseph would take Jesus's blood covered body, and then he cleaned and prepared it for his tomb, not the womb but the tomb that was also carved out of solid rock. This was Joseph of Arimathea, a Pharisee and member of the Sanhedrin, and he bravely took Jesus precious body and wrapped it in cloth.

He set him in the tomb and this tomb had never been defiled by a dead man. In that same way Mary's womb had not been defiled by dead men. And in both cases, Joseph gave this special place to Jesus.

Jesus was born out of that pure womb, but he was born again – so to speak – out of that pure tomb. He burst forth as the first fruits, from the house of bread, he was the first of a new life from the dead, the first of the second birth.

Back to 0 AD.

Mary and Joseph were in the manger with baby Jesus.

Joseph likely thought of the days he grew up here in Bethlehem. He would have remembered the stories his father told of his great, great grandfather, who was the shepherd boy David. He would have heard how he took care of his father's sheep and little lambs. He fed them, he watered them, he wrote the beautiful Psalms.

Joseph likely would have recalled Psalm 23. In this Psalm you see a good shepherd who leads and cares for his sheep. He even says that he restores his soul:

> *The LORD is my shepherd,*
> *I will not be in need.*

He lets me lie down in green pastures;
He leads me beside quiet waters.
He restores my soul;
He guides me in the paths of righteousness
For the sake of His name.
Even though I walk through the valley of the shadow of death,
I fear no evil, for You are with me;
Your rod and Your staff, they comfort me.
You prepare a table before me in the presence of my enemies;
You have anointed my head with oil;
My cup overflows.
Certainly goodness and faithfulness will follow me all the days of my
life,
And my dwelling will be in the house of the LORD forever.
(Psalm 23 NASB)

Joseph could have thought, "Perhaps David kept his little lambs in this same sheepfold."

Ruth, Boaz, and King David were all in Joseph and Mary's ancestry tree.

Then Joseph could see a warm glow, like the northern lights, over the next hill where the shepherds were watching their sheep by night.

Over that hill, a great and powerful light had shined down upon the shepherds. They could feel this light because it was heavy, yet it was warm with the love and peace of God.

Suddenly an angel appeared to them and said, "Do not be afraid, I bring you good news that will cause boundless joy for all the people. This night in the city of David, a Savior has been born to you; he is the Messiah, the Lord. This will be a sign to you: You will find a baby wrapped in cloths and lying in a manger.

Suddenly a great company of the heavenly host appeared with the angel, praising God, and saying, "Glory to God in the highest heaven, and on earth peace to those on whom his favor rests."

Then the angels disappeared, and these shepherds said to each other, "Let's go to Bethlehem and see this thing that has happened, which the Lord has told us about."

So, they wasted no time looking for him. They found the young couple, Mary and Joseph, and the precious baby just as the angel had told them.

Their hearts burned with the overflowing love of God.

These shepherds could not help but spread the good news all around. All who heard them would have been amazed. So, the shepherds returned to their work praising God and giving him all of the glory.

Forty days later, the young family took a trip from Bethlehem, north, about five to six miles to the magnificent city of Jerusalem.

According to the law of Moses, this forty-day was the time that they had to wait to go to the Temple and give the offering for the purification rites.

The book of Leviticus says what they were to do in detail.

When the right time came after the birth of her son, she was supposed to bring a lamb for the burnt offering.

But if she cannot afford a lamb, she can bring two doves. One was to be for the burnt offering and the other for the sin offering.

When they arrived in the great city of Jerusalem, they headed straight to the Temple. They bought two doves from the Temple merchants because they could not afford a lamb for the offering.

In those days, a priest would stand at the entrance and his job was to inspect and examine the lamb.

He would not inspect, or examine the worshiper, but just the lamb.

After the lamb was found faultless, the worshiper was free to go into the Temple court and freely worship the Lord.

Mary and Joseph were too poor to buy the choice lambs that were born and purchased from Bethlehem.

But in their hearts, and in their arms was the Lamb of God, the perfect one of God who takes away the sin of the world.

He was born in Bethlehem just as the Prophet Micah had penned it.

He was without blemish, there was no fault in him – later that would echo from the mouth of Pontius Pilate, "I find no fault in him."

Most importantly they held him, and they already adored him in their hearts. Their relationship with him was already there and growing stronger.

Any parent knows that our children are our very own heart outside of our own body.

Jesus was already born into their own hearts. David was a man after God's own heart and both Mary and Joseph understood this more than ever.

So, the two of them were perfectly suited to enter the Temple that day to worship God. They had no need of anything else because the God the Father approved the Lamb in their arms and in their hearts. The Son of God was truly with them. Immanuel – God with us.

The Father in Heaven looks down and sees two perfectly suited people, Mary and Joseph, suited in the righteousness of the one they held close. Yes, they were blemished, with fault, imperfect and in need, but what the Father sees is His perfect Son in their hearts as they held him close. He sees the Lamb without blemish.

They met a man named Simeon there in Jerusalem.

It had been revealed to him by God, by the Holy Spirit that he would not die before he had seen the Lord's Messiah.

He was suddenly moved by the Spirit and walked into the Temple courts. When he saw the two with their child, Simeon took the child in his arms and praised God.

Then this man Simeon said, "Sovereign Lord, as you have promised, you may now dismiss your servant in peace. For my eyes have seen your salvation, which you have prepared in the sight of all nations: and the glory of your people Israel."

Joseph and Mary marveled at what was said about their baby boy.

Perhaps they pondered what Simeon said, "For my eyes have seen your salvation..." because the name Jesus means salvation.

There was also a prophetess, named Anna, who was of the tribe of Asher. She was old and never left the Temple but worshiped night and day, fasting and praying.

She came up to them right after Simeon spoke and gave thanks to god and spoke about the child to all who were looking forward to the redemption of Jerusalem.

This prophetess spoke to those who were waiting for the Messiah. Can you imagine what she said? It must have been amazing.

Joseph and Mary saw something amazing forty days earlier when Jesus was born. They saw the fulfillment of the very name Bethlehem Ephrathah because it pointed to the redemption of Jerusalem and to all who open their hearts to him. They saw their savior born. They saw him and he was born into their hearts.

So, we see the little town of Bethlehem as a picture of a good, tender heart. It is where the rich, good soil produced golden grain for bread and the fruit of the vine.

Now you can see the picture.

When our hearts are humble and tender, like the little town of Bethlehem, that is when Jesus, the Lamb of God is born into our hearts.

Again, Bethlehem means House of Bread.

Jesus said, I am the Bread of Life.

Ephrathah means Fruitful. When we abide in him and he in us we produce good fruit.

Jesus said, "I am the vine".

Little, humble, Bethlehem was known as a place of good soil. The good tender soil is broken open and it allows the seed that the Lord sows to take root and grow. Then that seed is born into multiple grain for bread, or a vine into a cluster of sweet grapes which speaks of the sweet taste of communion. It also speaks of the trees of weighty olives which were pressed into oil for anointing and healing. The oil speaks of the Holy Spirit.

This little place is a picture of where Christ is born to this day. He can be born in your heart.

When you are "Born Again," just as Jesus said we must be in order to enter his Kingdom, then we become, Bethlehem Ephrathah, the very birthplace of Christ. It is he who is born in us and we are born in him.

This happens inside of us, where the heart and soul meet. What us mere humans see is the outside image of a person, but what God sees is the inside of the heart.

Imagine your heart as a candle. It is either lit and full of light, or it is unlit and dark.

In the darkness the lit candle is a source of light and warmth. The fire of the candle gives you light to your path.

The unlit candles cannot be seen in darkness, only the lit ones.

What God sees if you are born again through Jesus, is the glow of the light of Jesus in you, in your heart.

Jesus said, "I am the Light of the World."

Is his light inside of you?

Is he in your heart?

At this moment, these words are alive, asking you the question, "Are you born again?"

When the candle is lit the warmness, the burning in the heart of the candle causes the wax to be warm, tender, soft and pliable. A lit candle has a purpose and is doing what it was designed to do. Its purpose is to give light.

On the other hand, an unlit candle is dark, cold, and the wax is hard like a hard heart. It has no purpose and is lonely. It longs to be lit and give out warm rays of light, but it is not capable of lighting itself. It must be lit by someone who has the fire. Another candle can light the unlit candle because it has been lit. The lit candle is not the source of the fire, but it has received it.

I remember going through the US Army Ranger school in the middle of winter. I was wet and freezing all the time.

My Ranger buddy showed me a survival trick that helped me through the rigorous course.

He took a small survival candle, lit it, and then sat down with his poncho over himself. The top was open just enough to ventilate. Even though it was below freezing and windy he was warm. He was also able to read his map inside of this hasty shelter.

In this same way you and I need the Light of the world, Jesus. To warm our hearts, to light our paths, to save us from death.

So do not harden your heart but let the warm love of God fill your heart.

You can open your heart and allow the light in to soften it. He knocks on the door to your heart, but you must unlock and open it. All you must do is invite him in.

He was in Mary and Joseph's heart.

Is he in your heart?

Joseph and Mary knew Jesus.

Do you know him?

It is not a matter of what you know but who you know.

Know that you know him and open to let his Spirit live inside of you.

If today you hear His voice, do not harden your heart.

If you are broken hearted, then you are tender hearted and that is when the Holy Spirit will pour out his Living Water on that seed and you will be born into Christ.

So, what are you waiting for?

If you have not received Christ, can you think of any reason not to receive him now.

You can choose to pray this prayer with an open heart and receive him now. Just stop what you are doing and pray this from your heart:

Lord Jesus, I am a sinner.

I turn from my sin.

Please forgive me of my sins.

You are the Lamb of God and the Light of the World.

I believe you shed your blood and died on the cross to forgive me and save me.

I receive that saving forgiveness.

I choose to follow you as my Lord and Savior.

I pray this in Jesus name.

Amen.

CHAPTER TWENTY-ONE: ZECHARIAH

About everyone is familiar with the Zechariah twelve passage, "They will look upon Me whom they pierced", but there is more. This book of prophecy is chalked full of typology of Christ, and you will see a special connection between Joseph's story, and the Messiah.

Chapter three shows a scene of Joshua as the High Priest, standing before the Lord Yahweh and satan standing there accusing him.

Zechariah 3

Then he showed me Joshua the high priest standing before the angel of the LORD, and Satan standing at his right to accuse him.

First you see Joshua who was a son of Joseph of the tribe of Ephriam. There is a lot of Messiah language in that alone. The ancient scribes and sages were awaiting for the arrival of Messiah, son of Joseph.

If you read the name Joshua in Hebrew it's Yeshua, and the Greek, Jesus. You see him as the High Priest, and you know Jesus is our Great High Priest forever. We as followers of Yeshua are also called priests too. It makes perfect sense because we are Christ like, and we identify in Christ.

Satan's personality shows the opposite because he loves to accuse you and me day and night. He first will tempt you with sin, and when you fall for it, he accuses you before God. That is his personality, he is called the accuser of the brethren: *"Now the salvation, and the power, and the kingdom of our God and the authority of His Christ have come, for the accuser of our brothers and sisters has been thrown down, the one who accuses them before our God day and night. And they overcame him because of the blood of the Lamb..."(Revelation 12)*

Look at what satan is called in the Dead Sea Scroll of Zechariah: *He showed me Joshua the high priest standing before Yahweh's angel, and Satan standing at his right hand to be his adversary.*

He is Yahweh's enemy and our enemy too. Make no mistake about it. We are at war and have been since the beginning. This is why the world elites hate Israel because they take on the personality of their lord satan.

Zechariah 3

And the LORD said to Satan, "The LORD rebuke you, Satan! Indeed, the LORD who has chosen Jerusalem rebuke you!

That passage is God saying, "The LORD rebuke you, satan". Jesus did that very thing when he was being tempted by satan for forty days and nights. And Yeshua finally rebukes him and tells him to get behind him.

Look at the Dead Sea Scroll passage with the very name of God, Yahweh being used: *Yahweh said to Satan, "Yahweh rebuke you, Satan! Yes, Yahweh who has chosen Jerusalem rebuke you!*

Then you can see God saving Israel out of the heat of the tribulation period. Look at it in the Dead Sea Scroll: *Isn't this a burning stick plucked out of the fire?"*

If you look at the previous chapter of Zechariah, you can see that God saves Israel and brings them home from their exile. Some say that it speaks only of their freedom from the Babylonian captivity. In much of prophecy there is a near fulfillment and then a far side fulfillment. Also, you can see Babylon referenced in the Book of Revelation as the world system of today.

In this passage God takes tender care of Israel. He calls them the apple of his eye. They are still the apple of his eye because God's promises are forever.

Now look at the previous chapter:

Zechariah 2
Dead Sea Scroll

Come! Come! Flee from the land of the north,' says Yahweh; 'for **I have spread you abroad** *as the four* **winds of** *the sky,'* **says Yahweh.** *'Come,* **Zion!** *Escape, you who dwell with* **the daughter of Babylon.'** *For* **Yahweh of Armies** *says:* **'For** *honor he has sent me to the nations* **which plundered you;** *for he who touches you* **touches the apple of his eye.** *For, behold, I will shake my hand* **over them, and they will be** *a plunder to those who served them;* **and you will know that** *Yahweh of Armies has sent me. Sing* **and rejoice, daughter of** *Zion; for, behold, I come, and I will dwell within you,' says Yahweh.*

God says to Israel, he that touches you touches the apple of my eye. When the world pokes their accusing finger at Israel today, they poke their fingers into God's eye.

As I am writing this page, the International Criminal Court has accused Israel of war crimes even though they have proven to have conducted the most careful war to protect civilians in world history.

But that is not good enough for the world elites.

So what did they do?

They issued arrest warrants for Israel's good leader, Benjamin Netanyahu, and his staff.

What they did was poke the very pupil of God's eye.

Zechariah 3:8

Dead Sea Scroll

"...Joshua the high priest, you and your fellows who sit before you; for they are men who are a sign: for, behold, I will bring out my servant, the Branch."

Here God says that Joshua the High Priest was a sign of the servant.

What servant?

The suffering servant, the Messiah, Yeshua son of Joseph.

He then calls him, "the Branch" which has always been the language of the Messiah. Remember, he is the Branch the stem of Jessie. Jesus' mother Mary was of the line of Judah, Jessie, David and Nathan. Mary also had the line of Joseph as well when you look closely at her genealogy record.

Zechariah 3:9
Dead Sea Scroll

I will remove the iniquity of that land in one day. In that day,' says Yahweh of Armies…"

In one day, Jesus paid for the sins of Israel and the world. When he was on that cross God poured out all of his wrath on him.

On that one day, it was accomplished, and it was finished once and for all.

Even though you will fall into sin over and over throughout your life as a follower of Jesus, he paid for every single one of those sins in one day. Don't ever forget that. Do not listen to other voices that may say that you have finally done it, you committed too many sins and now God has run out of forgiveness.

No.

It was all paid for. All of it.

Zechariah 4

Then the angel who had been speaking with me returned and woke me, like a person who is awakened from his sleep.

And he said to me, "What do you see?" And I said, "I see, and behold, a lampstands all of gold with its bowl on the top of it, and its seven lamps on it with seven spouts belonging to each of the lamps which are on the top of it; also two olive trees by it, one on the right side of the bowl and the other on its left side." Then I said to the angel who was speaking with me, saying, "What are these, my lord?" So the angel who was speaking with me answered and said to me, "Do you not know what these are?" And I said, "No, my lord." Then he said to me, "This is the word of the LORD to Zerubbabel, saying, 'Not by might nor by power, but by My Spirit,' says the LORD of armies.

This speaks of the church. You know that in Revelation Jesus calls the seven golden lampstands the church. These lamps are taken care of by the High Priest because he keeps the olive oil poured into it so it will shine bright and hot.

You could see in that passage that Zechariah is asked if he knew what he saw. He gave the best answer and said, "No my lord".

Then he received an answer which is so powerful, *"Not by might nor by power, but by My Spirit,' says the LORD of armies".*

We, who are the church are not able to do anything by might, or by the power of humankind, but by the constant outpouring of God's Spirit. The Holy Spirit. He gives you the power you need daily. Even after you fail again, and again, you get back up and continue the race.

How?

By the power of God the Holy Spirit. He empowers you to follow Jesus.

This power comes from the Branch. The Branch that bears the ripe fruit of the olive from where the oil comes from. Jesus sends you the Holy Spirit and the Spirit always points you to the Branch.

Just like Joseph's prophecy of the branch reaching over the walls Jesus reaches out to you.

This Branch also builds the Temple of God. Jesus is preparing a place for you and me. And when it is complete, when it is finished his Father will say, "Go get your bride". What a glorious day that will be.

Zechariah 6

Then say to him, 'The LORD of armies says this: "Behold, there is a Man whose name is the Branch, for He will branch out from where He is; and He will build the temple of the LORD.

Yes, it is He who will build the temple of the LORD, and He who will bear the majesty and sit and rule on His throne. So He will be a priest on His throne, and the counsel of peace will be between the two offices."'

He will come back after the seven-year tribulation period and rule as the King on his throne. He will be Majestic, and as Priest.

He will be both King and Priest.

Zechariah 9

Rejoice greatly, daughter of Zion!
Shout in triumph, daughter of Jerusalem!
Behold, your king is coming to you;
He is righteous and endowed with salvation,
Humble, and mounted on a donkey,
Even on a colt, the foal of a donkey.

That prophecy spoke of his first coming. The next part of the prophecy speaks of his second coming and his reign as King.

And I will eliminate the chariot from Ephraim
And the horse from Jerusalem;
And the bow of war will be eliminated.
And He will speak peace to the nations;
And His dominion will be from sea to sea,
And from the Euphrates River to the ends of the earth.

When Jesus returns as King, he will bring his peace with him. There will finally be true peace, a world peace like there has never been. His kingdom will be from sea to sea which means over the entire globe.

Jesus will rule the nations and there will be no need for any other government because the government will be on his shoulders. He will be called Wonderful, Counselor, Mighty God, and Everlasting Father. Even though he is God the Son, he will be like the Father to us. This speaks of relationship.

Finally this world will have a good King.

Even creation itself will celebrate: *"For we know that the whole creation groans and suffers the pains of childbirth together until now. And not only that, but also we ourselves, having the first fruits of the Spirit, even we ourselves groan within ourselves, waiting eagerly for our adoption as sons and daughters, the redemption of our body."(Romans 8:22 NASB)*

Now you and I are about to dive into the heaviest chapter of prophecy in Zechariah, if not the Old Testament. You will see the Lord come back and save Israel from her enemies.

When this happens, the Lord reveals it to them. This is much like the story of Joseph. Imagine it, Joseph said to his brothers in Hebrew, "Ani Yosef" – I am Joseph, and they were in awe.

In that same way Jesus will reveal himself to Israel. Perhaps he will meet with them privately, just he and his brothers. He could say to them in Hebrew, "Ani Yeshua" and it will look just like the scene with Joseph and his brothers as they wept together.

You will see it in this chapter.

First you will see how the Lord comes as a warrior defending Israel.

We will look at this amazing passage in the Dead Sea Scrolls, which is the oldest manuscript.

Zechariah 12
Dead Sea Scroll

A revelation, Yahweh's word concerning Israel. Yahweh, who stretches out the heavens, and lays the foundation of the earth, and forms the spirit of man within him says: "Behold, I will make Jerusalem a cup of reeling to all the surrounding peoples, and it will also be on Judah in the siege against Jerusalem.

It will happen in that day, that I will make Jerusalem a burdensome stone for all the peoples. All who burden themselves with it will be severely wounded, and all the nations of the earth will be gathered together against it.

This speaks of today. Most of the world hates Israel. How else could you explain the protesters at the most elite universities in the world, where they stood in solidarity with the Hamas monsters of October 7th.

These are the future leaders of this world, and it shows just how this prophecy is fulfilled. Jerusalem is the burden on them, and they will attack the very bloodline people of Jesus.

In that day Yahweh will defend the inhabitants of Jerusalem. He who is feeble among them at that day will be like David, and David's house will be like God, like Yahweh's angel before them. It will happen in that day, that I will seek to destroy all the nations that come against Jerusalem.

Yahweh saves Jerusalem and he destroys all the nations that come against her. He rescues the inhabitants of Jerusalem, saves them, and makes them new.

Now you are going to see the most famous Zechariah prophecy. It fully speaks of Jesus, and it looks like Joseph's story.

I will pour on David's house, and on the inhabitants of Jerusalem, the spirit of grace and of supplication; and they will look to me whom they have pierced; and they shall mourn for him, as one mourns for his only son, and will grieve bitterly for him, as one grieves for his firstborn.

They see him whom they have pierced, and they mourn.

This looks a lot like Joseph's story when after he revealed to them that he was alive. They were in shock and in fear. But he speaks to them with lovingkindness and tender mercies.

God declares that he will personally pour into them the spirit of grace and supplication. Grace means getting something amazingly good that you did not earn. Supplication means mercy, and mercy means not getting what you do deserve.

This same scene was played out four thousand years ago, when Joseph finally revealed he was alive. He forgave them with supernatural love and mercy.

He showed them immense Hesed. He gave them loving kindness and tender mercies. They received life, and fellowship with the one whom they sold down the road many years ago. Yet, he loves them, forgives them, gives them life, food for them and their families, new clothing and even the best of the land.

In that passage you saw that they would look on him whom they pierced and then they will mourn for him. They mourn for him. Just like the Jewish people feel like they have betrayed Joseph, in a greater way they will finally realize that they have betrayed their own brother Yeshua.

They will weep just like Joseph wept with each brother, each tribe individually.

This was the greatest family reunion in history. But the one you see in Zechariah is the greater, and it is marvelous.

Look at how they weep with him individually by tribe.

Zechariah 12 (NASB)

In that day there will be great mourning in Jerusalem, like the mourning of Hadadrimmon in the plain of Megiddo. The land will mourn, every family by itself; the family of the house of David by itself and their wives by themselves; the family of the house of Nathan by itself and their wives by themselves; the family of the house of Levi by itself and their wives by themselves; the family of the Shimeites by itself and their wives by themselves; all the families that remain, every family by itself and their wives by themselves.

What a day that will be when Jesus they will see. What a wonderful day that will be.

At this same time, Jesus will come back down to this earth for the second coming. He left his disciples from the Mount of Olives as he ascended into the clouds. He said he would return in the same way.

He has been preparing a place for you and me for almost two thousand years now.

In Zechariah, you get the details of where and what his return to Jerusalem looks like.

Zechariah 14

Then the LORD will go forth and fight against those nations, as when He fights on a day of battle. On that day His feet will stand on the Mount of Olives, which is in front of Jerusalem on the east; and the Mount of Olives will be split in its middle from east to west forming a very large valley. Half of the mountain will move toward the north, and the other half toward the south...And on that day living waters will flow out of Jerusalem, half of them toward the eastern sea and the other half toward the western sea; it will be in summer as well as in winter.

Just like you saw in Ezekiel, this river flows from the house of God, the Temple, and the waters are healed because they are living water. They flow all year, including summer and winter.

Did you know that they have discovered a fault line that runs east and west right through the Mount of Olives? In that passage you see that the Mountain splits in two and a beautiful, lush valley is created. This valley is full of fruit trees and a beautiful river runs through it.

And the LORD will be King over all the earth; on that day the LORD will be the only one, and His name the only one.

Jesus will be the King and no other.

This is best because he is righteous and true. He knows the heart of man, the very motives and nothing is hidden from him.

All the land will change into a plain from Geba to Rimmon south of Jerusalem; but Jerusalem will rise and remain on its site from Benjamin's Gate as far as the place of the First Gate to the Corner Gate, and from the Tower of Hananel to the king's wine presses.

People will live in it, and there will no longer be a curse, for Jerusalem will live in security.

Jerusalem is finally restored and even greater than Solomon's time. It will be the desire of the entire world to see it. It will be the gem city of the world.

Years ago my wife and I loved to go to Seattle, which is called the Emerald city. Back then it was safe, and clean. We would walk off of the Ferry boat and walk the streets freely. We bought fresh food, chocolate, and flowers at the Pike Place market. It was so peaceful and clean.

Today, it is not the same place. The police are gone, the shops are boarded up, there is graffiti everywhere, and the urine odor is the only aroma. To be honest it looks like a Zombie Apocalypse due to the Fentanyl drug addiction crises. Used needles are now mixed in with the garbage on every street.

This is not what this new Jerusalem looks like. It is clean, with gemstones, and gold foundations. The pavers glisten because they are gold. Instead of walking on urine stained, garbage filled sidewalks and streets, you will walk on clean, pure gold pavers.

The smell of this city will be fragrant with flowers, fruit, fresh baked bread, and barbeque.

The street performers sing with voices so smoothly and beautifully. The stringed instruments, flutes, trumpets, and drums work in together in perfect harmony. The dancing reflects the music, and the joy of dancing fills the streets.

Children play freely and run around anywhere they wish.

There are places to eat, gardens, parks, streams, fruit trees, concerts, and best of all, Jesus' house, the Temple.

So, this Zechariah prophecy gives you great hope.

CHAPTER TWENTY-TWO: THE PSALMS – THE WRITINGS

The Psalms are chalked full of prophecies of Jesus. Psalm 22 stands out like a massive lighthouse in the dark. It was written as if David was looking through the eyes of Jesus on the cross. Psalm 22 is not the only place you can see Jesus in the Psalms because he himself quoted other Psalms that spoke of him. In this chapter you will also see Psalms that point to Joseph as a type of God the Son, Jesus.

It speaks of his first coming in humility, and the suffering servant, however, much of it speaks of the end of time, and his second coming through his rule in reign in Jerusalem, his kingdom here on earth.

In fact, the first mention of him is about his reign as King in Jerusalem. Look for yourself:

Psalm 2

Why are the nations restless
And the peoples plotting in vain?
The kings of the earth take their stand
And the rulers conspire together
Against the LORD and against His Anointed, saying,
"Let's tear their shackles apart
And throw their ropes away from us!"
He who sits in the heavens laughs,
The Lord scoffs at them.
Then He will speak to them in His anger
And terrify them in His fury, saying,
"But as for Me, I have installed My King
Upon Zion, My holy mountain."
"I will announce the decree of the LORD:
He said to Me, 'You are My Son,

Today I have fathered You.
'Ask it of Me, and I will certainly give the nations as Your inheritance,
And the ends of the earth as Your possession.
'You shall break them with a rod of iron,
You shall shatter them like earthenware.'"
Now then, you kings, use insight;
Let yourselves be instructed, you judges of the earth.
Serve the LORD with reverence
And rejoice with trembling.
Kiss the Son, that He not be angry and you perish on the way,
For His wrath may be kindled quickly.
How blessed are all who take refuge in Him!

Wow!

That looks a lot like today. The nations rage as if they are greater than God. You see people shaking their fists in the air in defiance against all authority.

The nations are raging against His Son, and he rules them with a Rod of Iron.

That language is connected to the Messiah's rule and reign throughout the Bible. Here you can see it from Jesus himself in the book of Revelation.

Nevertheless, what you have, hold firmly until I come. The one who overcomes, and the one who keeps My deeds until the end, I will give him authority over the nations; AND HE SHALL RULE THEM WITH A ROD OF IRON, AS THE VESSELS OF THE POTTER ARE SHATTERED, as I also have received authority from My Father; and I will give him the morning star. The one who has an ear, let him hear what the Spirit says to the churches.' (Revelation 2:25-29 NASB)

This is something you want. This world desperately needs the law and law enforcement. So the Messiah ruled with a rod of iron, speaks of law and order.

You and I have seen what happened to our cities in America since the police were defunded. The drug addiction homelessness problem, the riots, stores being robbed by mobs, it is all the result of no one ruling with authority.

In this next Psalm you will see the Messiah identified as the son of man. You see, Jesus is the Son of God, or you could say God the Son. But he is also the Son of Man. This means he is fully man and fully God.

Psalm 8

Dead Sea Scroll

When I consider your heavens, the work of your fingers,
the moon and the stars, which you have ordained;
what is man, that you think of him?
What is the son of man, that you care for him?
For you have made him a little lower than the angels,
and crowned him with glory and honor.
You make him ruler over the works of your hands.
You have put all things under his feet

Where it says you made him a little lower than the angels, it shows the humility of Jesus. He was already with the Father, sitting on the throne with his father and yet he humbled himself to become a man.

He is the son of man, yet, in this Psalm you see he is crowned with glory and honor.

He is both, man and God.

Later, you will see Psalm twenty-two. This is a powerful prophecy of the cross of Jesus. It was as if David was looking through the eyes of Jesus one thousand years before the event of the cross.

I have dedicated a whole chapter in this book to Psalm 22.

The next Psalm is one that will comfort you when you need help. It speaks of Jesus, the Good Shepherd, who watches over you and takes loving care of you.

Psalm 23
The LORD is my shepherd,
I will not be in need.

Just these opening words bring great comfort. The LORD is my shepherd.

I have heard pastors and elders refer to themselves as shepherds over the flock. And when I heard them say that I always reminded them that they are still sheep in need of the Shepherd too.

There really is only One Shepherd who watches over the flock.

Jesus preached humility. He said not to lord yourselves over others like the Gentile leaders do. If you are a pastor or church leader, remember that you are a sheep who is in need too.

Now you can see the rest of this comforting Psalm from the oldest manuscript.

Psalm 23

Dead Sea Scroll

He makes me lie down in green pastures.
He leads me beside still waters.
He restores my soul.
He guides me in the paths of righteousness for his name's sake.
Even though I walk through the valley of the shadow of death,
I will fear no evil, for you are with me.
Your rod and your staff,
they comfort me.
You prepare a table before me
in the presence of my enemies.
You anoint my head with oil.
My cup runs over.
Surely goodness and loving kindness shall follow me all the days of
my life,
and I will dwell in Yahweh's house forever.

Each sentence is loaded with healing and encouragement. I love how it is David, who was the king, of Israel and yet he calls on the Lord as his own Shepherd. He knew how much he needed Yahweh.

You can see David penning this with a growing glow of a smile as each sentence spills onto the parchment. Remember this is anointed Holy Scripture. These words came from God.

This Psalm speaks of Jesus and remember Jesus said, *"I am the Good Shepherd who lays his life down for the sheep."*

Look at these statements.

He restores my soul. This would have made David's heart warm because of the great sin he committed when he slept with Uriah's wife and then had him killed. But when he finally stopped hiding, and repented to God, his soul was restored.

I will fear no evil, for you are with me. Often we sheep tend to fear evil in this world. It can be scary at times, but you can stand firm in that statement because it says you are with me. God is with you, and he does not miss a thing.

My cup runs over. That speaks of the overflowing power of being filled with the Holy Spirit. Back in the Jesus Revolution or Jesus Movement times in the 1970's, this was normal. It was a revival, and it seemed like everyone was being filled and overflowed with God's Spirit.

One guy was teaching, and he took a cup and held it upside down, and then sideways asked, if the living water (Holy Spirit) poured into this cup, would it keep this water? The answer was no. Then he turned the cup upright and talked about how we sheep tend to look down and not up. Then he poured the water into the cup and overflowed it and showed how important it is for us to keep looking to God for help.

The last words of that Psalm are uplifting, *Surely goodness and loving kindness shall follow me all the days of my life, and I will dwell in Yahweh's house forever.*

Look at that. Goodness and loving kindness shall follow you all the days of your life.

That is like being pursued by someone but not in a bad way. You are being followed by the Lord, the Good Shepherd's love and kindness until your last breath.

Finaly you see the closing statement, *and I will dwell in Yahweh's house forever.* That means after you breathe your last, or Jesus returns for you, you will dwell with him in his house forever and ever. Hallelujah.

The apostle John directly quoted the next Psalm. He was at the cross, the only one of the twelve closest men who followed Jesus and was standing there next to Jesus' mother Mary at the scene of the cross.

Psalm 34:20
Dead Sea Scroll
He protects all of his bones.
Not one of them is broken.

John looks up as he comforts Mary and remembers this Psalm. Imagine it. He was the closest disciple of Jesus, and he sees his pain and agony. He would have had tears flowing down his face but at the same time he was taking in the scene.

Jesus died on that cross before the two criminals that were crucified with him. The soldiers were ordered to break their legs so that all three of them would die (it means they could not push up with their legs to take a breath).

But they found Jesus already dead, so they skipped him. That was a fulfillment of this Psalm.

John 19

"...they came to Jesus, when they saw that He was already dead, they did not break His legs. Yet one of the soldiers pierced His side with a spear, and immediately blood and water came out. And he who has seen has testified, and his testimony is true; and he knows that he is telling the truth, so that you also may believe. For these things took place so that the Scripture would be fulfilled: "NOT A BONE OF HIM SHALL BE BROKEN..."

John signifies this passage as a fulfillment in Jesus.

You can see this was also true for the lambs that were prepared for the Passover. In Exodus chapter twelve, God says not to break the bone of the lamb.

They pierced his side and water mixed with blood came out. That speaks right into the New Temple that Ezekiel sees. Water flowed out from the house of the Lord, and continued down through the south side of the East Gate.

That water is described as living water in Zechariah, and it heals the waters of the earth.

Jesus' death on the cross and resurrection from the dead changed everything. Living water from the Holy Spirit is available to all who receive Jesus as their Lord and Savior.

Psalm 41

Even my close friend in whom I trusted,
Who ate my bread,
Has lifted up his heel against me.
But You, LORD, be gracious to me and raise me up

Jesus directly references this Psalm as speaking about his betrayer, Judas Iscariot: *I am not speaking about all of you. I know the ones whom I have chosen; but this is happening so that the Scripture may be fulfilled, 'HE WHO EATS MY BREAD HAS LIFTED UP HIS HEEL AGAINST ME.'(John 13:18 NASB)*

Even though Jesus knew he would betray him, he still loved him and treated him as a friend. Judas chose this for himself. He was not coerced into doing it, he chose it. You and I have a choice too. You can be loyal to Jesus and follow him, or you can choose to turn you back on him.

Either way he still loves you and wants the best for you.

What is the best?

A life that has a close relationship with the creator of all things who humbled himself to die in your place so that you could have a good life forever.

The next Psalm is about the Messiah, and it was taught that way throughout the centuries.

It speaks of a King who is righteous, the promised One of Israel, the Messiah who was to come. Jewish commentators of old, although confused about this king, but they recognized him to be the Messiah.

Rabbis Radak and Ibn Ezra both maintained that this song was dedicated to the Messiah.

This is without a doubt about the Messiah.

Inside of it you discover a wedding feast with a bride dressed in beautiful clothing that is interwoven with gold. Then you see that the virgins follow her. The Psalm declares to these brides that He is their Lord and for them to bow down to him.

This speaks of the bride of Christ near the end of time, and you can see the specially selected ones who are sealed by God during the tribulation. They are called, "Virgins" in the book of Revelation.

First, look at the Psalm and see it for yourself.

Imagine the scene of a King's wedding in his palace and it is glorious.

Psalm 45

My heart is moved with a good theme;
I address my verses to the King;

SEE JESUS IN THE OLD TESTAMENT

My tongue is the pen of a ready writer.
You are the most handsome of the sons of mankind;
Grace is poured upon Your lips;
Therefore God has blessed You forever.
Strap Your sword on Your thigh, Mighty One,
In Your splendor and majesty!
And in Your majesty ride on victoriously,
For the cause of truth, humility, and righteousness;
Let Your right hand teach You awesome things.
Your arrows are sharp;
The peoples fall under You;
Your arrows are in the heart of the King's enemies.
Your throne, God, is forever and ever;
The scepter of Your kingdom is a scepter of justice.
You have loved righteousness and hated wickedness;
Therefore God, Your God, has anointed You
With the oil of joy above Your companions.
All Your garments are fragrant with myrrh, aloes, and cassia;
From ivory palaces stringed instruments have made You joyful.
Kings' daughters are among Your noble women;
At Your right hand stands the queen in gold from Ophir.
Listen, daughter, look and incline your ear:
Forget your people and your father's house;
Then the King will crave your beauty.
Because He is your Lord, bow down to Him.
The daughter of Tyre will come with a gift;
The wealthy among the people will seek your favor.
The King's daughter is all glorious within;
Her clothing is interwoven with gold.
She will be brought to the King in colorful garments;
The virgins, her companions who follow her,
Will be brought to You.

They will be brought with joy and rejoicing;
They will enter into the King's palace.
In place of your fathers will be your sons;
You shall make them princes in all the earth.
I will make Your name known among all generations;
Therefore the peoples will praise You forever and ever.

You just saw a wedding feast for a King. This bride arrives and suddenly she is told to forget her father's house.

That statement is because you can see it in Joseph's story after he is given a Gentile bride.

Remember, Joseph had two sons, the first one he named Manasseh which means, "God has made me forget all my trouble and all of my father's household."

Joseph then has a second son, and he named him Ephraim. His name means, "Fruitful."

In Jeremiah chapter thirty-one, it speaks of the people of Israel being saved near the end. In it you see Ephraim mentioned as the Israeli's who are saved and shepherded by God. You also see these same people being called, "Virgins" by God.

Look at Jeremiah 31 in the Dead Sea Scroll: ***At that time," says Yahweh, "I will be* the God of all the families of *Israel, and they will be my people... "Yes, I have loved you with an everlasting love.***

You can see that it starts with Yahweh bringing his own people back to his fold.

Why?

He said it himself, he said, "...I have loved you with an everlasting love." God's promises are forever and ever. This should bring you great hope because you can see that the God of Abraham, Isaac, and Jacob does not change his mind.

This amazing Jeremiah prophecy continues, and it fits right into Psalm 45. Now you will see how Ephraim and the word Virgin are tied together.

Jeremiah 31
Dead Sea Scroll
Therefore I have drawn you with loving kindness.
I will build you again,
and you will be built, O virgin of Israel.
You will again be adorned with your tambourines,
and will go out in the dances of those who make merry.
Again you will plant vineyards on the mountains of Samaria.
The planters will plant,
and will enjoy its fruit.
For there will be a day that the watchmen on the hills of Ephraim
cry,
'Arise! Let's go up to Zion to Yahweh our God.'"
For Yahweh says,
"Sing with gladness for Jacob,
and shout for the chief of the nations.
Publish, praise, and say,
'Yahweh, save your people,
the remnant of Israel!'
"...they will come with weeping.
I will lead them with petitions.
I will cause them to walk by rivers of waters,
in a straight way in which they won't stumble;
for I am a father to Israel.
Ephraim is my firstborn.

That not only fits Psalm 45, but it has a direct connection into the book of Revelation where you see the special Israelis who are chosen and sealed by God.

Jesus comes to Mount Zion, and they follow Jesus wherever he goes. He is their Shepherd and king.

What is amazing is that they are called, the virgins, and the first fruits to God. They are Jesus brethren by blood, and he is there to fight for them.

Revelation 14
(NKJV)

*Then I looked, and behold, a Lamb standing on Mount Zion, and with Him one hundred and forty-four thousand, having His Father's name written on their foreheads. And I heard a voice from heaven, like the voice of many waters, and like the voice of loud thunder. And I heard the sound of harpists playing their harps. They sang as it were a new song before the throne, before the four living creatures, and the elders; and no one could learn that song except the hundred and forty-four thousand who were redeemed from the earth. These are the ones who were not defiled with women, for **they are virgins**. These are the ones who follow the Lamb wherever He goes. These were redeemed from among men, being **firstfruits** to God and to the Lamb.*

In that Psalm you saw a wedding feast and the King. Look at the sequence, *She will be brought to the King in colorful garments; The virgins, her companions who follow her, Will be brought to You. They will be brought with joy and rejoicing; They will enter into the King's palace.*

That Revelation passage fits into the Psalm like a glove. They complement each other and that is why it is so important to see Jesus in the Old Testament. When you do that, you gain more understanding of who God is, and what he will do next.

Psalm69

This highly quoted Psalm gives insight into Jesus like no other. It is quoted in Matthew, Mark, Luke, John, Acts and Romans.

You can see direct quotes in the New Testament.

There are also many references to it other than direct quotes. Some of it seems to be describing the early years of Jesus, a glimpse into "the silent years," as they are often called, of Christ's childhood and his young manhood of which the Gospels tell us practically nothing.

Luke recorded a scene when Jesus was twelve years old and in the Temple.

Luke 2

Now the Child continued to grow and to become strong, increasing in wisdom; and the favor of God was upon Him.

His parents went to Jerusalem every year at the Feast of the Passover.

And when He was twelve years old, they went up there according to the custom of the feast; and as they were returning, after spending the full number of days required, the boy Jesus stayed behind in Jerusalem, but His parents were unaware of it. Instead, they thought that He was somewhere in the caravan, and they went a day's journey; and then they began looking for Him among their relatives and acquaintances. And when they did not find Him, they returned to Jerusalem, looking for Him.

Then, after three days they found Him in the temple, sitting in the midst of the teachers, both listening to them and asking them questions. And all who heard Him were amazed at His understanding and His answers. When Joseph and Mary saw Him, they were bewildered; and His mother said to Him, "Son, why have You treated us this way? Behold, Your father and I have been anxiously looking for You!" And He said to them, "Why is it that you were looking for Me? Did you not know that I had to be in My Father's house?" And yet they on their part did not understand the statement which He had made to them. And He went down with them and came to Nazareth, and He continued to be subject to them; and His mother treasured all these things in her heart.

Other than what Luke recorded, we know truly little about his childhood. This Psalm fills in the details. We will gain insight into his darker days in Nazareth and his dark hours on the cross in this Psalm.

Imagine it. You are in the north of Israel, in Nazareth around the first part of the first century. You hear the heart sob of a small boy, a teenager, and a young man: ***Don't let those who wait for you be shamed , Lord Yahweh of Armies. Don't let those who seek you be brought to dishonor , God of Israel. Because for your sake, I have borne reproach. Shame has covered my face. I have become a stranger to my brothers, an alien to my mother's children. (Psalm 69 Dead Sea Scroll)***

Jesus was raised with his mother's other children, and they may have treated him like a stranger. They would have hated him because of who he was, the perfect one. So, in that same way the sinner hates you and me, if you bear the mark of Jesus, because you are righteous in him.

Paul quoted this Psalm, and he gave you more insight into it. he signifies that the old Testament is here for your instruction and hope: *For Christ did not please himself, but as it is written, "The reproaches of those who reproached you fell on me." For whatever was written in former days was written for our instruction, that through endurance and through the encouragement of the Scriptures we might have hope. (Romans 15:3-4 ESV)*

"For the zeal of your house consumes me…" (Psalm 69:9 Dead Sea Scroll) That verse is quoted in the New Testament when Jesus cleared the Temple courtyard of merchants and money changers.

John 2

And within the temple grounds He found those who were selling oxen, sheep, and doves, and the money changers seated at their tables. And He made a whip of cords, and drove them all out of the temple area, with the sheep and the oxen; and He poured out the coins of the money changers and overturned their tables; and to those who were selling the doves He said, "Take these things away from here; stop making My Father's house a place of business!" His disciples remembered that it was written: "ZEAL FOR YOUR HOUSE WILL CONSUME ME."

Jesus had zeal or fire in his heart to stand against the corruption of the merchants in the temple.

This Psalm is such a treasure. In that same verse his zeal ignites hot toward the sin he saw at the Temple. Then you see that the sin or the reproach is on him: ***The reproaches of those who reproach you have fallen on me. (Psalm 69:9 Dead Sea Scroll)***

He is saying that their sin would fall upon him. Remember he ended up taking the sin of the world upon his own shoulders, *He became sin who knew no sin.*

You can well imagine Jesus would fast as a young man. You can imagine his brothers would ridicule him for it. They would have assumed that he was just putting on an act. You can imagine they made fun of him because he was different: ***And surely when I fasted, that was to my reproach. When I made sackcloth my clothing, I became a byword to them.***

Jesus was used to the mocking, backbiting, and slandering. He was able to take it, but it still hurt. He was fully man as well as God the Son.

The Psalm continues: ***Those who sit in the gate talk about me. The drunkards make songs.***

This was the song the drunks would sing in the tavern of Nazareth. You know that word got around about Mary and Joseph's first son.

Later, as a grown man in his early thirties, Jesus was being made fun of as an illegitimate son by the religious leaders. You can see it in the gospel of John.

Jesus is tangling with the Pharisees, and they say, *"We were not born of fornication...." (John 8: 41-48)*

They threw his apparent illegitimacy in his face.

How did Jesus respond? Or what would Jesus do?

He responds by telling them that their father is satan.

Wow. That does not sound nice. That does not sound like the meek and mild Jesus.

Jesus was not here to please people and that needs to be a lesson for us today. Sometimes being a Christian means that you speak the hard truth even if it makes others angry.

Those who hate me without a cause are more than the hairs of my head. (Psalm 69:4 Dead Sea Scroll)

If I had not come and spoken to them, they would not have sin; but now they have no excuse for their sin. The one who hates Me hates My Father also. If I had not done among them the works which no one else did, they would not have sin; but now they have both seen and hated Me and My Father as well. But this has happened so that the word that is written in their Law will be fulfilled: 'THEY HATED ME FOR NO REASON.' (John15:24-25 NASB)

Now look at the scene of the cross.

"...and for my thirst they gave me vinegar to drink. (Psalm 69:21 NASB)

The soldiers also ridiculed Him, coming up to Him, offering Him sour wine, and saying, "If You are the King of the Jews, save Yourself!" (Luke 23:36 NASB)

John recorded how this Psalm was fulfilled. Remember he stood there at the foot of the cross and saw it all. He recorded it in detail: *they put a sponge full of the sour wine on a branch of hyssop and brought it up to His mouth. Therefore when Jesus had received the sour wine, He said, "It is finished!" And He bowed His head and gave up His spirit. (John 19:28-30 NASB)*

It was finished!

What was finished?

Our failures, our wrong doings, our selfishness, our record of payment to God for sin was paid in full. All of it! That is why Jesus cried out "It is finished!"

Is it finished in your heart and mind? If you are a believer and follower of Jesus, you need to know and remind yourself daily that it is finished.

You do not go on probation for 30 days after you have failed and fell into sin. You cannot do anything to pay it off. It had already been paid for by Jesus.

So, get back up and get back into the race, the marathon to Heaven.

Now you can see a prophecy in that Psalm of what happened to the people of Israel after their rejection of Jesus. *"May their table before them become a snare; And when they are at peace, may it become a trap. May their eyes grow dim so that they cannot see..." (Psalm 69:22-23 NASB)*

Paul, who describes himself as *"...Hebrew of the Hebrews" (Phil. 3:5)*, wrote Romans chapter eleven, and in it he shows this Psalm describing the state of the Jewish people during the church age.

However, the church age will end, and when it does the blindness will be gone and they will see Jesus for who he really is. God will save all of Israel as stated in Romans eleven, verse twenty-five.

Paul shared insight into this time of the Gentiles, and he quotes this Psalm: *And David says,*

"MAY THEIR TABLE BECOME A SNARE AND A TRAP,
AND A STUMBLING BLOCK AND A RETRIBUTION TO THEM.
"MAY THEIR EYES BE DARKENED TO SEE NOT,
AND BEND THEIR BACKS CONTINUALLY."
I say then, they did not stumble so as to fall, did they? Far from it! But by their wrongdoing salvation has come to the Gentiles, to make them jealous. Now if their wrongdoing proves to be riches for the world, and their failure, riches for the Gentiles, how much more will their fulfillment be! (Romans 11:9-12 NASB)

He continues and explains that when that last number of Gentiles comes to Christ, all of Israel will be saved. This must be the heart of every Christian because it is the heart of God.

You cannot have it both ways. You cannot claim Jesus and hate the Jewish people and Israel. Something is verry wrong deep down in your soul if that speaks of you.

Paul hammers this point home in Romans 11. You must not be arrogant and think that God has cut off Israel from the tree and put you there in place of Israel forever. Paul even warns you not to believe that or God will cut you off too.

Those are serious words and must be heeded. Especially today when you have witnessed Israel miraculously becoming a nation again after two-thousand years. You have seen the hatred of the world against them. This speaks of their connection to God. The world hates God because the god of this world is satan.

Jesus himself explained that satan would not attack his own. Remember how Jesus drove out demons from someone and the Religious leaders accused him of doing that with the power of Beelzebub (satan).

Jesus told them in so many words, how stupid that statement was because satan would not fight against himself. A kingdom divided will not stand and satan knows that.

God still has the most amazing plan to save Israel.

This warms my heart, and it should warm yours too.

The next part of Psalm 69 speaks directly into what Judas Iscariot fate was and what happened to that piece of land, the field of blood:

And it became known to all the residents of Jerusalem; as a result that field was called Hakeldama in their own language, that is, Field of Blood. For it is written in the book of Psalms:
'MAY HIS RESIDENCE BE MADE DESOLATE,
AND MAY THERE BE NONE LIVING IN IT';
and,
'MAY ANOTHER TAKE HIS OFFICE.'
(Acts 1:20 NASB)

Did you know that you can visit Israel today and see this very field?

If you go there, you will see that no home or business is built on it. This is prime real estate, but no one lives on it. Everyone believes it is cursed to this day.

Psalm 78

You can see Jesus the Rock, the Stone of Israel in this Psalm. Not only is he called their Rock, but he is called their redeemer.

This clearly speaks of Jesus.

They remembered that God was their rock, the Most High God, their redeemer. But they flattered him with their mouth, and lied to him with their tongue. (Psalm 78 Dead Sea Scroll)

Psalm 81

This is a special Psalm because it links Old Testament Joseph as a type of Jesus:

Blow the trumpet at the time of the New Moon,
At the full moon, on our solemn feast day.

For this is a statute for Israel,
A law of the God of Jacob.
This He established in Joseph as a testimony

That word, "Testimony" in the Old Testament, is always in reference to God himself. So Joseph shows you God the Son, and how he was a foreshadowing of him.

You can look at the chapter on Joseph in this book and see the details of Joseph and Jesus compared.

Psalm 110

The LORD says to my Lord:
"Sit at My right hand
Until I make Your enemies a footstool for Your feet."
The LORD will stretch out Your strong scepter from Zion, saying,
"Rule in the midst of Your enemies."
Your people will volunteer freely on the day of Your power;
In holy splendor, from the womb of the dawn,
Your youth are to You as the dew.
The LORD has sworn and will not change His mind,
"You are a priest forever
According to the order of Melchizedek."
The Lord is at Your right hand;
He will shatter kings in the day of His wrath.
He will judge among the nations,
He will fill them with corpses,
He will shatter the chief men over a broad country.
He will drink from the brook by the wayside;
Therefore He will lift up His head.

Jesus directly quoted this Psalm to the religious leaders: *"How is it that the scribes say that the Christ is the son of David? David himself said in the Holy Spirit, 'THE LORD SAID TO MY LORD, "SIT AT MY RIGHT HAND, UNTIL I PUT YOUR ENEMIES UNDER YOUR FEET."' David himself calls Him 'Lord'; so in what sense is He his son?"* (Matthew 22:41-46)

He silenced them with this. Whenever Jesus asked them a question they could not answer. However, he was able to answer their questions when he wanted to.

His wisdom was boundless and deep. He was the greater than Solomon, and you know that Solomon was the wisest man in history.

This Psalm continues into what looks like the Millennial reign on earth. You can see it as he stretches his scepter out over Zion, he is a priest forever after the order of Melchizedek, and he will judge among the nations.

There is only One who can fulfill that Psalm, and his name is Jesus.

Psalm 118

A stone which the builders rejected
Has become the chief cornerstone.
This came about from the LORD;
It is marvelous in our eyes.
This is the day which the LORD has made;
Let's rejoice and be glad in it.

By now, you know that this stone is a picture of the Messiah. Jesus himself said so to the Pharisees and they perceived he was talking about themselves.

He first tells them a story that illustrates who they were and who he is. Take a look.

Matthew 21

*But when the vine-growers saw the son, they said among themselves, 'This is the heir; come, let's kill him and take possession of his inheritance!' And they took him and threw him out of the vineyard, and killed him. Therefore, when the owner of the vineyard comes, what will he do to those vine-growers?" They *said to Him, "He will bring those wretches to a wretched end and lease the vineyard to other vine-growers, who will pay him the fruit in the proper seasons."*

Jesus said to them, "Did you never read in the Scriptures,

'A STONE WHICH THE BUILDERS REJECTED,

THIS HAS BECOME THE CHIEF CORNERSTONE;

THIS CAME ABOUT FROM THE LORD,

AND IT IS MARVELOUS IN OUR EYES'?

Therefore I say to you, the kingdom of God will be taken away from you and given to a people producing its fruit. And the one who falls on this stone will be broken to pieces; and on whomever it falls, it will crush him."

When the chief priests and the Pharisees heard His parables, they understood that He was speaking about them. And although they sought to arrest Him, they feared the crowds, since they considered Him to be a prophet.

Yes, he was The Prophet. The one that Moses spoke of. But he was much more than just a prophet. He was the Son of God.

In Islam they say Jesus was a prophet, but not the Son of God. They claim that God has no son.

Inside of the Dome of the Rock, on the upper wall of the dome, pointed toward the Golden Gate or East Gate are the words, "Far be it removed from His transcendent majesty that He should have a son."

Those false words are pointed at the very place where Jesus entered Jerusalem on Palm Sunday and where he will return at his second coming.

He was the Stone that the builders rejected, and he is the Chief Cornerstone.

CHAPTER TWENTY-THREE: PSALM 22 – THE CROSS

Jesus was on the cross and it was as dark as the darkest night. Then he suddenly cries out the beginning words of the Psalm: "My God, My God why have you forsaken Me." Jesus shouted this out for all to hear, and suddenly light shown just like the dawn of a new day.

This is how the Rabbis instructed the students of scripture in those days. They would announce the opening words to a passage of scripture and the students would turn or scroll to it because they did not have chapter numbers and verse numbers like we do today. That was installed by our Bible translators.

Back in those days of ancient Israel and the time of Jesus, the teachers would say the opening words.

So here we see Jesus the Great, the greatest Rabbi of all, announcing the opening words to this powerful Psalm, "My God, My God why have you forsaken Me." He proclaimed it from the cross, right at what looked like the dawn of a new day.

David penned Psalm twenty-two one thousand years before Christ was born. And it was as if he were looking through the eyes of Jesus while on the cross.

Imagine the scene.

Jesus is nailed to the middle cross, between two criminals. Suddenly and unexpectedly, darkness falls on everyone like a heavy blanket. It fell in the middle of the day, at high noon, and it lasts for three hours, all the way to three o'clock.

This darkness was recorded in the Bible, but it was also recorded by secular historians from the same day. They said it was so dark you could feel it. That is how the darkest nights can feel.

When I lived in Santa Cruz, California, my dad, and I would go steelhead fishing in the San Larenzo river, deep in the coastal Redwood mountains. These massive, towering redwood trees created great shade by day, but at night they can cause deep darkness.

One late, winter afternoon, I was fishing in the river and catching these amazing sea run rainbow trout called steelhead. I wanted to keep fishing, and it was getting dark. I found myself miles down this deep gorge and now it was dark.

As I started the steep hike up the gorge, my flashlight died. It was a complete blackout. There was no moon that night. It was cloudy and so the stars gave no light. On top of that, the massive redwood trees blocked any light that might have come.

I remember feeling this darkness. I had to feel my way up the mountain and out of this thick dark forest. It took hours and it only takes thirty minutes with light.

This darkness at the cross was a supernatural darkness, and it would cause everyone there to tremble.

This is when one of the two criminals reconsidered and believed in Jesus.

This is when the Roman soldier realized this was the Son of God.

It could be that this is when Joseph of Arimathea and Nicodemus realized it without a doubt, that Jesus was in fact the Messiah. They knew the Scriptures and they knew the Psalms. They could have said the rest of the Psalm under their breath as they watched it play out right before their own eyes.

The darkness ended with Jesus crying out the beginning words of Psalm 22, "My God, My God, why have you forsaken Me" and suddenly light began to grow.

This Psalm is titled "Aijeleth[1] Hashshahar[2]" which means "The Dawn", this is exactly what was happening, at this very moment when Jesus cried out those words.

---

1.   https://www.blueletterbible.org/search/preSearch.cfm?Criteria=Aijeleth&t=NASB20

Jesus announced the opening words of this Psalm and then the title of the Psalm was being fulfilled right before everyone's eyes. The title of "The Dawn" was displayed for all to see. It was like a live painting, the light slowly emerged in the middle of the day. It was the dawn of a new day, a new era, a new covenant.

There was still another dawn, in three days, it would be the dawning day of his resurrection from the dead. That would fully complete the mission.

But here, at the cross, this amazing Psalm was being fulfilled right before the eyes of the religious leaders who hated him, the ones who defended him, the soldiers, the regular common people, the weeping women who followed Jesus, his own mother, Mary, and his closest disciple John.

Psalm 22

For the music director; upon Aijeleth Hashshahar. A Psalm of David.
My God, my God, why have You forsaken me?
Far from my help are the words of my groaning.
My God, I cry out by day, but You do not answer;
And by night, but I have no rest.

The music director was giving it the worship music of Aijeleth Hashshahar. This was a tune and a chant by the worship leaders.

We do not have this song today, but if you could, listen to your favorite worship song while reading it and studying it. Perhaps listen to, "Were You There," "Old Rugged Cross," or "Jesus Paid It All."

Listening to worship music in the background immerses it deep into your soul. That is why God had them do it in so many of these Psalms.

When you get to verse six, I suggest listening to a new song by Michael W. Smith, called "Crimson Dust." This song speaks right into the Psalm about the Crimson worm of verse six.

---

2.   https://www.blueletterbible.org/search/
preSearch.cfm?Criteria=Hashshahar&t=NASB20

But for now we need to go in order from the top.

Start with the music, I am listening to all three of those songs of the cross as I am typing this part of the chapter now.

This was written down by David, one thousand years before this scene took place. He could have been listening to worship music, and was penning this through the power of the Holy Spirit.

He was writing in the first person, just as if he were suffering on the cross and seeing through the eyes of Jesus.

Mark 15

Those who were crucified with Him were also insulting Him. When the sixth hour came, darkness fell over the whole land until the ninth hour. At the ninth hour Jesus cried out with a loud voice, "ELOI, ELOI, LEMA SABAKTANEI?" which is translated, "MY GOD, MY GOD, WHY HAVE YOU FORSAKEN ME?"

Jesus was being insulted and mocked by both criminals who were being crucified with him.

Then the darkness fell upon everyone at high noon (sixth hour), and it was thick. People trembled in fear. The mockers may have held their tongues. This could have been a time of great silence as it was oily dark.

After this long three hours of deep darkness over the whole land, the dawn came. It was not like a normal dawn because it was three o'clock in the afternoon (ninth hour).

As the light emerged, the crowd was in awe of this supernatural event and Jesus shouts out the opening words to Psalm 22, *"My God, my God, why have You forsaken me?"*

The religious leaders knew exactly what that meant. Nicodemus and Joseph of Arimathea knew it was this Psalm. They knew new it as the Psalm of the Messiah.

They would have had it memorized, and could have whispered the following verses as they watched it played out before their eyes.

"Far from my help are the words of my groaning." Nicodemus could have repeated these words as he watched Jesus groan in severe pain.

"My God, I cry out by day, but You do not answer" Joseph of Arimathea could have said that realizing it was day as Jesus cried out to his Father, *"Father, forgive them for they know not what they are doing",* and then it was dark as night, and still Jesus found no rest, *"And by night, but I have no rest.".* He would have realized this Psalm was being fulfilled line by line, in sequence right in front of him.

Now we will be seeing the Psalm from the Dead Sea Scroll, and still imagining it from the eyes of those who stood there.

Psalm 22

Dead Sea Scroll

But you are holy,
you who inhabit the praises of Israel.
Our fathers trusted in you.
They trusted, and you delivered them.
They cried to you, and were delivered.
They trusted in you, and were not disappointed.

Jesus could have been praying this Psalm in his own mind. He had the scriptures in his heart and soul because he knew it as he is called, the Word. He was there when David penned it. He knew it before it was penned.

Here he could find hope in his darkest hour. He could trust his Father even though he was being separated from him.

Psalm 22

Dead Sea Scroll

Verse six

But I am a worm, and no man;
a reproach of men, and despised by the people.

What you just saw was an "I AM" statement.

I am a worm.

How is this a statement about the Messiah?

What was David thinking?

You can be sure that the two Pharisees, Joseph of Arimathea and Nicodemus knew exactly what this meant.

In the Torah, the first five books of the Bible, God detailed how to use the red dye for the Tabernacle fabrics, the Priests garments, and the yarn for the Scapegoat.

The red dye stuff was a worm called Tola'at Shani.

Tola'at is translated as "Worm." The word Shani is translated as, "Scarlet" or "Crimson."

You can see it combined as, "Tola'at Shani" to mean, Scarlet Worm, or Crimson Worm.

These teachers of the Law in Jesus time knew what this was. They knew the Torah.

Nicodemus could have said that part of the Psalm, "...I am a Tola'at Shani and no man," as he looked at the red blood of Jesus staining the wood of the cross.

You can call it the Crimson Worm of Psalm 22.

This is where you can listen to the worship song by Micael W. Smith, "Crimson Dust" and feel the scene in a deeper way.

This Hebrew word is amazing, and God placed it there for a time such as this.

Today, in Israel, the Temple Institute is making sure that they gather everything needed to build the Jewish Temple. The Institute is committed to the ancient text, to the Law of Moses, by meticulously gathering each item just as the Ancient Israelites did thousands of years ago.

Their goal is to have all the elements ready for the quick set up of the Jewish Temple. Just as in king Solomon's day, no hammer or chisel will be heard that day, in the heart of Jerusalem, as they erect the Temple. So, as they constructed and gathered the goods such as; the lamp stand called the Menorah, the table for the showbread, the stones, the gold vessels, the incense, and the priestly garments, something amazing was rediscovered.

This is Israel's mysterious discovery, and this is how they found it. They needed to make the scarlet red dye for the veil, and for the High Priest garments just like the times of Moses and King Solomon, when suddenly they discovered the Tola'at Shani.

The Tola is translated "Worm" in Hebrew. It is also called the "Tola'at Shani," translated "Scarlet Worm" or "Crimson Worm." This worm was found on trees, then gathered and crushed to make the crimson red dye for the temple fabrics.

The making of the Temple veil and priestly garments requires knowledge of the materials and methods commanded by Torah (the first five books of the Bible written by Moses). So, the knowledge was lost over two thousand years and had to be researched and relearned.

Only years ago, a professor in Israel rediscovered the Tola'at Shani. He said in his own words that it was part of, "the redemptive process of the Jewish people today."

On a hot July day, the Temple Institute organized this historic event: the first Tola'at Shani harvest in the land of Israel in over two thousand years. The location of the harvest was a hilltop village in Samaria north of Jerusalem. This was the land of the ancient tribe of Ephraim.

The reason for this historical event was the need to gather the crimson-red worms for creating the belt for the priestly garments now being produced by the Temple Institute.

The long-term goal of the event was to educate a new generation in Israel about the elusive Tola'at Shani, how to harvest it, and how to produce the crimson dye prescribed in the Torah.

You see, the Tola'at Shani was used for Temple related purposes, which included the priests' belts, the scarlet wool tied onto the scapegoat on Yom Kippur, and the massive Veil of the Temple.

The lecture about the Tola'at Shani was given by a Professor of a University in Israel. He is a researcher and a world expert in the ancient dye in the Middle East. As he kept the theme focused on the Holy Temple, the professor described his own odyssey with the Tola'at Shani, which he has been intensely researching for ten years.

Studying ancient texts, including the Torah and Talmudic, as well as ancient Greek, Latin and Aramaic works, the professor began to re-identify and re-discover the unique properties and characteristics of the Tola'at Shani. He travelled the world in search of the scarlet worm, and so he discovered the crimson worm being harvested in the mountains of Turkey.

Then something mysterious happened. It was only after his travels abroad that he discovered this Tola'at Shani, were a "stone's-throw-away" from his own front door.

The common Israeli oak trees fill the hillside land of Israel, and so the tiny crimson Tola'at Shani bodies were attached to them. So he had a revelation and realized this discovery was just outside his window.

Later the professor explained to the students and representatives from the Temple Institute the art of identifying and removing the Tola'at Shani from the bark of the oak trees to which it attaches itself.

The Tola'at Shani attaches itself to the trunk and branches of the oak when it is ready to give birth to its young, this parent Tola'at Shani grows from the size of a pinhead to a maximum of seven millimeters in diameter, which is about the size of a pea.

The thousands of tiny crimson eggs develop during the early summer, and it is essential to harvest them at this point, before the red eggs hatch and leave the parent, taking with them their crimson-red pigment. The mature parent looks like a miniature Pomegranate fruit when it is ripe.

After the professor finished his lecture, he began to demonstrate by dissolving the Tola'at Shani worms previously harvested and dried into a glass of boiling water. The results were seen immediately as the glass of clear water turned pink, to dark crimson red like pomegranate juice or red wine.

In fact, the Tola'at Shani is much like a Pomegranate fruit. When the fruit is ripe for harvest, it is full of tiny red seeds (like Tola'at Shani eggs) marked by the same exterior color of the sweet parent fruit. The Pomegranate was used to make, "Spiced Wine." This is found in King Solomon's Song of Solomon.

Also, the first Temple in Jerusalem was beautifully decorated with Pomegranates. The High Priest also had the Tola'at Shani –dyed yarns made in the shape of the pomegranates sewn onto the hem of his robe.

Interestingly, both the crushed Tola'at Shani, and Pomegranate juice are known for their good medicinal purposes for the heart.

Now, back to our modern-day story in Israel. The time came to harvest the Tola'at Shani. Although worms were gathered, it was still short of the amount needed for the dying of the wool to be embroidered onto the belts of the 120 priestly garments that the Temple Institute is currently producing.

To supplement the supply of Tola'at Shani needed, the Institute sent a group of Israeli's to Ankara, Turkey, to purchase the scarlet worms because they are native to the mountains of Turkey.

Not only was it used as the red dye for ancient Israel, but the life cycle of this Crimson worm tells you a story.

This little creature tells the story of the cross.

One time in its life it climbs up a tree or piece of wood, attaches itself to it as it swells up and turns Crimson red. It is stuck firmly to that wood. Then it dies and gives birth to its offspring. They offspring eat of the flesh of the parent Tola'at Shani, and they turn Crimson red too. After three days, the blood-red stain on that wood turns as white as snow.

I am listening to the worship song by Micael W. Smith, "Crimson Dust" right now as I type this.

Imagine it. You are one of the Jewish residents of Jerusalem. You see a common Kermes Oak tree, near the site of the cross. You are focused on the cross of Jesus and you see his body swollen so much, that he was not recognizable. His skin was a dark crimson color as he was attached to that tree, that crimson stained wood of the cross.

Then your focus changes and the cross is blurred as the sharpness of the tree next to you becomes clear.

You see a Tola'at Shani, the Scarlet worm attached to the wood of the tree. The wood around it is dyed crimson -blood-red. The body is swollen and crimson red. Then it dies and it bursts open at its death, and you can see what looks like thousands of its tiny offspring birthed. They are all dyed the same rich crimson color as the parent Tola.

They live as it died.

Then you notice the wood is stained the same color as the cross. Your focus goes back out to the cross and then back to the stain on the tree.

You see Jesus taken down from the cross by Nicodemus and Joseph. They take his body away and Joseph wraps Jesus's body in white cloth. Then he took him over to his tomb and the stone was rolled in front of it to seal it shut.

Three days later, you come back to that tree. You look at that spot that was stained crimson red and you are shocked. You see it now as white as snow. It is pure white and looks like frost or like a snowflake.

Then a warm wind arises, and that white substance falls to the ground like a snowflake.

Immediately you remember the Manna, the Bread of Heaven that looked like frost on the ground. Then you remember Jesus words, "I am the Bread of Life."

The Romans called this same dye stuff, "Grain."

Jesus said, *"The hour has come for the Son of Man to be glorified. Truly, truly I say to you, unless a grain of wheat falls into the earth and dies, it remains alone; but if it dies, it bears much fruit..." (John 12 NASB)*

Then a fresh spring breeze lifts the snow-white flaky substance, and it is picked up and it ascends into the sky.

Then the scripture in Isaiah flashes in your mind and heart: **"Come now, and let's reason together," says Yahweh: "Though your sins be as scarlet, they shall be as white as snow. Though they be red like crimson, they shall be as wool." (Isaiah 1:18 Dead Sea Scroll)**

Your heart is set ablaze at this point. It is burning with the love of God. Tears of joy run down your face as you know Jesus is the Messiah.

Then you look out to the cross. You see the crimson stain is gone and it is empty and clean.

It is morning and you look back over to the tomb of Joseph, and you see the stone is rolled away. You walk over to it, and you see the seal was broken open.

Peeking in, you see the white cloth that Joseph used to wrap Jesus's body. The blood is gone, but the cloth is marked with a brilliant outline of Jesus' face and body. You take this shroud and save it as a precious treasure.

That story was meant to tell you how the Crimson worm ties into the gospel.

Now, let us go back to the Psalm and the scene of the cross.

Psalm 22

Dead Sea Scroll
All those who see me mock me.
They insult me with their lips. They shake their heads, saying,
"He trusts in Yahweh.
Let him deliver him.
Let him rescue him, *since he delights in him."*

Joseph of Arimathea sees his fellow Pharisees mocking Jesus. He sees the Sadducee's shake their heads and saying, *"He trusts in Yahweh. Let him deliver him. Let him rescue him, since he delights in him."*

This would have broken his heart as he remembers Jacob's most favored and loved son, Joseph, and how his own brothers hated and mocked him.

He continues to remember the Psalm and says it as he looks at Jesus on the cross.

I am poured out like water.
All my bones are out of joint.
My heart is like wax;
it is melted within me.
My strength is dried up like a potsherd.
My tongue sticks to the roof of my mouth.
You have brought me into the dust of death.

He sees Jesus cry out, "I thirst."

One of the worst things about being crucified is the extreme dehydration. This speaks of his tongue sticking to the roof of his mouth.

Joseph realizes that Jesus is brought to the edge of death.

For* dogs *have surrounded me.
A company of evildoers have enclosed me.
They have pierced my hands and feet.

He could see this in his mind, from memory, and in person. He realizes it is clearly a fulfillment of Psalm 22.

This is how the Dead Sea Scroll reads it, *"They have pierced my hands and feet"*

The Masoretic Text says, "like a lion" rather than "they have pierced." There is a one letter difference between the two. However, the Dead Sea Scroll reads **"they have pierced."**

> ***I can count all of my bones.***
> ***They look and stare at me.***
> ***They divide my garments among them.***
> ***They cast lots for my clothing.***

Perhaps Nicodemus was remembering this Psalm passage, and he looks over to the soldiers that were near the cross, and he see this, *"Then the soldiers, when they had crucified Jesus, took His outer garments and made four parts: a part to each soldier, and the tunic also; but the tunic was seamless, woven in one piece. So they said to one another, "Let's not tear it, but cast lots for it, to decide whose it shall be." This happened so that the Scripture would be fulfilled: "THEY DIVIDED MY GARMENTS AMONG THEMSELVES, AND THEY CAST LOTS FOR MY CLOTHING." (John 19:23-24 NASB)*

Perhaps this is the garment his mother Mary made for him. It was special to him; it was like the special coat that Joseph son of Jacob wore.

Nicodemus may have looked over to Mary, and could have seen how heartbroken she was. She may have looked over to her son's clothing and remembered the day she gave it to him. She could have remembered the day she gave the cloak to Jesus and how thankful and happy he was when he tried it on and how he hugged her.

Mary was so heartbroken; it was worse than a sword piercing her heart. She saw her perfect little baby boy when she looked at Yeshua.

Psalm 22

> *Yet You are He who brought me forth from the womb;*
> *You made me trust when upon my mother's breasts.*

I was cast upon You from birth;
You have been my God from my mother's womb.

John surely held Mary close at this point. Even he knew the Psalms and he may have recalled this passage where it says, *"You have been my God from my mother's womb."*

Then John saw this, *"Now beside the cross of Jesus stood His mother, His mother's sister, Mary the wife of Clopas, and Mary Magdalene. So when Jesus saw His mother, and the disciple whom He loved standing nearby, He said to His mother, "Woman, behold, your son!" Then He said to the disciple, "Behold, your mother!" And from that hour the disciple took her into his own household." (John 19:25-27 NASB)*

Jesus tells John to take his mother in as his own. What an honor for John. This shows how deeply Jesus loved and honored his own mother.

History shows us that John did in fact take Mary into his home. They ended up in Ephesus together where John ended up pastoring.

Both Nicodemus and Joseph would have seen how Jesus looked upon his own mother and they too remembered the Psalm, *"You made me trust when upon my mother's breasts...*

But don't be far off, Yahweh.

You are my help: hurry to help me.

Deliver my soul from the sword,

my precious life *from the power of* the dog.

Jesus continues to pray to his Father while in great agony. He had great trust in him and says, "You are my help."

Save me from the lion's mouth;
From the horns of the wild oxen You answer me.

Now you can see a huge shift in this Psalm. First he says, "*Save me from the lion's mouth...*"

Remember Peter said that satan goes about like a roaring lion seeking whom he may devour. Here, Jesus has been spiritually gnawed on by satan and his followers. And furthermore he asks to be saved from the horns of the wild oxen. Back in those days, there were wild oxen that were huge. They were known as being powerful and extremely aggressive. Here Jesus is feeling the pain of the horns of the wild oxen.

However, there is a massive shift in the Psalm. He says, "You answer me."

From this moment forward it is no longer the suffering of the cross but now the Victory.

John could have noticed this shift when he saw this, *"After this, Jesus, knowing that all things had already been accomplished, in order that the Scripture would be fulfilled… when Jesus had received the sour wine, He said, "It is finished!" And He bowed His head and gave up His spirit. (John 19:28,30 NASB)*

John saw how things shifted, especially when Jesus said, "It is finished."

The Psalm continues in a song of great victory. It becomes greater and greater to the end.

Psalm 22

I will proclaim Your name to my brothers;
In the midst of the assembly I will praise You.
You who fear the LORD, praise Him;
All you descendants of Jacob, glorify Him,
And stand in awe of Him, all you descendants of Israel.
For He has not despised nor scorned the suffering of the afflicted;
Nor has He hidden His face from him;
But when he cried to Him for help, He heard.
From You comes my praise in the great assembly;
I shall pay my vows before those who fear Him.
The afflicted will eat and be satisfied;

Those who seek Him will praise the LORD.
May your heart live forever!
All the ends of the earth will remember and turn to the LORD,
And all the families of the nations will worship before You.
For the kingdom is the LORD'S
And He rules over the nations.
All the prosperous of the earth will eat and worship,
All those who go down to the dust will kneel before Him,
Even he who cannot keep his soul alive.
A posterity will serve Him;
It will be told of the Lord to the coming generation.
They will come and will declare His righteousness
To a people who will be born

This victorious part of the Psalm starts with his brothers. Jesus first met with the women and then with the two on that road to Emmaus. Then he came to all his closest brothers, his disciples.

Then the Psalm speaks to all his descendants of Jacob. In other words, to all of Israel.

These are like excentric circles, growing as they expand outward.

Then it is proclaimed to the assembly.

Next it is proclaimed to, "*All the ends of the earth will remember and turn to the LORD.*"

Then to the dead, and then, "*It will be told of the Lord to the coming generation...To a people who will be born.*" That speaks of you and me.

The last word of this Psalm is magnanimous and magnificent.

He has performed it.

The Hebrew word is עָשָׂה. It is Asa: aw-saw'; a primitive root; to do or make, in the broadest sense and widest application:—to accomplish!

To Accomplish!

"After this, Jesus, knowing that all things had already been accomplished, in order that the Scripture would be fulfilled... when Jesus had received the sour wine, He said, "It is finished!" And He bowed His head and gave up His spirit. (John 19:28,30 NASB)

It is finished. It is accomplished. It is done!

Thank you, Jesus!

CHAPTER TWENTY-FOUR: PROVERBS 30 – HIS SON

Solomon primarily authored the book of Proverbs, and it provides you with wisdom for living a good life. However, there is one that stands out differently than the rest. It bursts off of the pages and says, "The Son of God."

Proverbs thirty was not written by Solomon, but God made sure it was included in Holy scripture.

It is called an oracle or prophecy.

Proverbs 30 (ESV)

The words of Agur son of Jakeh. The oracle.
The man declares, I am weary, O God;
I am weary, O God, and worn out.
Surely I am too stupid to be a man.
I have not the understanding of a man.
I have not learned wisdom,
nor have I knowledge of the Holy One.
Who has ascended to heaven and come down?
Who has gathered the wind in his fists?
Who has wrapped up the waters in a garment?
Who has established all the ends of the earth?
What is his name, and what is his son's name?
Surely you know!

Wow!

Did you see that?

What is his name and what is his son's name?

He is asking and then he says, surely you know.

We do know God's name today. His name is Yahweh. That is the name.

The Hebrew word, for the name is, "Hashem." This is what they use to say God.

The Jewish people started a tradition of not saying the name of God because they have so much reverence for his name. They took the command not to take his name in vain very seriously.

However, the Dead Sea Scrolls and other Archeological findings have shown you the name. The name of God is, Yahweh, and the name of his son is Yeshua.

As a Christian we are adopted children of God and we can call him, "Abba", which means Father or Dad. If we can do that, we can also call him Yahweh.

The opening statement shows how burdened he was. He was weary and he is talking to God about it: *The man declares, I am weary, O God; I am weary, O God, and worn out.*

Remember Jesus said, *"Come to Me, all who are weary and burdened, and I will give you rest. Take My yoke upon you and learn from Me, for I am gentle and humble in heart, and YOU WILL FIND REST FOR YOUR SOULS. For My yoke is comfortable, and My burden is light." (Matthew 11:28-30 NASB)*

This wise man named Agur, is weary.

Why is he weary?

Because he craves a relationship with God. He has wisdom from God, but he wants to know him.

He also says, "I am too stupid..." This is meant to show that he is humble before the wisdom of God. In other words, compared to how smart God is, we are all stupid.

> *I have not the understanding of a man.*
> *I have not learned wisdom,*
> *nor have I knowledge of the Holy One.*

Here he says that he has no real understanding, and he has not learned true wisdom. He is a wise man, otherwise he would not have written a Proverb. But he is looking for a different kind of wisdom.

The wisdom he wants is from the Holy One, whom he says he has no knowledge of. In other words, he does not know him intimately like he desires to know him.

This whole proverb is a revelation of God, and it shows that he had a Son.

Today, people say, "But we are all sons of God because he made all of us." That may sound true and wise on a human level, but it is false.

The truth is, we are not children of God. That is why Jesus had to come and die for us. When you receive Jesus, who is God's only Son, you then get to become adopted sons and daughters to God.

If we were all children of God, then Jesus would not have had to come and sacrifice his own life to save you and me.

So, there is a need for you and me to know God deeply and personally.

Agur understood this and it made him weary. He then asks a series of questions.

Who has ascended to heaven and come down?

He is asking who has done this. In other words, who can simply go up into Heaven and hang out with God, then come back down. Angels get to do this, but they are not human.

The only one who could do this is the pre-incarnate Lord Jesus. He visited with Abraham, Jacob, Moses, Joshua, and others. However, this was limited, and they could not go up and spend time with him in Heaven.

This is the problem Agur is talking about. He wants to know God. This is humankind's greatest need; it is to know God.

Jeremiah chapter thirty-one gives you a peak into what would come: "*They will not teach again, each one his neighbor and each one his brother, saying, 'Know the LORD,' for they will all know Me, from the least of them to the greatest of them,*" declares the LORD, "*for I will forgive their wrongdoing, and their sin I will no longer remember.*" (*Jeremiah 31:34 NASB*)

The solution will come, and that is God's Son Jesus. Through him we get to know him and have an intimate relationship with him. We will get to that later in this Proverb.

Who has gathered the wind in his fists?

The answer to all his questions in this Proverb: "God." Here he knows that only God has the wind in his fists. This holding of the wind in his fists not only speaks of creation, but that God has control over the winds now, in the present.

Remember how Jesus rebuked the winds of the storm? And his disciples were in awe: *They came up to Jesus and woke Him, saying, "Master, Master, we are perishing!" And He got up and rebuked the wind and the surging waves, and they stopped, and it became calm. And He said to them, "Where is your faith?" But they were fearful and amazed, saying to one another, "Who then is this, that **He commands even the winds** and the water, and they obey Him?" (Luke 8:24-25 NASB)*

Who has gathered the wind in his fists?
Who has wrapped up the waters in a garment?
The answer is only God can.
The answer is Jesus did it.
Who has established all the ends of the earth?
Again, only God has done that. He created everything and gave limits to the earth, the land, the sea, and the atmosphere.

Now we get to the final question from Agur. This is the main point of the Proverb. This is like nothing else you will find in the book of Proverbs.

Remember the obvious answer to his questions so far has been God. Only God can do any of those things he asked.

What is his name, and what is his son's name?
Surely you know!

Again the obvious answer to all the questions was God. And now he is asking something personal.

He first asks, what is his name?

Any Jewish man or woman of that time could answer it. They would say, Yahweh.

It was all that was asked, this would be easy. But the next question would have been puzzling to them. It was like an unsolvable riddle.

"...what is his son's name?"

In other words, you really do not know God if you do not know his son. If you cannot name the name above all names, Jesus, or Yeshua, then you do not know God.

This is the big idea of this Proverb.

The theme is this: I am too stupid, I do not know anything, all because I do not know God intimately and personally, and I cannot know God intimately until I know his Son.

Without the arrival of Jesus and the New Testament, this riddle in the heart of Proverbs 30 would have never been solved.

His Son's name

His name is above all names. You know his name, Yeshua and it means Salvation, which means he saves. He saves you!

Look at all the names of Jesus, the Son of God:

Advocate (1 John 2:1)
Almighty (Rev. 1:8; Mt. 28:18)
Alpha and Omega (Rev. 1:8; 22:13)

Amen (Rev. 3:14)
Apostle of our Profession (Heb. 3:1)
Atoning Sacrifice for our Sins (1 John 2:2)
Author of Life (Acts 3:15)
Author and Perfecter of our Faith (Heb. 12:2)
Author of Salvation (Heb. 2:10)
Beginning and End (Rev. 22:13)
Blessed and only Ruler (1 Tim. 6:15)
Bread of God (John 6:33)
Bread of Life (John 6:35; 6:48)
Capstone (Acts 4:11; 1 Pet. 2:7)
Chief Cornerstone (Eph. 2:20)
Chief Shepherd (1 Pet. 5:4)
Christ (1 John 2:22)
Creator (John 1:3)
Deliverer (Rom. 11:26)
Eternal Life (1 John 1:2; 5:20)
Everlasting Father (Isa. 9:6)
Gate (John 10:9)
Faithful and True (Rev. 19:11)
Faithful Witness (Rev. 1:5)
Faith and True Witness (Rev. 3:14)
First and Last (Rev. 1:17; 2:8; 22:13)
Firstborn From the Dead (Rev. 1:5)
God (John 1:1; Heb. 1:8; Rom. 9:5; 2 Pet. 1:1;1 John 5:20; etc.)
Good Shepherd (John 10:11,14)
Great Shepherd (Heb. 13:20)
Great High Priest (Heb. 4:14)
Head of the Church (Eph. 1:22; 4:15; 5:23)
Heir of all things (Heb. 1:2)
High Priest (Heb. 2:17)

Holy and True (Rev. 3:7)
Holy One (Acts 3:14)
Hope (1 Tim. 1:1)
Hope of Glory (Col. 1:27)
Horn of Salvation (Luke 1:69)
I Am (John 8:58)
Image of God (2 Cor. 4:4)
King Eternal (1 Tim. 1:17)
King of Israel (John 1:49)
King of the Jews (Mt. 27:11)
King of kings (1 Tim 6:15; Rev. 19:16)
King of the Ages (Rev. 15:3)
Lamb (Rev. 13:8)
Lamb of God (John 1:29)
Lamb Without Blemish (1 Pet. 1:19)
Last Adam (1 Cor. 15:45)
Life (John 14:6; Col. 3:4)
Light of the World (John 8:12)
Lion of the Tribe of Judah (Rev. 5:5)
Living One (Rev. 1:18)
Living Stone (1 Pet. 2:4)
Lord (2 Pet. 2:20)
Lord of All (Acts 10:36)
Lord of Glory (1 Cor. 2:8)
Lord of lords (Rev. 19:16)
LORD [YHWH: Yahweh] our Righteousness (Jer. 23:6)
Man from Heaven (1 Cor. 15:48)
Mediator of the New Covenant (Heb. 9:15)
Mighty God (Isa. 9:6)
Morning Star (Rev. 22:16)
Offspring of David (Rev. 22:16)
Only Begotten Son of God (John 1:18; 1 John 4:9)

Our Great God and Savior (Titus 2:13)
Our Holiness (1 Cor. 1:30)
Our Husband (2 Cor. 11:2)
Our Protection (2 Thess. 3:3)
Our Redemption (1 Cor. 1:30)
Our Righteousness (1 Cor. 1:30)
Our Sacrificed Passover Lamb (1 Cor. 5:7)
Power of God (1 Cor. 1:24)
Precious Cornerstone (1 Pet. 2:6)
Prince of Peace (Isa. 9:6)
Prophet (Acts 3:22)
Resurrection and Life (John 11:25)
Righteous Branch (Jer. 23:5)
Righteous One (Acts 7:52; 1 John 2:1)
Rock (1 Cor. 10:4)
Root of David (Rev. 5:5; 22:16)
Ruler of God's Creation (Rev. 3:14)
Ruler of the Kings of the Earth (Rev. 1:5)
Savior (Eph. 5:23; Titus 1:4; 3:6; 2 Pet. 2:20)
Son of David (Lk. 18:39)
Son of God (John 1:49; Heb. 4:14)
Son of Man (Mt. 8:20)
Son of the Most High God (Lk. 1:32)
Source of Eternal Salvation for all who obey him (Heb. 5:9)
The One Mediator (1 Tim. 2:5)
The Stone the builders rejected (Acts 4:11)
True Bread (John 6:32)
True Light (John 1:9)
True Vine (John 15:1)
Truth (John 1:14; 14:6)
Way (John 14:6)

Wisdom of God (1 Cor. 1:24)
Wonderful Counselor (Isa. 9:6)
Word (John 1:1)
Word of God (Rev. 19:13)

CHAPTER TWENTY-FIVE: RUTH AND BOAZ

Benjamin Franklin read the story of Ruth to a group of unbelievers, and they were amazed.

Franklin served from 1776 to 1778 on a commission to France charged with the critical task of gaining French support for American independence. French aristocrats and intellectuals embraced Franklin.

He was the United States Ambassador to France, and he occasionally attended the Infidels Club—a group that spent its time searching for and reading literary masterpieces.

On one occasion Franklin read the book of Ruth to the club when it was gathered, but changed the names in it so it would not be recognized as a book of the Bible.

When he finished, they were unanimous in their praise. They said it was one of the most beautiful short stories that they had ever heard, and demanded that he tell them where he had run across such a remarkable literary masterpiece.

It was his great delight to tell them that it was from the Bible, which they professed to regard with scorn and derision, and in which they felt there was nothing good.

The book of Ruth is certainly a literary masterpiece. It is a beautiful story of restoration and love.

Ruth is one of the only two books in the Bible named after a woman.

What is the other one?

That is right, the book of Esther.

The name Ruth means friendship. She becomes, in this story, a close friend, a loyal Gentile friend to her Israeli mother-in-law Naomi. It is a beautiful story of God's love between these two women.

It is a beautiful story; it is also the story behind the story that is simply fascinating.

The book of Ruth is one of those beautiful Old Testament pictures that is designed by God himself to illustrate the dramatic truths of the New Testament. It is a word picture in the Old Testament illustrative of the truth we find in the New Testament.

It is very unusual that you have a mother-in-law and a daughter-in-law relationship, and they love each other well, consistently, and permanently.

It is also a love story between Ruth and her husband-to-be named Boaz.

Not only is it one of the two books in the Bible named after a woman, but it is also the only book in the Bible named after a woman who becomes the ancestor of the Lord Jesus Christ.

It is also the only book in the Old Testament that is named after a non-Jewish woman, non-Jewish person because Ruth is a Gentile. She was from the other side of Israel, the eastern side, the area of Moab.

Ruth 1
Dead Sea Scroll

Elimelech, Naomi's husband, died; and she was left with her two sons. They took for themselves wives of the women of Moab. The name of the one was Orpah and the name of the other was Ruth. They lived there about ten years. Mahlon and Chilion both died, and the woman was bereaved of her two children and of her husband. Then she arose with her daughters-in-law, that she might return from the country of Moab; for she had heard in the country of Moab how Yahweh had visited his people in giving them bread.

Naomi not only lost her husband but then lost her only sons. She was wounded, hurt and sorrowful. The only glimmer of hope for her was to return to her father's land.

Just like Joseph's story, there was a great famine and Jacob heard that there was bread in Egypt. But this time there was bread in Bethlehem, in the land of Israel.

If you stood on the east side, on a hill in Bethlehem, on a cloudless day, you could look down and see the Dead Sea. And then on the other side of the Dead Sea, the hills rise, and you see the plains, the plateau of Moab.

In Moab, the highest hills are about 3,500 feet. The lowlands are about 2,500 feet. The soil is very porous, it brings in good amounts of the rainwater from that high plateau, because it sits opposite to the low desert. So, it is lush and is good for farming.

This is why her husband Elimelech went there when there was a famine. But God wanted the Israelites to stay in their own land.

The Moabites were the descendants of Lot. And they were false worshippers, or idol worshippers. They worshipped god called Chemosh, and he is found written in the Bible, in the Old Testament. Chemosh was a very fierce, angry god, whom they believed required blood and sacrifice.

So he was worshipped by killing people-especially children-as part of their worship to this false god.

Naomi knew this about the Moabites and so it was another reason she knew it was best to get out of there.

Naomi said to her two daughters-in-law, "Go, return each of you to her mother's house. May Yahweh deal kindly with you, as you have dealt with the dead, and with me.May Yahweh grant you that you may find rest, each of you in the house of her husband." Then she kissed them, and they lifted up their voices, and wept.

They said to her, "No, but we will return with you to your people." Naomi said, "Go back, my daughters. Why do you want to go with me? Do I still have sons in my womb, that they may be your husbands? Go back, my daughters, go your way, for I am too old to have a husband."

She had nothing to offer these two women and tells them to go and start a new life without her.

The trip back to Bethlehem would be long and dangerous. She would have to go alone and would be a target of the wild animals and the bandits.

Both of these young Gentile women would have known that.

Psalm 1:19 says, *"Before I was afflicted, I went astray. But now, I keep Your word."*

So, here you see two daughters-in-law with a choice. They can stay in Moab or follow Naomi and protect her as she goes back to the land of her fathers.

And they raised their voices and wept again; and Orpah kissed her mother-in-law, but Ruth clung to her.
Then she said, "Behold, your sister-in-law has gone back to her people and her gods; return after your sister-in-law." But Ruth said, "Do not plead with me to leave you or to turn back from following you; for where you go, I will go, and where you sleep, I will sleep. Your people shall be my people, and your God, my God. Where you die, I will die, and there I will be buried. May the LORD do so to me, and worse, if anything but death separates me from you."

This young Moabite woman makes a resolution to follow her Jewish mother-in-law to the land of her ancestors, the land of Judah, the area of Bethlehem, the land of Israel.

She tells Naomi that your people will be my people, and your God my God.

So they both went on until they came to Bethlehem. And when they had come to Bethlehem, all the city was stirred because of them, and the women said, "Is this Naomi?" But she said to them, "Do not call me Naomi; call me Mara, for the Almighty has dealt very bitterly with me. I went away full, but the LORD has brought me back empty. Why do you call me Naomi, since the LORD has testified against me and the Almighty has afflicted me?"

So Naomi returned, and with her Ruth the Moabitess, her daughter-in-law, who returned from the land of Moab. And they came to Bethlehem at the beginning of barley harvest.

Her name, Naomi means "My Delight".

Here she says, call me Mara, and it means bitter.

Her they arrive at the first harvest, for the barley.

Barley and wheat were planted in the autumn and ripened in spring. Barley matured faster and would be harvested sooner. So, the first fruits of grain offered during the Festival of Unleavened Bread would have been barley.

That puts it right around Passover and the Feast of First Fruits. That would mean, it was around the time of Jesus death on the cross, and his resurrection as the First Fruit.

Ruth 2

Now Naomi had a relative of her husband, a man of great wealth, of the family of Elimelech, whose name was Boaz.

And Ruth the Moabitess said to Naomi, "Please let me go to the field and glean among the ears of grain following one in whose eyes I may find favor."

In the Old Testament law of the Jewish people, there was, in Leviticus chapter 23, the laws of the harvest. And there was a welfare law that God instituted known as gleaning. And gleaning was this: when the harvesters go through and take the crops at harvest time, they do not go through a second time.

They only go through once and they move quickly so that they would leave the grain behind. In fact, this kind of farming, where you would speedily go to harvest crops, could sometimes leave as much as one fourth of the harvestable crop in the field.

God said, leave it that way. Do not go back and get the rest. Let the poor of the land go in and glean whatever is left, and take it home for themselves.

It was a beautiful, gracious way that God cared for the poor. So the poor could glean in the fields, according to Leviticus chapter 23.

So she left and went and gleaned in the field after the reapers; and she happened to come to the portion of the field belonging to Boaz, who was of the family of Elimelech.

God was working behind the scene here. Ruth just so happens to glean from this man. "*...she happened to come to the portion of the field belonging to Boaz*".

Now behold, Boaz came from Bethlehem and said to the reapers, "May the LORD be with you." And they said to him, "May the LORD bless you."

What a wonderful thing for a boss to say to you. And the workers response showed how they were also followers of the Lord God. They knew that every crop was a blessing from Yahweh, and they heard their leader say, *"May the LORD be with you.."*

Naomi witnessed this and felt something quite different than what she saw in Moab.

Then Boaz said to his servant who was in charge of the reapers, "Whose young woman is this?"

Boaz was already attracted to this young woman who was working hard to glean these crops, the leftover crops.

And the servant in charge of the reapers replied, "She is the young Moabite woman who returned with Naomi from the land of Moab. And she said, 'Please let me glean and gather after the reapers among the sheaves.' So she came and has remained from the morning until now..."

The manager who oversaw the reapers, said to Boaz that she is the young Moabite or Gentile woman who returned with Naomi. He also told him how she said please let me glean. She was gracious and humble.

Then Boaz said to Ruth, "Listen carefully, my daughter. Do not go to glean in another field; furthermore, do not go on from this one, but join my young women here. Keep your eyes on the field which they reap, and go after them. Indeed, I have ordered the servants not to touch you. When you are thirsty, go to the water jars and drink from what the servants draw."

Boaz shows her grace and tells her to stay in his field. She was to get all her bread from him, and he offers here good drinking water for when she is thirsty.

He called her, "daughter."

Boaz is starting to look like Jesus.

Remember Jesus with the woman at the well? He offered her living water.

Jesus also said, *"If anyone is thirsty, let him come to Me and drink. The one who believes in Me, as the Scripture said, 'From his innermost being will flow rivers of living water.'" (John 7)*

What was Ruth's response to Boaz who was a great Gentlemen, and who was showing her grace?

She bows down to him in great thankfulness and shows humility:

Then she fell on her face, bowing to the ground, and said to him, "Why have I found favor in your sight that you should take notice of me, since I am a foreigner?"

She realizes his grace. She was humble and asks why she has favor in his eyes, since she was a Gentile, a foreigner.

His response to her is key. It is key for every Christian today, and it speaks of how you and I treat the least of those who are related to Jesus.

Boaz replied to her, "All that you have done for your mother-in-law after the death of your husband has been fully reported to me, and how you left your father and your mother and the land of your birth, and came to a people that you did not previously know. May the LORD reward your work, and may your wages be full from the LORD, the God of Israel, under whose wings you have come to take refuge."

He says to her, in so many words, it is because of all that you had done for the least of these, who is my kin, Naomi, my Jewish relative.

Jesus also said something to that effect.

He gave a story to show what it will be like in the end, when his kingdom finally comes to this earth: And the King will answer and say to them, *'Truly I say to you, to the extent that you did it for one of the least of these brothers or sisters of Mine, you did it for Me.'(Matthew 25 NASB)*

Ruth is being rewarded for watching over the least of one of the Jewish relatives of Boaz.

Then Ruth returned to Naomi and gave her the roasted grain she had from Boaz. She then told her about what had happened, and she told her his name.

In that same way, Gentile Christians tell their Jewish friends about the One who has been kind to them. They tell of this Jewish King, who has blessed them and saved them.

"...Naomi said to her, "The man is our relative; he is one of our redeemers."

Naomi is warming up to this man who has been so kind and gentle to Ruth. She even tells Ruth that he is our relative. In other words, he is Jewish.

Today there is a movement among the Palestinians, and other Muslims to claim that Jesus was a Palestinian. They claim that he is not for Israel and is against her. This is propaganda. It is a lie straight from the pit of hell.

In response to this new claim, the Israeli's, including the Rabbis are angry about this. They are now claiming Jesus as one of theirs. They are now saying that Jesus was a Jewish man in their own history, who was also an Israeli through and through.

God has caused them to be jealous over the Jewishness of Jesus. This is his plan spelled out in Romans 11, in order to save them.

Just as it was in Joseph's story, they did evil to him, but after years of denying him, they discover he is alive and that he loves them.

They meant it for evil, but God can use it for good to bring them back to him and save them.

Yeshua loves Israel.

Naomi also said to Ruth that this relative is our redeemer.

Jesus is the Redeemer. He has paid the price for any who would receive his gift of life.

Then Naomi gave Ruth advice on how to properly draw closer to this good man who is their redeemer.

She slept at his feet one night and when he woke, the matter of redemption was discussed. He produces a plan on how he would redeem both her and Naomi. He had to settle the matter with a relative who was closer to Naomi. And if that man did not want to pay the price, then Boaz would.

He then blessed her with more grain to take home. Then Ruth went back and told Naomi everything.

The timing of all of this is so perfect.

The place was perfect too.

She just happened to glean in the field of Boaz. There were hundreds of fields in Bethlehem, but she just so happened to work here.

Bethlehem is a Hebrew name that we Gentiles talk about around Christmas. Most do not know that the Hebrew word for bread is לֶחֶם, lehem, pronounced LE-ḥem, and it means grain or bread.

The Hebrew word for house is בַּיִת, Beyt. So, Bethlehem means the house or the place of bread.

Why?

Because it was called the breadbasket of Judah. It is where Israeli farmers had healthy crops, and Boaz happened to have one of those where Ruth just happened to be gleaning. So it was the right timing, and it was the right place.

First, the two ladies needed redemption.

Boaz made sure to make this transaction with the elders of his people. He told him you will redeem it or buy it back; if you will not redeem it, then tell me that I may know. First it is on you to redeem it, and then I am next after you.

When Jewish people had a piece of property, they had a title deed.

If they lost the property or had to sell the property, they needed a title deed. Often, there was a scroll that was kept by the seller, and one that was for public records, for the buyer.

So the buyer and the seller had access to the deed. The deed was this scroll sealed with wax seals. On the inside, and sometimes even on the outside, the details of the transaction were written.

For somebody to redeem that lost land, there were qualifications. You had to be related. This was a Goel, a kinsman redeemer. You also had to be willing. Lastly, you had to be able. You had to have the money.

Then Boaz said to the elders and all the people, "You are witnesses today that I have bought from the hand of Naomi all that belonged to Elimelech and all that belonged to Chilion and Mahlon. Furthermore, I have acquired Ruth the Moabitess, the widow of Mahlon, to be my wife in order to raise up the name of the deceased on his inheritance, so that the name of the deceased will not be eliminated from his brothers or from the court of his birth place; you are witnesses today."

This redemption was fulfilled. This Christlike man had purchased back the Gentile woman and her friend, this woman of Israel.

The story continues and the Kinsmen Redeemer marries the Gentile woman. He then had a Gentile bride, who was grafted into the family tree of Israel.

So Boaz took Ruth, and she became his wife, and he had relations with her. And the LORD enabled her to conceive, and she gave birth to a son. Then the women said to Naomi, "Blessed is the LORD who has not left you without a redeemer today, and may his name become famous in Israel.

He was their redeemer. Jesus is our redeemer.

Now you can see how God placed Ruth, in the line of David. And you know that Jesus is in that same line.

And the neighbor women gave him a name, saying, "A son has been born to Naomi!" So they named him Obed. He is the father of Jesse, the father of David.

Now these are the generations of Perez: Perez fathered Hezron, Hezron fathered Ram, and Ram fathered Amminadab, and Amminadab fathered Nahshon, and Nahshon fathered Salmon, and Salmon fathered Boaz, and Boaz fathered Obed, and Obed fathered Jesse, and Jesse fathered David.

This is the Royal line.

This is one of the most powerful stories of Jesus, his Gentile bride, and Israel.

The kinsman redeemer is one of the clearest pictures of Jesus in the Bible. You saw a bridegroom who buys a Gentile bride, and prepares her to be his wife.

The Gentile bride is the church. Jesus gave a parable in which he said, *the kingdom of Heaven is like a treasure hidden in the field, which a man found and hid, and for the joy over it, he goes and sells all that he has, and he buys the field.*

Revelation 5

I saw in the right hand of Him who sat on the throne a scroll written inside and on the back, sealed up with seven seals.

And I saw a strong angel proclaiming with a loud voice, "Who is worthy to open the scroll and to break its seals?" And no one in heaven or on the earth or under the earth was able to open the scroll or to look into it. Then I began to weep greatly because no one was found worthy to open the scroll or to look into it. And one of the elders said to me, "Stop weeping; behold, the Lion that is from the tribe of Judah, the Root of David, has overcome so as to be able to open the scroll and its seven seals...Worthy are You to take the scroll and to break its seals; for You were slaughtered, and You purchased people for God with Your blood from every tribe, language, people, and nation.

God sold everything he had by giving his son, to purchase that treasure in the field. That treasure looks just like Ruth and Neomi. Boaz looks like Jesus.

He paid a heavy price for his bride and for Israel.

CHAPTER TWENTY-SIX: DANIEL

Jesus referenced Daniel when he spoke about the end of time. Jesus made sure that future generations, people like you, would understand that Daniel recorded the Abomination of Desolation as a future event near his return.

Daniel was also given the exact number of days until Jesus first coming on Palm Sunday.

He also prophesied that the Messiah would be cut off, or killed.

Jesus directly quoted Daniel when he was speaking about the end times, and he called Daniel a prophet.

Daniel as a Type of Christ

Not only did Daniel pen prophecy about Jesus, but he was also pictured as a type of Christ.

The evil leaders wanted Daniel dead because of envy. This is like Joseph's brothers had envy toward Joseph over his most favored status and for his prophetic dreams. They surely hated Daniel because of his promotion and his God-given gift with dreams.

Daniel 6

Daniel began distinguishing himself among the commissioners and satraps because he possessed an extraordinary spirit, and the king intended to appoint him over the entire kingdom. Then the commissioners and satraps began trying to find a ground of accusation against Daniel regarding government affairs; but they could find no ground of accusation or evidence of corruption, because he was trustworthy, and no negligence or corruption was to be found in him.

Then they decided to trick the king of Persia into making a law that would force Daniel to be sentenced to death. They hated this young Jewish man, who was blameless. They conspired to murder him.

This is how the religious leaders saw Jesus.

Then these men said, "We will not find any ground of accusation against this Daniel unless we find it against him regarding the law of his God."

Then these commissioners and satraps came by agreement to the king and spoke to him as follows: "King Darius, live forever! All the commissioners of the kingdom, the prefects and the satraps, the counselors and the governors, have consulted together that the king should establish a statute and enforce an injunction that anyone who offers a prayer to any god or person besides you, O king, for thirty days, shall be thrown into the lions' den.

They conspired together and they thought they had found the perfect solution. They made up a new law to entrap Daniel. They consulted together the scripture says.

The scriptures tell us to obey the authorities, however, if obeying them violates what God wants us to do, then we are to disobey. Daniel shows us right here how this is done.

Now when Daniel learned that the document was signed, he entered his house (and in his roof chamber he had windows open toward Jerusalem); and he continued kneeling on his knees three times a day, praying and offering praise before his God, just as he had been doing previously.

What was his crime?

He prayed to Yahweh daily even though it was against the new law of the land. He was not ashamed of praying to God, even if others saw it.

So, then the king was forced to have Daniel arrested and sentenced to death. He did not want to do that. Remember, even Pilate did not want to crucify Jesus.

Daniel was innocent, but condemned.

They sent him down into the pit full of hungry lions. And like Joseph, he was down in a pit even though he was innocent.

So, he was put in the death cave, with the hungry lions, and they rolled a stone over the entrance. That totally speaks of the tomb of Jesus.

Those who hated Jesus were happy he was dead. They thought they had won.

And a stone was brought and placed over the mouth of the den; and the king sealed it with his own signet ring and with the signet rings of his nobles, so that nothing would be changed regarding Daniel.

Jesus was falsely accused and placed in the Tomb with the stone rolled in front of it and it was also sealed: *So they went and made the tomb secure by sealing the stone and setting a guard. (Matthew 27 ESV)*

Daniel was falsely accused and put into the Lion's den, to be killed, as they placed the stone and seal on him.

In Psalm twenty-two, you see the suffering Messiah, and he prays to be delivered from the mouth of the lion, *"Save me from the mouth of the lion!"(Psalm 22 ESV)*

When Jesus was raised from the dead, the stone was rolled away by the Angel, and Jesus was found to be alive. When did this happen? It was early in the morning, at dawn.

You can see the same thing in Daniel's story. It was at dawn, at the break of day, and he was alive.

Then the king got up at dawn, at the break of day, and went in a hurry to the lions' den.

In Daniel's story the Angel shut the mouths of those hungry Lions.

The king called for Daniel, and he found him alive just like Jesus was found alive.

And when he had come near the den to Daniel, he cried out with a troubled voice. The king began speaking and said to Daniel, "Daniel, servant of the living God, has your God, whom you continually serve, been able to rescue you from the lions?" Then Daniel spoke to the king, "O king, live forever! My God sent His angel and shut the lions' mouths, and they have not harmed me, since I was found innocent before Him; and also toward you, O king, I have committed no crime."

This was good news. It made the king happy. He was so filled with joy and gave glory to the God of Daniel.

Then the king was very glad and gave orders for Daniel to be lifted up out of the den. So Daniel was lifted up out of the den, and no injury whatever was found on him, because he had trusted in his God.

Then the king was furious with those who conspired together against Daniel. He commanded that they be thrown down into the Lion's den. Those who are the enemies of Jesus, will have to face God's wrath just like Jesus did.

The king then gave orders, and they brought those men who had maliciously accused Daniel, and they threw them, their children, and their wives into the lions' den; and they had not reached the bottom of the den before the lions overpowered them and crushed all their bones.

Their children, and wives?

I understand how you feel.

Remember this was a record of what happened. God did not command it. However, it does show you how fathers and husbands who conspire to do malicious deeds to the innocent can lead their families into severe consequences.

Then the king gave a new order:

Then Darius the king wrote to all the peoples, nations, and populations of all languages who were living in all the land:

"May your peace be great! I issue a decree that in all the realm of my kingdom people are to tremble and fear before the God of Daniel; For He is the living God and enduring forever,

And His kingdom is one which will not be destroyed,
And His dominion will be forever.
"He rescues, saves, and performs signs and miracles
In heaven and on earth,
He who has also rescued Daniel from the power of the lions."
So this Daniel enjoyed success in the reign of Darius, and in the reign
of Cyrus the Persian.

He rescues, he saves, and his kingdom will be forever.

This powerfully speaks of Jesus.

Where else can you see Jesus in the book of Daniel?

In the first dream of King Nebuchadnezzar there is an image, and this image represents the world empires, all the way from Daniel's time to the end of time.

Daniel 2

Now in the second year of the reign of Nebuchadnezzar,
Nebuchadnezzar had dreams; and his spirit was troubled and his sleep
left him.
Then the king gave orders to call in the soothsayer priests, the conjurers,
the sorcerers, and the Chaldeans, to tell the king his dreams. So they
came in and stood before the king. The king said to them, "I had a
dream, and my spirit is anxious to understand the dream."

This king was troubled by his dreams. This looks similar to the story of Joseph.

There are only two men in the Bible, other than Jesus, who had no recorded sin. One was Joseph and the other is Daniel. Were they sinless? Of course not. The Bible also says that all have sinned. But it is interesting that both of these two guys were interpreters of dreams, promoted to the right hand of the throne, and had no recorded sin.

So, here in Babylon, the king had dreams, and they troubled him.

He desperately wanted to understand what the dreams meant.

Then the Chaldeans spoke to the king in Aramaic: "O king, live forever! Tell the dream to your servants, and we will declare the interpretation." The king replied to the Chaldeans, "The command from me is firm: if you do not make known to me the dream and its interpretation, you will be torn limb from limb and your houses will be turned into a rubbish heap.

Not only did he demand to interpret the dreams, but he also insisted they tell him what he saw in the dream. This would require something supernatural because no one can tell you what you saw in your dream.

This king gave them an impossible task and their very lives depended on doing it.

So what was his dream and what does it have to do with Jesus?

His dream was of a great statue, which represents the kingdoms of this world, or the empires of the world in our history. Daniel tells him the dream, then he interprets it. At the end of time, a Stone comes and destroys all of these world kingdoms all at once.

This Stone is the Stone of Israel, Yeshua. Yes, that's right Jesus.

He will arrive on this earth one day and the kingdoms of this world will be destroyed, and his kingdom will be established here on earth as it is in Heaven.

Daniel 2
Dead Sea Scroll

Daniel answered before the king, and said, "The secret which *the king has demanded can't* be shown to the king by wise men, enchanters, magicians, or soothsayers; *but there is a God in heaven who reveals* secrets, and he has made known to the king Nebuchadnezzar what will be in the latter days..."

In the latter days. God reveals secrets, and has made it known to us today through this amazing Old Testament book of prophecy and New Testament books like Revelation.

"You, O king, saw, and behold, a great image. This image, which was mighty, and whose brightness was excellent, stood before you; and its appearance was terrifying. As for this image, its head was of fine gold, its breast and its arms of silver, its belly and its thighs of bronze, its legs of iron, its feet part of iron, and part of clay. You saw until a stone was cut out without hands, which struck the image on its feet that were of iron and clay, and broke them in pieces. Then the iron, the clay, the bronze, the silver, and the gold were broken in pieces together, and became like the chaff of the summer threshing floors. The wind carried them away, so that no place was found for them. The stone that struck the image became a great mountain, and filled the whole earth.

You see this great image. Its head is gold, arms of silver, belly and thighs of bronze, two legs of iron, and feet of iron and clay.

So what does that mean?

The scripture in Daniel tells you.

Daniel tells this mighty king of Babylon, king Nebuchadnezzar, that he is the head of gold.

You are the head of gold.

Then Daniel continues on and shows you the next kingdom or empire, and then the next and so on.

After you, another kingdom will arise that is inferior to you; and another third kingdom of bronze, which will rule over all the earth. The fourth kingdom will be strong as iron, because iron breaks in pieces and subdues all things; and as iron that crushes all these, it will break in pieces and crush all the earth.

Whereas you saw the feet and toes, part of potters' clay, and part of iron, it will be a divided kingdom; but there will be in it of the strength of the iron, because you saw the iron mixed with miry clay. As the toes of the feet were part of iron, and part of clay, so the kingdom will be partly strong, and partly broken.

He shows them these world empires in sequential order from the top down. Then he finally gets to the last one and it is partly strong and partly broken.

You still might be asking; how do I know which kingdoms these are?

The kingdom that followed the head of gold, the Babylonian Empire, were the two arms of silver, the Medo-Persian Empire.

The Medo-Persians conquered Babylon in 539 B.C.

According to fifth-century B.C. historian/storyteller Herodotus, the Medo-Persians developed a vast system of taxation heavily dependent on silver during the reign of Darius the Great (522–486 B.C.)

After the two arms of silver you see the belly and thighs of bronze, and this speaks of the Empire of Greece. The Greeks had mastered the art of bronze-working, making it a logical choice for them. The technology to work with iron, which would lead to the later Iron Age, was not yet developed or widespread. Bronze, an alloy of copper and tin, was strong and durable enough for effective protection in battle.

Then you see the two legs of Iron, and that represents the Roman Empire. This Empire lasted much longer than the rest of them. It also was divided into the Eastern and Western Roman Empires. This would speak of those legs.

Also, the Roman Spears, swords, daggers, and palstaves, were originally made of bronze, but later the Romans turned entirely to iron.

The entire image that Daniel saw is actually the entire world system moving forward in time from top to bottom.

Today, you cans see the influence of Babylon. The elites of this world want a world with no borders. Even progressive Christians want that. They want to unite the world into one unified government.

The intent of the people of the world in the original Babylon was to come together and build their own way to Heaven, so they built the tower of Babel. They were working to create Heaven here on Earth.

There is even a ministry today called: Redeeming Babel. This is what you can see at the top of their website: *Christians are called to serve as signposts to the coming Kingdom of God, when Jesus will finally repair all brokenness. In a culture afflicted by division and confusion–a condition depicted by the story of Babel in Genesis 11:1-9–Redeeming Babel equips Christians to navigate the chaos with timeless Biblical truths.*

That all sounds good until you look at the actual scripture they reference.

Genesis 11

Now all the earth used the same language and the same words.

And it came about, as they journeyed east, that they found a plain in the land of Shinar and settled there. Then they said to one another, "Come, let's make bricks and fire them thoroughly." And they used brick for stone, and they used tar for mortar. And they said, "Come, let's build ourselves a city, and a tower whose top will reach into heaven, and let's make a name for ourselves; otherwise we will be scattered abroad over the face of all the earth."

Now the LORD came down to see the city and the tower which the men had built. And the LORD said, "Behold, they are one people, and they all have the same language. And this is what they have started to do, and now nothing which they plan to do will be impossible for them. Come, let Us go down and there confuse their language, so that they will not understand one another's speech."

So the LORD scattered them abroad from there over the face of all the earth; and they stopped building the city. Therefore it was named Babel, because there the LORD confused the language of all the earth; and from there the LORD scattered them abroad over the face of all the earth.

The context of this passage was that God did not want them to come together, to be unified as one world, and to build their own way to Utopia or Heaven.

It was the Lord God who purposefully confused their languages so that they would spread out and start nations.

This so-called ministry called Redeeming Babel is funded by the elitists who work with the World Economic Forum and other organizations like them. The elitists have been working to infiltrate the church.

And how do they do it?

They find these weak pastors and leaders who hate nationalism, the nation of Israel, and conservatives, and they create these study groups like the "After Party" to trick Christians into thinking like them.

So this spirit of Babel or Babylon is alive and well in this giant image that moves forward in time.

It moves from top to bottom, and then you see the two arms of silver, representing the next Empires, the Medo-Persians.

Then the Greeks defeated them. It was Alexander the Great who conquered them and the world. You can see the influence of Greek culture in our governments today. Democracy originally came from Athens, and it was used in the next Empire too.

After the Greeks came the Romans. They would crush any who stood against them with the crushing force of iron. The Roman Empire lasted longer than any other. It was divided into the Eastern and Western Empires which explains the two legs of iron.

You can see the influence of the Roman Empire to this day.

During the time of Nazi Germany, Hitler and his minions were fascinated with the Romans.

It was the Roman government who crucified Jesus.

The Romans hated the Jewish people of the land of Israel. They wanted to crush Israel and wipe it off the map.

Emperor Hadrian was like Haman and Hitler.

Around 135 A.D. he sold all Jewish prisoners into slavery, forbade the teaching of the Torah, renamed the land of Judea and Israel, Syria Palaestina. This is where the Palestine name came from. He changed Jerusalem's name to Aelia Capitolina. He even replaced synagogues with Roman temples.

That Empire may have changed its names, but it is still here in Europe and throughout the world.

The whole image that Daniel saw is still moving down, and forward in time.

The last kingdom or Empire is the feet.

This one will have the shortest time, and it will be partially strong like iron and partially weak like clay. This is the least valuable as far as metals go. And clay tends to corrode iron.

Daniel 2
Dead Sea Scroll

And whereas you saw the iron mixed with miry clay, they will mingle themselves with the seed of men; but they won't cling to one another, even as iron does not mix with clay.

After this great stone is cut out without human hands and it destroys the image, it becomes the greatest of all kingdoms and fills the earth. In other words, not by the world coming together.

This stone becomes the Kingdom of God.

You saw until a stone was cut out without hands, which struck the image on its feet that were of iron and clay, and broke them in pieces. Then the iron, the clay, the bronze, the silver, and the gold were broken in pieces together, and became like the chaff of the summer threshing floors. The wind carried them away, so that no place was found for them. The stone that struck the image became a great mountain, and filled the whole earth.

God wins in the end. Jesus wins. You win if you are one of his. This Stone crushes the world system. That Stone is Jesus the Messiah. He is that Stone that builders rejected and has become the Chief Cornerstone.

"...the God of heaven will set up a kingdom which will never *be destroyed, nor will its sovereignty* **be left to another people;** *but it will break in pieces and consume* **all these kingdoms,** *and it will stand forever."*

His Kingdom is forever and ever, amen.

If you enjoyed this book, please consider leaving a positive review as it will help get the message out to the entire world that Jesus is in the Old Testament. Thank you, and may the Lord bless you.

SEE JESUS IN THE OLD TESTAMENT

ABOUT THE AUTHOR: GEORGE AARON CRABB

George was born in Santa Cruz, California and raised by loving parents who were saved during the Jesus revolution of the 1970's. His family moved to Albuquerque, New Mexico where they attended Calvary Albuquerque when it started in 1982. It was during that time that "Seeds" were planted by hearing the Word of God taught by Pastor Skip Heitzig.

It was a year later in Tucson, Arizona that he gave his life to Jesus and was "Born Again".

His family moved back to Santa Cruz when he was 14 and he became an avid surfer. Surfing became his life and slowly he drifted away from close relationship with Jesus.

At twenty-one years old, he knew that living to surf was a dead end. So, he volunteered to become an Army Ranger. During this time in the Rangers he learned how to be a man. Though he learned much, he was still a lost son to God. The party life was everything until he met the love of his life, Christina. Later they married and they moved back to his hometown of Santa Cruz.

His wife, work and surfing were his priority until they had their first child in 2002. Later they decided that it would be better to raise their son in Washington State. He started to go to church again and turn back toward the Lord.

It was a men's conference at Calvary Fellowship in Seattle that he re committed his life to Jesus. Greg Laurie was preaching, and he felt the touch in his heart from the Holy Spirit to stand up for the prayer of re-dedication.

Since that time, he has been on fire for God, as he began to teach and preach at his local Church and his first teaching was on Old Testament Joseph. He turned this teaching into a book. Then other Sunday sermons and teachings became books.

OTHER BOOKS BY THE AUTHOR: TOLA'AT SHANI, ROAD TO
EMMAUS, JOSEPH, AND THE SAME TODAY
All available at Amazon, Barnes & Noble, and Apple iBooks

This short book takes you deep into Psalm 22 and it focuses in on
the Crimson worm of verse six. This has been sold all over the world
and hundreds have been blessed by it. I hope you will be blessed by
it as well.

ROAD
TO
EMMAUS

GEORGE CRABB

This short book will give you the big picture of where you can see
Jesus in the Old Testament.

This Book takes you deep into Old Testament Joseph and how he was a picture and a type of Jesus.

The
Same
Today
GEORGE CRABB

This book is the story of my life. In it you will see what it was like as a little boy during the Jesus Revolution. You will also see miracles and adventure. From being a local Santa Cruz surfer, to a Sergeant in the elite 75th Army Rangers. But the greatest adventure of all, is discovering the love and grace that God has shown to me.

THE AUTHOR'S YOUTUBE CHANNEL: THE WHOLE BIBLE WITH GEORGE CRABB

You can subscribe to my channel for free and watch everything.

Don't miss out!

Visit the website below and you can sign up to receive emails whenever George Crabb publishes a new book. There's no charge and no obligation.

https://books2read.com/r/B-A-XHIEB-YLXVE

Connecting independent readers to independent writers.